SATURDAY MILLIONAIRES

HOW WINNING FOOTBALL
BUILDS WINNING COLLEGES

SATURDAY MILLIONAIRES

HOW WINNING FOOTBALL BUILDS WINNING COLLEGES

KRISTI DOSH

WILEY

Turner Publishing Company / Wiley General Trade

200 4th Avenue North • Suite 950 • Nashville, Tennessee 37219

445 Park Avenue • 9th Floor • New York, NY 10022

www.turnerpublishing.com

Saturday Millionaires: How Winning Football Builds Winning Colleges

Cover design: Jose Almaguer

Book design: Lissa Auciello-Brogan

Library of Congress Cataloging-in-Publication Data

Dosh, Kristi.
 Saturday millionaires : how winning football builds winning colleges / Kristi Dosh.
   pages cm
 ISBN 978-1-118-38665-1 (hardback)
1. Football--Economic aspects--United States. 2. College sports--Economic aspects--United States. 3. Universities and colleges--United States--Finance. I. Title.
 GV956.4.D67 2013
 796.332'63--dc23
                              2013024461

Printed in the United States of America

13 14 15 16 17 18 0 9 8 7 6 5 4 3 2 1

To Chadd—the best part about my life is you.

CONTENTS

FOREWORD

The late great Beano Cook told me years ago if college football ever changed its postseason format it would be for all the wrong reasons. It's never because the powerbrokers want to make it right. No matter how much money is made, there's always an appetite for more money, and it's that need that challenges administrations in these institutions of higher learning.

As I've grown older, I've noticed that my old original *College GameDay* partner was as I used to say, a "college football soothsayer."

The rich will continue to get richer, but they'll throw enough breadcrumbs behind them to keep the have-nots from starving. You see, while the new playoff might bring more opportunity on the field (the full extent of which remains to be seen), their share of the pie will increase only enough to stave off their hunger. Those schools will continue to rely largely on student fees to compete at college football's highest level.

It's not all bad though. Some schools are operating with a surplus of great amounts, actually enabling them to give cash back to the academic side, as Kristi will detail in the book. Others are funding athletics to act as a billboard for the university, reaping the rewards when their team plays on national television.

Fans are more sophisticated now and usually want to know why certain decisions are made. Trust me when I say it's always a business decision. These institutions have the mission to educate, but they are also in the business of making money.

Kristi knows that better than anyone I know.

Many times I've wondered if anyone would step up and go through what it takes to investigate the business of intercollegiate athletics. In addition to my studio and play-by-play work, I also host a nationally syndicated radio show. A few years ago, my agent made me aware of Kristi Dosh. She was a guest on my show one summer day, and since then she's been my go-to resource anytime we talk the business of college sports.

In this book, she will detail how the incredible growth of college sports has led to tremendous success for some while inspiring others to compete beyond their means. Does that mean we'll eventually see a new division emerge as the powerbrokers separate from the pack?

Television is funneling more money into intercollegiate athletics than ever before, but has it reached its full market share?

Will universities ever be compelled to share that money with the student athletes?

This author is best suited to answer those questions.

The business of college football has changed dramatically in the past twenty years, and her understanding of why schools decide what they do separates her from anyone else I know in my industry. This is a book I've been waiting to read for years.

In the following pages you learn that Kristi Dosh is indeed the "SportsBizMiss."

—Tim Brando, host of the *Tim Brando Show*

SATURDAY MILLIONAIRES

INTRODUCTION

When I say Boise State University, what's the first thing you think of? Unless you're part of the small minority who attended school there, I'm guessing it's the blue football field. Or perhaps the Statue of Liberty play the Broncos used to win the 2007 Fiesta Bowl. As sure as I am that it wasn't their 13th-ranked public undergraduate engineering program that caught your eye, I'm positive it was something football-related, and not just because this book is about college football.

Most of you will think football first, because football has made Boise State part of the national conversation. And no doubt football is a reason that in just six years, from 2006 to 2011, the percentage of freshman enrolling at Boise State from out-of-state has jumped from 13.5 percent to 34 percent. Considering out-of-state tuition was $10,400 higher per student for the 763 non-resident freshman entering in the fall of 2012, that could translate into nearly $8 million dollars more annually than if those students were in-state enrollees. Multiply that by the non-resident students at Boise State in their second year and beyond, and by the number of years each of those students spends at Boise State to get their degree, and we're talking hundreds of millions of dollars, assuming those students don't become state residents during their tenure.

Out-of-state students translate directly into dollars, but Boise State has experienced other positive enrollment trends. Following the football team's 2007 and 2010 Fiesta Bowl appearances, the university experienced enrollment increases of 9.1 percent and 5.6 percent, respectively. However, the university also used the increased applications to become more selective. Over 70 percent of new freshman applicants were admitted in 2006, but only 54 percent were admitted in 2011. The percentage of students who scored in the top quarter on their ACTs grew from 28 percent to 40 percent over the same five-year period.

While these numbers can't be solely attributed to football, they also aren't merely indicative of a nationwide trend, or even a regional trend. Fellow state school, University of Idaho, which played football at the FBS level as a member of the WAC during this time period, saw its numbers fall while Boise State's rose. From 2006 to 2011, the average GPA of University of Idaho's freshman fell from 3.42 to 3.33, while Boise State saw an increase from 3.28 to 3.34. While Boise State's out-of-state enrollment for freshman surged from the aforementioned 13.5 percent to 34 percent, Idaho's fell from 34 percent to 24 percent.

At many universities, those on the academic side will use their dying breath to tell you that football has no positive impact on academics. In fact, some are adamant college football has corrupted universities. They'll tell you about US News and World Report rankings and research grants, but they'll deny their football team's BCS bowl appearance had anything to do with increased applications or more selective enrollment.

Boise State, however, embraces its football success. This is perhaps most evident in the website it created to highlight faculty and university achievements outside athletics—it's called "Beyond the Blue," an acknowledgment that the blue football field on the East side of campus is the most-recognized feature of the university.

The fact is, football creates publicity in a way few schools could duplicate with a more traditional marketing campaign. A study in 1992, when national football coverage was far less than what it is today, found 70 percent of all articles written about Northwestern University in major newspapers were about athletics. Just 5 percent were written about university research at the prestigious university. A visit from ESPN's College Gameday has been found to have a $5 million publicity impact according to current Texas A&M athletic director Eric Hyman, who said the topic was studied when he presided over the athletic department at University of South Carolina. An appearance in the national championship game? Malcolm Turner of Wasserman Media Group says it's worth tens of millions of dollars. That's advertising a university simply cannot buy.

Let's say you're University of Alabama. Are you going to receive more applicants from a billboard on the side of I-85 in Atlanta or from knocking LSU out of national championship contention with a big win on Saturday night on primetime television? I think we all know the answer to that.

Instead of fighting it, more universities need to embrace the role big-time college football plays in the overall university picture. The leaders at Boise State have figured this out. Football success can lead to more applications. More applications allow the university to be more selective. Students with better academic profiles attract better professors. Top professors mean more research grants and academic recognition. A better academic reputation leads to a higher ranking. A higher ranking attracts higher-profile students and professors, and so on. And it all started with football.

In this day and age, there is no one type of university and one path to success. Some, like Harvard University, have been around for centuries and can stand on their academics alone (although, let's not forget they also choose to field a football team). Others, like Boise State, started as a junior college and have been awarding four-year degrees for fewer than 50 years. The latter will never be the former, no matter how much they prioritize academics. A kid in California doesn't grow up knowing about Boise State's engineering program. He grows up watching Boise State play football on national television.

No one ever got anywhere trying to swim against the tide. So, instead of focusing on what college football isn't, this book illustrates what it is and how universities can use it to their advantage. As you'll see in Chapter 1, football can provide dividends far greater than any subsidy it might receive from the university. Besides, the university pays less than you think. The "direct institutional support" USA Today annually likens to a disease infecting athletic departments when it produces its NCAA financial database can be anything from waiving out-of-state tuition up-charges to state lottery funds meant to support Title IX. Not exactly the scandalous story it's made out to be.

Throughout the book I'll show you how many of the flashy headlines declaring college football synonymous with big business and corruption are more about grabbing your attention than helping you understand reality. For example, it was easy to hear a $3.6 billion television contract announced for a conference like the Atlantic Coast Conference (ACC) in 2012 and be overwhelmed at the dollars generated by big-time college sports. What most people, media members included, don't do is break that number down: $240 million per year, $17.1 million per school per year, $1.1 million per sport (if each school carried the NCAA-mandated minimum of 16 sports, which most exceed).

The average sport at ACC member Georgia Tech, which sponsors 17 sports, costs $3.2 million to run, according to its 2010-2011 NCAA financial disclosure. That leaves an average of $2.1 million per sport to cover *after* applying television revenue. Amazing how far the money doesn't go. Like most schools, Georgia Tech only turns a net profit on football and men's basketball, which means those two sports must generate enough revenue to support all the rest if the athletic department is to cover its own expenses.

Georgia Tech is one of the schools berated in the press for taking university money to balance its budget. The athletic department's 2010-2011 NCAA financial disclosure shows $1.7 million in direct institutional support. The university isn't writing the athletic department a check, however. The money you see listed as direct institutional support is actually a reflection of money *not* changing hands. It's the amount of money the athletic department saved by paying in-state tuition for out-of-state student athletes. Oh, the horror—the university isn't slapping the athletic department with an up-charge.

There are plenty of stories out there about universities covering athletic department expenses (which, as I've illustrated, is often misunderstood), but few about the amount of money athletic departments send back to their universities.

Nearly 11 percent of the University of Alabama athletic department's expenses went toward paying the university for the tuition, room and board for scholarship athletes. You read that right—the athletic department cut a check to the university to cover tuition, room and board for scholarship athletes. Over 22 percent went to facilities, including the cost of utilities, maintenance and any building leases (and at some schools, it's the university receiving rent as landlord). Team travel cost another 5 percent of the expense budget. Nick Saban, one of the highest-paid coaches in the country in 2010-2011, accounted for just 4.1 percent of Alabama's total athletic department expenses. Yet, it's his salary you'll hear about the most.

Outside of football and men's basketball, most sports don't even produce enough revenue to cover the cost of tuition, room and board for its athletes. As you'll see in Chapter 2, gymnastics at University of Florida only produces enough revenue to cover 39 percent of the student aid it provides for gymnastics athletes. Then there's still a host of other expenses to cover, including travel, medical, coaching salaries, facilities, equipment and the like. The first two chapters will break down actual budgets and look at several schools individually to give a clearer picture of where all the money goes and why it's impossible to judge an athletic department's financial situation without looking at the university as a whole.

If seeing the breakdown of where all the money goes doesn't convince you that athletic departments can't afford to pay student athletes above and beyond what is already provided, Chapter 3 will finish the job.

Articles like Taylor Branch's highly publicized "The Shame of College Sports" in *The Atlantic* would lead you to believe that the millions in television money and contributions athletic departments receive only serve to pay higher coaching salaries and build new facilities. They never mention that Florida fielded 21 varsity sports in 2010-2011, seven more than the NCAA minimum, or that the Gators athletic department spent $9.2 million on grants-in-aid for student athletes in 2010-2011, more than twice the $4 million required by the NCAA.

Don't think it's fair that football and men's basketball generate the money used to fund opportunities for athletes in other sports? Ask the NCAA to change its requirements, and then start calling your Congressman and asking for a repeal of Title IX. Don't get sucked into salacious rants that dare compare student athletes to slaves. How many slaves were housed in a multimillion dollar facility, fed regularly, attended to by top-notch trainers and medical staff and received a degree allowing them to expect median lifetime earnings of $2.3 million?[1] The comparison is preposterous.

Even if you think student athletes should be paid above and beyond their tuition, room and board and the other amenities and services they receive free of charge, Chapter 3 will show you there's a big difference between *should* and *could*.

One of the most serious untold truths you'll learn in this book is that paying college athletes is virtually unfeasible. First, there are Title IX issues that would effectively force all student athletes, not just those in revenue sports, to be paid. Second, and most damning, there could be serious issues with nonprofit status and tax treatment—and not just for the athletic department, but for the entire university. In short, it's a risk no university can afford to take.

What universities can do for student athletes is continue to find new ways to fund additional scholarships and create more opportunities. They can use the attention football brings the university to collaborate with the athletic department on university-wide sponsorships and other initiatives that benefit the entire student body. They can hire someone like Tom Jurich as athletic director, who, as you'll see in Chapter 7, helped reshape the University of Louisville far beyond the confines of the athletic department.

As conferences and schools take control of their future in athletics, they can't help but influence the course for the entire university, as examples like Boise State and University of Louisville will show you. We'll end the book like we started, with a discussion of the impact college football can have on the university as a whole.

Certainly that impact is not always positive, as the recent academic scandal at UNC and booster improprieties at Miami and Ohio State have shown. College football is not without flaws. Some universities are doing a better job harnessing its power than others, who seem to let the football program run unbridled. This book is meant to pass along the knowledge I've gained while visiting campuses, speaking with athletic directors and reviewing athletic department and university financial statements and allow you to examine news stories with a critical eye.

In the end, I think you'll see that college football can't be viewed independently of the athletic department or the university, and that it can be an important catalyst for the success of each.

NOTES

[1] Luminafoundation.org, "New study finds that earning power is increasingly tied to education: a college degree is critical to economic opportunity," Last accessed on October 1, 2012, from http://www.luminafoundation.org/newsroom/news_releases/2011-08-05.html.

DOES FOOTBALL PAY FOR ITSELF
(Even If the School Pays for Football)?

Much attention is given to the money generated by athletic departments. It's not hard to see why considering the Pac-12 conference announced a $3 billion, 12-year television deal with ESPN and Fox in the fall of 2011. In fact, the five power conferences (ACC, Big-12, Big Ten, Pac-12 and SEC) all have television contracts that average over $200 million per year, primarily driven by football and men's basketball programming.

With each individual school averaging over $17 million per year from these contracts, pundits ask why many athletic departments still need student fees or funds from the university (often referred to as "direct institutional support") to balance their budgets.

Chapter 2 will take you inside actual athletic department budgets to show exactly how all those tens of millions of dollars from football are spent, but this chapter will take a wider view and examine overall athletic spending and why so much money is invested in football.

Athletic department expenditures can run upwards of $130 million and averaged $52 million across all public FBS programs in 2010-2011, large sums for sure. How much is it in the grand scheme of things though? In 2006, operating expenses in athletics accounted for an average 6 percent of total higher education spending for schools competing at the FBS level. Only a few years prior, the number was even lower at 3.8 percent. The jump is attributed in part to a change in reporting methods.[1]

The University of Florida's financial statements for 2010-2011 show total operating expenses for the university and its component units (which include athletics, Shands Hospital, Health Science Center affiliates and other direct support organizations) of $4.2 billion. Athletic department expenses for the same time period totaled $113.5 million, 2.7 percent of total university expenditures. It's also worth noting athletic revenues fully cover those expenses.

While big-time college sports come with an implied minimum on the expense side, revenues can vary greatly. Take athletics at the University of Memphis for example, which accounted for 10.3 percent of total university operating expenses in 2010-2011. At that time, Memphis was not in an AQ conference and did not produce enough revenue to cover expenses without student fees and direct institutional support.

According to a report commissioned by the Knight Commission, athletics spending nationally spiked 50 percent per student athlete at public institutions with an FBS program from 2005-2009, while academic spending per student grew just 22 percent.[2] This ignores that athletic departments, which generally have fewer than 1,000 student athletes, are being compared to entire universities with sometimes tens of thousands of students.

A look at athletics alone shows average athletic department revenues at public FBS institutions have risen by 49 percent, from $35.3 million to $52.3 million, while average expenses have only risen 45 percent from $34.2 million to $49.2 million, according to financial disclosures provided by the institutions to the NCAA (referred to hereinafter as NCAA disclosures).

At the FBS level of Division I, television contracts for football and basketball upwards of $1 billion signed by the top five conferences have led to a growing sentiment amongst the public and those in academia that athletic departments should be self-supporting.

Each year a handful of public FBS programs are applauded for being self-sustaining, meaning no revenue in the form of direct institutional support, government support or student fees is necessary to show a net profit on their NCAA financial disclosure. For the 2011-2012 school year, just 23 public schools made that list, all of which were in the five conferences with the largest television contracts.

The media has a field day with this story every year, particularly *USA Today*, which publishes a portion of each public university's NCAA financial disclosure annually. Fewer than 10 percent of all public FBS institutions are running their athletic department in the black, these writers shout! But are they really educating fans about athletic department finances or throwing around words like "subsidy" and "dependence" to spark debate about the place of athletics in higher education?

There are two separate issues worth addressing here. First, the very idea that athletic departments should be self-sustaining. Second, the method of accounting used in computing athletic department budgets.

It's certainly an enviable position for a university when the athletic department is not only self-sustaining, but showing a net profit. Schools like Ohio State, Louisiana State, Michigan and Florida field more than the number of teams required by the NCAA, fully fund to NCAA scholarship limits, and show a net profit even after donating funds back to the university.

But is this model realistic for every FBS institution? Should it be considered a failure when an athletic department cannot independently support itself?

No one complains about the English department not producing enough revenue to cover its expenses. Those same people will tell you that it's because the English department is part of the university's mission. A fair argument, although the U.S. has a long history of athletics as part of the educational experience, starting with the academically elite Ivy League schools.

Following the line of thinking that the athletic department is not the same as the English department, the question then is whether or not to have athletics at all, not whether or not the department is being appropriately funded.

Due to a number of indirect benefits, discussed in part in Chapter 10, many universities choose to have athletics. It's important to understand that a certain baseline of expenses is required in order to compete at the Division I level. First, the NCAA requires each school competing at the FBS level to sponsor 16 sports. Second, each FBS athletic department must offer a minimum 200 grants-in-aid or spend a minimum of $4 million on grants-in-aid for student athletes.

From the outset then, running an athletic department can be a losing proposition. As you'll see in the next chapter, football and men's basketball are generally the only sports whose revenues exceed their expenses. That leaves the net profit from those two sports as the only significant way to fund the minimum of 14 other sports without having to rely on the student fees, direct institutional support or government support that put the department out of the running for the self-sustaining title.

Transfer Pricing

The problem with understanding the true financial picture of an athletic department becomes complicated as you examine the transfer pricing practices between universities and athletic departments. Transfer pricing is terminology that refers to the analysis, documentation and adjustment of charges made between related parties for goods, services or use of property.

Facilities Rental

One example of transfer pricing is when a facility is owned by the university but leased by the athletic department, meaning the athletic department pays the university rent.

At Ohio State University, the athletic department paid over $2 million to rent the Jerome Schottenstein center for the 2011-2012 school year for men's and women's basketball and men's ice hockey and $1.2 million for their share of operational expenses for the McCorkle Aquatics Center. In addition, the athletic department paid rent for two additional buildings used for academic services for athletes: the Younkin Success Center at a cost of $501,338 and the Fawcett Center at $76,613. Another $986,000 in rent was paid by the athletic department for use of the Fawcett Center for athletic offices.

This isn't something generally seen between academic departments and the university. The biology department isn't paying the university to rent classroom space.[3] Of course, not all athletic departments pay rent to the university for athletic facilities—some fund all of the facilities completely on their own. The biology department definitely isn't funding the construction of its own buildings.

As an example of the amount of transfers that are made from athletic departments to the university, see the following chart, which represents all university transfers to be made by Ohio State's athletic department to the university for the 2011-2012 school year:

University Overhead $5.200,000
A 5.9 percent university overhead charge on athletic department
revenues for the department's share of University services, such
as insurance, payroll services, purchasing and accounting.

Physical Plant Assessment $456,000
Annual maintenance and custodial service of the Ice Rink,
St. John Arena and French Field House by Facilities Operations
& Development.

Cost Containment $1,090,000
Annual cost containment assessment since its inception in
1986 due to University-wide cost cuts ($590,000).
Annual $500,000 assessment on OSU Golf Course
operations since 1997.

Grants-in-Aid $15,702,000
Tuition, room and board and fees for scholarship athletes.

WOSU $350,000
Fund transfer to WOSU to pay for salaries and operational
costs responsible for the production of Big Ten Network
academic programming.

Transportation and Parking $165,000
Annual assessment imposed to financially support Transportation
and Parking in the maintenance of parking lots supporting the
Schottenstein Center and other athletic venues.

School of Music/OSU Marching Band $100,000
Additional financial support for the School of Music and the
OSU Marching Band (in addition to the Band's $200,000 operating
budget funded by the athletic department).

University Development $855,000
Estimated assessment levied by the University's fundraising arm.

Office of Legal Affairs $175,000
Estimated salary and benefits for athletics' legal counsel.

Office of Financial Aid $35,000

Office of Academic Affairs $20,000

Jerome Schottenstein Center Operating Transfer $2,090,030
Facility rent paid to the Schottenstein Center for men's and women's
basketball, men's ice hockey, TeamShop and Ticket Office space.

McCorkle Aquatics Center Operating Transfer $1,200,000
Annual share of facility operational expenses paid to RPAC (Student Life) for
men's and women's swimming, men's and women's diving, and synchronized
swimming athletic programs.

Student-Athlete Support Services Office Funding $2,384,421
Fund annual budget for student-athlete support services sent to
Office of Academic Affairs (Operating: $1,806,471; Younkin Rent:
$501,338; Fawcett Rent: $76,613).

Fawcett Center $986,000
Administrative office rent.

Library Renovation $1,000,000
The fifth installment of a nine-year commitment to the University's renovation
efforts at the William Oxley Thompson Memorial (Main) Library.

LifeSports $250,000

The LifeSports program is one of the University's largest outreach programs to the local inner-city community. LifeSports has been hosted by the athletic department since 1968 and is an instructional program for boys and girls from low-income households using sports and education. The athletic department subsidizes the $250,000 annual cost of the four-week summer program.

In total, Ohio State's athletic department sent over $32 million back to the University for the 2011-2012 school year, more than 25 percent of its total budget.

Student Aid

Another area examined by several studies is the practice of athletic departments paying the university the full value of tuition, room and board and fees for each scholarship athlete. The total cost to the athletic department can range from school to school both because of the varying price tags and the number of student athletes.

Ohio State University is home to one of the largest athletic departments in the country in terms of the number of student athletes. For the 2010-2011 school year, Ohio State had 1,000 student athletes. Tuition, room and board and fees for an in-state student was $22,258, while it was $36,442 for an out-of-state student. In total, these expenses accounted for $15.1 million of the athletic department's expenses.

On the smaller end, an athletic department still spends several million dollars paying the university for student-athlete tuition, room and board and fees. The University of North Texas had far fewer student athletes than Ohio State in 2010-2011 with just 348. It also has cheaper rates with in-state students at $14,758 and out-of-state students at $21,926. At the end of the day, it still had to send over $3.3 million back to the university to cover the costs of grants-in-aid.

Several studies have found the practice of athletic departments paying "list price" for grants-in-aid skews the department's true financial picture. Brian Goff, a professor of economics at Western Kentucky University, attempted to adjust athletic department financials to account for some of the transfer pricing, including the "list price" practice.

Goff reasons that a university only spends a fraction of the "list price" to house and instruct student athletes. His study states, "The incremental instructional expense is nearly zero because at universities, where even small amounts of excess capacity exists, few, if any, additional faculty or staff must be employed to accommodate the additional student athletes."[4]

In addition to the fact that the list price allows for the university to realize some margin of profit, up-charges for out-of-state students can significantly increase the expenses for an athletic department. Is the university making money off the athletic department or are those student athletes taking the place of other students who would have been admitted in their place and paying full list price? It's not a question easily answered. All we do know is that student aid is a huge expense for athletic departments.

Direct Institutional Support

Since out-of-state tuition is largely an up-charge, and not indicative of additional costs to the university, some universities provide tuition waivers to allow out-of-state student athletes to be treated as in-state students. This can show up in a couple of different ways on athletic department financials: as a payment (a sort of refund) to the athletic department from the university or as a reduction in expense for the athletic department if the money is deducted before payment is sent to the university. Almost all athletic departments that receive these waivers use the former method, showing it as revenue categorized as direct institutional support.

For example, the University of Illinois planned to provide $920,000 in tuition waivers to the athletic department to ensure Title IX compliance for the 2011-2012 school year. Rather than a reduction in the athletic department's scholarship expenses, these monies are reported as revenue into the athletic department from the university under the direct institutional support category.

As mentioned at the start of the book, Georgia Tech is in a similar situation. The athletic association's audited financial report shows $1,667,213 in institutional support for fiscal year 2011. Nearly $1.3 million of that reflects out-of-state tuition not charged to the athletic department—shown as revenue instead of a reduction in expenses. The remainder is the University's share of the athletic director's salary, as he is part of the University's senior management team and reports directly to the University president.

Many commentators simply see monies attributed to direct institutional support and go no further. As you've seen, that money isn't always a transfer of funds from the university to the athletic department. Is institutional support in this manner, especially given Goff's "list price" theory, a negative reflection on an athletic department's financial situation?

Government Support

Similarly, athletic departments which report government support are criticized without discussion of the funding being received.

Title IX presents additional complications when it comes to evaluating athletic departments. In the instance of University of Illinois, detailed above, tuition waivers are provided for female athletes and reported as direct institutional support. In addition, some state legislatures have decided to support Title IX by providing funding to athletic departments earmarked for women's athletics programs. This can show up on a school's NCAA disclosure as government support.

One of the most comprehensive state laws regarding Title IX compliance was enacted by the State of Washington. Under state law, institutions can grant tuition waivers amounting to up to a specified percent of total operating income.[5] One percent of those tuition waivers can be dedicated to gender equity initiatives in the athletic department.

The specified percentage for University of Washington is 21 percent. Based on fiscal year operating revenue of $3.39 billion, the university could provide discounts and waivers of up to $711.9 million, $7.1 million of which could be for athletics. The total amount provided for athletics in fiscal year 2011 was $2.5 million.

Many other states have similar laws. In Illinois, state law allows for up to 1 percent of total tuition revenue at a public university to be used to support tuition waivers for female student athletes. In Louisiana, state law allows for 50 tuition waivers per year for female student athletes at public universities.

University of Oregon showed $959,779 in direct state/government support for fiscal year 2011 on its NCAA disclosure document. Over half of that represents funds forwarded to the athletic department from the state lottery. Under Oregon law, a portion of state lottery proceeds are allocated to the athletic departments at the seven public universities in an effort to reduce the need for athletic departments to be supported by the university's general fund.

The athletic department cannot simply refuse these funds, and the university has no discretion to reallocate these funds. Is it the athletic department then that should be criticized for using state funds in its budget?

Florida A&M University recorded $263,036 in government support on its 2010 NCAA disclosure document. The athletic department confirmed those were funds received from the State of Florida for Title IX purposes. As is the case at Oregon, these funds cannot be reallocated by the University to other areas; these are funds directly appropriated by the State of Florida to the athletic department for a specific use.

Both Title IX and the NCAA's requirement that Division I schools sponsor 16 sports force athletic departments to operate at a minimum level. No matter how well-run or efficient an athletic department is, these two realities create a certain cost of doing business.

A study mentioned at the beginning of the chapter found athletic spending represents 6 percent of total higher education spending. However, the percentage of total higher education spending attributed to athletics varies greatly depending on the size of the institution. Smaller schools generally spend 5-10 percent of total spending on athletics, but some go so high as 15 percent. Meanwhile, a school with total spending over $1 billion only spends 5 percent on athletics on average, and a school with total spending over $2 billion allocates less than 3 percent to athletics.[6]

The authors of the study conclude the variance in these numbers reflects the minimum cost of doing business for athletic departments, largely due to NCAA and Title IX requirements.

While the television deals for the top five conferences are large on the surface, they deplete when you break them down by school and then by sport. Each school in those five conferences average at least $17 million per year from television contracts. All of these schools sponsor more than the NCAA minimum 16 sports, but assuming they each had the minimum, that's only a little over $1 million in revenue per sport.

As you'll see in the next chapter, sports outside of football and men's basketball generally do not generate net revenue, so it's the television contracts, ticket sales and contributions generated by those two sports that fund all of the other 14 plus sports.

Studies have also found athletic-produced revenues are often attributed to non-athletic accounts, particularly in the areas of merchandise sales, concession revenues, parking receipts and related revenues. Another example of transfer pricing, this reduces revenue shown for the athletic department, revenue which is actually generated in part or in whole by athletics.

Licensing

Now that we've looked at some of the ways transfer pricing can seemingly *increase* an athletic department's revenue, an example from Boise State University will help illustrate how transfer pricing can *reduce* an athletic department's revenue. The Boise State Bookstore returns all proceeds from the sale of Bronco insignia merchandise to the University, despite the fact that athletics clearly has an impact on the popularity of the school's logo.

In 2005, prior to the Broncos' big appearances in the 2007 and 2010 Fiesta Bowl games, Boise State had approximately 100 merchandise licensees through the Collegiate Licensing Company and generated about $210,000 in royalties. In 2012, Boise State had grown to over 350 licensees and generated more than $1 million in royalties. Coincidence? I think not.

University of Oregon is another example. Until 2009-2010, the University kept all licensing revenue and allotted the athletic department $200,000 per year. Currently the University shares 50 percent of net revenue from licensing with the athletic department, although a significant portion of sales are attributed to athletic sportswear and Nike apparel. Total licensing revenue for the University has grown from $750,000 to $2.25 million from fiscal year 2005 to fiscal year 2011, coinciding with successful football seasons.

Other schools have similar practices when it comes to licensing, which can account for multiple millions of dollars. At LSU, the University also keeps approximately 50 percent of all licensing revenue. Prior to its first national championship in football in 2003, LSU had never taken in more than $1 million in licensing revenue in a single year. After the win, licensing revenue increased by 208 percent, to $3 million, in just one year. By 2007, when the Tigers brought home another national championship, licensing was up to $5 million a year. With a 50/50 split, it wasn't only the athletic department cashing in on the football team's success.

The Royalties/Licensing/Advertising/Sponsorship category on an NCAA disclosure can also include "in-kind products and services provided as part of the sponsorship." University of Minnesota, under its contract with Nike, will receive $1 million in product for the 2013-2014 school year. The value of that product is included as revenue but obviously isn't cash that can be spent by the athletic department. Based on a survey of business officers at FBS athletic departments, the practice of reporting products and services received in conjunction with an apparel contract in this revenue category varies from school to school.

That same revenue category on the NCAA disclosure can also be boosted by the value of automobiles provided by local dealerships to coaches. Courtesy car programs are common at many FBS schools, and some include the value of the cars in this revenue category.

UTEP's Miners Club provides the following explanation of a courtesy car program on its website:

> The UTEP Athletics Department allows area auto dealers and donors the opportunity to directly impact the success of the UTEP athletics program and to promote and enhance its sports program through recruiting, scouting and public relations. Courtesy Car Program member can also assist the department in attracting and retaining quality coaches and athletics personnel by providing a personal benefit for them common to most NCAA Division I athletic programs.[7]

Some universities, like Purdue University, report the value of the vehicles leased under these programs in the Royalties/Licensing/Advertising/Sponsorship category. However, it's not the case everywhere, and simply reading the NCAA disclosure will not distinguish for you which does and which does not.

Before Ohio State's athletic department opted for stipends in place of courtesy cars in 2012, 80-85 members of the athletic department, including the head coaches of all 36 varsity sports, upper-level athletic department administrators and select assistant coaches and support staff, received courtesy cars from as many as 65 different auto dealers.[8]

However, Ohio State did not include the value of these vehicles under Royalties/Licensing/Advertising/Sponsorship. Instead, each dealer paid $2,500 per year to be a member of the Buckeye Club, Ohio State's fundraising arm, which shows up under Contributions. The cars were considered taxable income and were included on the W2s of individual coaches based on the lease value of the vehicle they received.

It just goes to show there's more to a school's story than simple numbers reported on an NCAA disclosure.

Gift Assessments

Oregon is a good illustration of another transfer pricing practice. The University assesses a 5 percent fee on each gift that comes through the University of Oregon Foundation for athletics. Assessments on gifts made to athletics account for approximately 50 percent of all assessments collected by the University, which the University uses to fund central development personnel and operating costs throughout the University. In addition, the athletic department directly funds expenses related to athletic development.

Oregon is not unique in its assessment practices. While not a practice at every FBS school, others do assess gifts to athletics. UCLA, for example, has an even higher assessment at 6.5 percent. This fee is taken off the top before contribution revenues are reported on UCLA's NCAA disclosure, which means the amount you see is actually 93.5 percent of all contributions made to athletics.

On the United States Military Academy's NCAA disclosure, you're seeing only 88 percent of contributions, as the University assesses a 12 percent fee to fund central development, even though athletic foundation employees are employees of the athletic department.

Discounted Tickets

In addition to some of the transfer pricing highlighted above, the widespread practice of offering discounted tickets to football and basketball games can reduce athletic department revenue. For example, at Oregon faculty and staff are offered a 20 percent discount on season tickets, representing approximately $80,000 in revenue loss each season. Students receive an approximate 50 percent discount on football and basketball tickets, accounting for approximately $1.9 million in lost revenue.

It's important to note, however, that many schools offer these discounts, or even free tickets, in exchange for student fee allocations to the athletic department, which averaged $5.2 million per school in fiscal year 2011 for the 69 public schools at the FBS level that reported student fees as revenue. At some schools, students vote on these student fees in campus-wide referendums. At others, a select group of students vote on student fee allocations to the athletic department. In yet other instances, students have no direct involvement in the amount or allocation of student fees.

Examining athletic department financials in their entirety by taking into account the various transfer pricing practices requires access to detailed university financials. Two studies prior to Goff's had such access at Utah State University and Western Kentucky University and used that access to estimate what the athletic department's financials would look like if transfer pricing hadn't skewed the picture. The Utah State study showed the athletic department had a net profit of $366,000, whereas publicly reported figures showed a $700,000 loss.[9] The Western Kentucky study had similar results, showing a loss of $300,000, far less than the reported $1.2 million in losses.[10]

These numbers did not include merchandise revenue, which could have a much larger impact on more well-known universities where licensing revenue runs into the multiple millions of dollars.

Based on these previous studies and others, Goff reasons a conservative amount that can be added to the finances of an athletic department at a public university to account for transfer pricing is $800,000 and $1.5 million for private universities. Using this methodology, he finds that a mere 10 percent of athletic departments lose money. Furthermore, he finds 79 percent of schools exceed $1 million in net profits and 72 percent exceed $2 million.

Another factor that must be taken into consideration, according to Goff, is the not-for-profit environment of universities and athletic departments.

As in other not-for-profit settings, unit directors in universities (e.g., department chairs, deans, athletic directors) do not typically have an incentive to maximize profits (budget surpluses). If surpluses are experienced or anticipated, most unit directors increase expenditures in order to fully utilize their budgets. As a result, expenses rise to match, and often exceed, budgets regardless of revenue. So it should come as no surprise that expenses for even the largest revenue producers in college sports are frequently reported as equal to, or greater than, revenues, especially when relying on self-reported figures.[11]

Goff's theory is backed up by a study suggesting every $1.00 in increased spending by athletic departments corresponds with an average $1.10 increase in revenue. The study's authors say in statistical terms they are 95 percent confident every $1.00 in increased spending corresponds with increased revenue of $0.90 to $1.30, which is largely what we see in practice: athletic department revenue hovering very closely to athletic department expenses, with some slightly below breaking even and some slightly above.[12]

Another important thing to understand when discussing athletic department financials is the relationship between the university and the athletic department. For example, the University of Florida's athletic department is a separate corporate entity from the university. It is a 501(c)(3) corporation organized in the State of Florida under the name: The University Athletic Association, Inc.

In some instances, being a separate corporate entity allows the athletic department to operate without budgetary approval from the university. However, under Florida law, The University Athletic Association, Inc. is a "direct support organization," meaning it is organized and operated exclusively to receive, hold, invest and administer property and to make expenditures for the University of Florida.[13] As such, its budget must be approved by the President of the University, who has considerable influence and power.

The situation is very different at Ohio State University, whose athletic department is not a separate 501(c)(3) corporation, but instead an auxiliary unit. Auxiliary units at universities are generally self-sustaining units that provide goods or services to individuals, such as students, faculty/staff and the public, for a charge.

The budget for athletics at Ohio State does not require approval from the university president. Although the university's chief financial officer is kept apprised of the budget, it is approved by an athletics council comprised of eight faculty members, one staff member, four students and two alumni.

College administrators who discussed the subject estimated 30-40 percent of FBS programs are in a situation like Ohio State's where university-level budget approval is not required.

On the other end of the spectrum, Vanderbilt University has tried a model where there is no separate athletic department (and, for a few years, no athletic director). In 2003, then–chancellor of the university Gordon Gee folded the athletic department into the division of student life. There was no divide, real or perceived, between the university and athletics. Needless to say, the chancellor and other university administrators were involved in the athletics budgeting process.

The University of Notre Dame, a private school like Vanderbilt, has an athletic department but also participates in the university's budget process, meaning the university must approve the budget. Thomas J. Nevala, the senior associate athletic director for business operations at Notre Dame, says the athletic department has a net revenue target set by the University each year.

"Our budget only grows if we get approval to grow and we can meet the revenue target," Nevala explained. As you'll see in Chapter 10, the revenue target includes earmarking approximately $20 million in revenue for the University each year.

Due to the varied nature of the relationship between athletic departments and universities, the president may or may not have direct oversight of athletics budgets. Depending on that relationship and state law, the athletic department may be immune to state budget cuts, which sometimes impact the academic side of universities profoundly.

Unfortunately, all too often media reports compare academic budget cuts and athletic budget increases. Much more must be known about the circumstances of the university's relationship to the athletic department and state laws and regulations before those comparisons can be made, but all too often that research is not completed.

There is more to an athletic department's financial story than you see in black and white on an NCAA disclosure or EADA report. As you've seen, transfer pricing practices can change an athletic department's financial picture dramatically. In addition, apparel and services reported as revenue aren't revenue in the cash-in-the-bank sense.

Contributions, which would seem to be a straightforward category, can also be deceiving. Discussed earlier, some universities assess a fee on donations to athletics. In most cases, these fees are deducted before being reported as revenue on the NCAA disclosure, meaning the value you see is less than what was actually given by donors.

However, the contribution revenue you see might also be higher than the actual cash received by the department. A number of athletic departments include the value of in-kind merchandise—from apparel to complimentary hotel rooms to courtesy cars—as contributions. Others include it under the Licensing/Royalties/Advertising/Sponsorship category, as discussed earlier.

In addition, practices differ in terms of how funds are transferred from the fundraising arm to the athletic department.

For example, Mississippi State reported $0 for this category in 2009-2010. Does that mean the Bulldog Club, the athletic department's fundraising arm, didn't collect a single dime from donors that year?

Of course not. The athletic department simply didn't take a distribution from the Bulldog Club that year. Steve Corhern, the Assistant AD for Business Operations at Mississippi State at that time, credited the SEC's new television contract for covering the athletic department's needs that year. In 2009, the SEC began its first year of two new television deals: a 15-year $825 million deal with CBS and a 15-year $2.25 billion contract with ESPN. Per school conference distribution jumped from $11.0 million for the 2008-2009 school year to $17.4 million for 2009-2010.

The Bulldog Club undoubtedly raised millions of dollars that year, but because it's a separate entity its revenues are kept off the athletic department's NCAA disclosure. Some athletic departments only take what they need each year, while others receive all net revenue produced by the fundraising arm. Simply looking at the NCAA disclosure won't tell you which is the case for a particular university.

You now see that athletic department financials are far more complicated than what appears on an NCAA disclosure or EADA report. Beyond the question of whether athletic departments should be self-sustaining is the question of whether it's even possible to judge self-sustainability without full knowledge of an individual institution's transfer pricing practices.

As Chapter 1 has shown you, the athletic department doesn't always get the full benefit of the revenue it produces. So, perhaps the more surprising feat isn't that so many athletic departments aren't self-sustaining (by the traditional definition), but that any are.

NOTES

[1] Jonathan M. Orszag and Mark Israel (2009). *The Empirical Effects of Collegiate Athletics: An Update Based on 2004-2007 data.* Unpublished study commissioned by the National Collegiate Athletic Association.

[2] The Delta Cost Project. *Football Bowl Subdivision (FBS): Athletics spending and institutional funding to athletics growing faster than academic spending.* Retrieved November 11, 2011, from http://www.knightcommission.org/images/pdfs/2011_fig_fbs_10.19.11.pdf.

[3] A small number of universities are moving toward "responsibility-centered management," or the idea that each department should act as a separate business unit. The CFO of a large FBS institution says it's very difficult to implement in a pure form and is usually done as a hybrid model, attempting to allocate revenue and expenses by academic and auxiliary department. A university using this model might allocate building expenses to an academic department.

[4] Goff, Brian, "*Effects* of University Athletics on the University: A Review and Extension of Empirical Assessment," *Journal of Sport Management*, 96-97 (2000).

[5] RCW 28B.15.910

[6] Orszag and Israel, op.cit.

[7] University of Texas-El Paso, Miner's Club. Retrieved February 16, 2012, from http://www.utepathletics.com/sports/MAC/spec-rel/courtesy-car.html.

[8] May, Tim. "At OSU, coaches to get stipend, not car," *The Columbus Dispatch*, March 8, 2012. Available at: http://www.buckeyextra.com/content/stories/2012/03/08/at-osu-coaches-to-get-stipend-not-car.html.

[9] Skousen, C.R. & Condie, F.A., "Evaluating a sports program: Goalposts v. test tubes," *Managerial Accounting*, 60 (1988): 43-49.

[10] Borland, M.V., Goff, B.L. & Pulsinelli, R.W., "College athletics: Financial burden or boon?" In G. Scully (Ed.), *Advances in the Economics of Sport* (Greenwich, CT: JAI Press), 215-235.

[11] Goff, op.cit.

[12] Orszag and Israel, op.cit.

[13] Florida Statute 1004.28.

2

ARE COACHES OVERPAID AND BOWL APPEARANCES OVERRATED?

ebates over whether athletic departments should be self-sustaining focus almost exclusively on universities playing football at the highest level. Others in Division I, the Ivy League, Division II and Division III are rarely the focus of these debates, although none of them are known to generate net revenue independent of university assistance. It's simply accepted that athletics are part of the educational experience and funding is provided much as it would be for an arts or music program.

Perhaps if FBS schools were spending on the same level as the others, the debate would not have evolved to its current level. For example, the average salary for the head coach of a men's team at Division II school Georgia Southern University was $100,657 in 2010-2011. The average at a state school at the FBS level, University of Georgia, was $841,657.

That average is nowhere near what some FBS head football coaches are receiving. Bobby Petrino, who was fired from his post at University of Arkansas in early 2012 following the revelation he had hired his mistress to work in the athletic department, was averaging $3.53 million per year.

It can be argued Arkansas experienced an enormous return on its investment.

From former coach Houston Nutt's final season in 2007 to the 2010 season under Petrino, the Razorbacks saw donations to the football program rise a whopping 359 percent, with growth of more than 80 percent from 2009-10 to 2010-11, to $15.4 million. No other SEC school saw such growth in that time period: Auburn's donations increased by 15 percent, while Florida saw a 9.7 percent increase. Georgia came in lower at 3.9 percent, and LSU saw donations decrease by more than 13 percent.

While it's important to note that every athletic department handles donations differently —some schools only taking what they need each year from their fundraising pots—there's no arguing Arkansas saw a huge influx of cash during Petrino's tenure.

Football revenue overall rose by 54 percent during Petrino's first three years, to $61.1 million. Auburn, which won a national title during that time period, saw a 30 percent increase. LSU's revenue growth came in at 13 percent to $69.1 million.

Some of that success is attributed to Petrino putting teams on the field that had fan-friendly high-powered offenses.

"Under Petrino, the team averaged 94 percent capacity for home games. It was only 91 percent under [Houston] Nutt," said Scott Prather, one of the founders of CoachesbytheNumbers.com, a website dedicated to gathering statistical data on football coaches. "If you figure each ticket at an average of $50 per ticket, that's nearly $600,000 per year."

During Petrino's tenure the athletic department also saw licensing revenue jump from $2.3 million in 2007-2008 to $8.0 million in 2010-2011. Arkansas became part of the IMG College family in 2009, a company that manages the Razorbacks' athletic publications, sponsorships and licensing, and signed a new contract with Nike in 2010.

Not convinced of the difference a coach can make? With virtually the exact same team as the previous season, the 2012 Razorbacks football team started the season with a stunning defeat at the hands of Louisiana-Monroe (a so-called have-not in the world of big-time college football). By the end of the season, the Razorbacks were a disappointing 4-8, after beginning the season ranked 8th in the nation in the AP Poll.

Besides a humiliating finish to what was billed as a season with the potential to produce a BCS bowl appearance, what other costs were associated with the loss? As you'll see in Chapter 10, a study has shown that a top 10 finish in the AP Poll at the end of the season translates to a 4.4 percent increase in enrollment. Even if the Razorbacks had slipped past the top 10, a top 20 finish would be predicted to increase enrollment by 3.4 percent.

Using Arkansas' 19,027 undergraduate enrollment for the fall of 2011, a 4.4 percent increase would mean 837 students. Assuming enrollment increased such that the percentage of residents vs. non-residents vs. foreign students stayed the same as Arkansas' 2011 fall enrollment, those additional 837 students would mean about $9.6 million more in tuition and fees for each year those students remained enrolled.

Does Petrino's $3.53 million a year salary still sound exorbitant to you?

The sword cuts both ways sometimes, as University of North Carolina found out following NCAA violations for improper benefits and academic misconduct. Although head football coach Butch Davis survived the NCAA investigation, the University decided too much damage had been done to its reputation to keep Davis. Unlike Petrino, Davis was fired without cause, which meant the University could end up owing him over $2.7 million. In addition, commentators believe UNC will experience decreases in donations and ticket sales, money it was counting on when a $70 million renovation project began on Kenan Stadium in 2010.[1]

Davis' initial contract with UNC was worth $1.86 million per year. As is the case with many coaches, very little of that was being directly paid by the University: $286,000 per year plus a $25,000 expense account. The Rams Club, the athletic department's fundraising arm, covered $1-1.3 million per year, and supplemental contracts with Learfield Communications and Nike amounted to $400,000 per year.

At the end of his second season at UNC, Davis was being credited with attendance increases that averaged 9,000 per game, leading to a $3 million increase in ticket sales in 2008.

So, while Davis seemed to be producing more than he cost while he was head coach, his dismissal impacted the athletic department's finances negatively in a way that still has yet to be fully calculated so soon after his departure.

In the end, are FBS head coaches overpaid, particularly at the top level? It's a more complicated question than is intended to be answered here. It has been estimated that on average only 25 percent of a head coach's salary is paid for by the university, with the bulk coming from outside sources as in Butch Davis' contract.[2]

It seems cyclical: an athletic department pays more to hire a coach who can increase revenue streams, then as the athletic department makes more money it spends more money to keep the coach or hire better assistants.

Perhaps this goes back to Goff's theory on nonprofit functionality. When an athletic department makes more money, it's going to spend more money. The myth, however, is that it spends all that money on football. As you'll see in this chapter, that's not true.

Revenue Sports

Each FBS institution must sponsor at least 16 sports per NCAA guidelines. Only rarely do sports other than football and men's basketball produce a net profit, meaning at least fourteen sports are producing net losses at virtually every school. Many in non-AQ conferences don't even produce a net profit in football or men's basketball without student fees, meaning every sport produces a net loss.

Why are most sports losing money? Many of those sports see little demand for tickets, either generating very little revenue or offering contests free to the public.

For example, University of Florida reported revenue for seven men's sports and ten women's sports in 2010-2011. Only four men's sports (football, basketball, baseball and track and field/cross country) and four women's sports (basketball, gymnastics, track and field/cross country and volleyball) generated ticket revenue. A total of $20.9 million of Florida's revenue was attributed to ticket sales, but just $509,974 of it was from sports other than football and men's basketball.

The majority of contributions received by an athletic department are generated from donation requirements tied to ticket purchases, sometimes referred to as ticket-related contributions. As you've seen, not many sports produce demand for tickets, which translates to a lack of contributions for those programs.

Sticking with our University of Florida example, only four men's sports and four women's sports generated contributions in 2010-2011. Men's and women's swimming account for two of those sports and only generated a combined $1,000. Not surprisingly, 94 percent of the $39.4 million in donations received that year for a specific sport were for football. An additional $2.6 million was donated without a specific sport designation.

Just because football brought in the money doesn't mean it spends all the money. At Florida, total expenses for football were far less than the contributions received that year at $26.5 million. The football program had a net profit of $46.5 million after figuring in all operating revenue and expenses. That money wasn't deposited away until the next football season, it was spent on other department expenses.

Athletic departments that show net revenue on the books have one thing in common: a football program with net profits great enough to cover the operating expenses of every other sport. Below is a look at the net profit or loss of each sport at University of Florida for the 2010-2011 school year.

University of Florida

Men's Sports

	Revenue	Expense	Net Profit
Football	$73,007,236.00	$26,463,539.00	$46,543,697.00
Basketball	$10,155,796.00	$9,293,107.00	$862,689.00
Baseball	$1,164,619.00	$2,863,976.00	($1,699,357.00)
Tennis	$160,858.00	$853,770.00	($692,912.00)
Golf	$164,903.00	$679,393.00	($514,490.00)
Swimming	$143,966.00	$1,442,280.00	($1,298,314.00)
Track and Field/X-Country	$67,822.00	$1,784,425.00	($1,716,603.00)

Women's Sports

	Revenue	Expense	Net Profit
Golf	$38,438.00	$510,794.00	($472,356.00)
Basketball	$178,990.00	$3,043,356.00	($2,864,366.00)
Tennis	$147,274.00	$1,088,770.00	($941,496.00)
Soccer	$234,947.00	$1,615,044.00	($1,380,097.00)
Volleyball	$546,468.00	$2,187,283.00	($1,640,815.00)
Softball	$235,584.00	$1,785,564.00	($1,549,980.00)
Gymnastics	$167,987.00	$1,680,268.00	($1,512,281.00)
Lacrosse	$459,792.00	$1,403,427.00	($943,635.00)
Swimming	$143,963.00	$1,546,089.00	($1,402,126.00)
Track and Field/X-Country	$67,821.00	$1,884,577.00	($1,816,756.00)

As you can see, most sports at University of Florida do not produce enough revenue to sustain themselves. Taking football and men's basketball out of the equation, each sport loses $1.4 million, on average.

It might also be helpful to see a breakdown of revenue and expenses for a non-revenue producing sport. Let's take gymnastics at Florida, for example:

REVENUE

Ticket Sales	$23,849
Student Fees	$0
Guarantees	$0
Contributions	$0
Compensation and Benefits Provided by a Third Party	$0
Direct State or Other Government Support	$0
Direct Institutional Support	$0

Indirect Facilities and Administrative Support	$0
NCAA/Conference Distributions (including all tournament revenues)	$0
Broadcast, Television, Radio and Internet Rights	$0
Program Sales, Concessions, Novelty Sales and Parking	$6,613
Royalties, Licensing, Advertisements and Sponsorships	$0
Sports Camp Revenues	$137,525
Endowment and Investment Income	$0
Other Operating Revenue	$0
TOTAL	$167,987

EXPENSE	
Athletic Student Aid	$427,120
Guarantees	$0
Head Coaching Salaries, Benefits and Bonuses Paid by University and Related Entities	$264,515
Assistant Coaching Salaries, Benefits and Bonuses Paid by University and Related Entities	$219,584
Coaching Other Compensation and Benefits Paid by a Third Party	$0
Support Staff/Administrative Salaries, Benefits and Bonuses	$53,798
Severance Payments	$0
Recruiting	$39,843
Team Travel	$189,768
Equipment, Uniforms and Supplies	$58,056
Game Expenses	$70,210
Fund Raising, Marketing and Promotion	$113,836
Sports Camp Expenses	$71,316
Direct Facilities, Maintenance and Rental	$105,907
Spirit Groups	$0
Indirect Facilities and Administrative Support	$0
Medical Expense and Medical Insurance	$27,427
Memberships and Dues	$0
Other Operating Expenses	$38,888
TOTAL	$1,680,268

NET REVENUE	($1,512,281)

The total revenue gymnastics produces is only enough to cover 39 percent of the student aid the athletic department must remit to the university to cover the tuition and room and board of gymnastics athletes. Like most sports, its revenue doesn't even cover the aid for its own athletes, much less the cost of coaches, traveling, hosting meets, medical insurance and other necessary expenses.

This is where football comes into the financial picture. At many, but not all, FBS schools, football absorbs the losses of at least a portion of the other sports. Schools like Florida produce enough net revenue from football to cover the operating expenses of all other sports. At other schools, student fees or direct institutional support must carry a larger share of the burden when football net revenues aren't enough.

We all talk about the "business" of college athletics, but many make the mistake of analyzing it as if it's a for-profit business. College athletics has very little in common with a for-profit company.

To illustrate, what would a for-profit company look like if it was run like a college athletic department?

Let's say The Coca-Cola Company is a college athletic department. Coca-Cola brand is football and Diet Coke is men's basketball. Mr. Pibb, Fanta and all the other Coca-Cola Company brands represent gymnastics, soccer, lacrosse and every other collegiate sport.

In this analogy, all of the sodas except Coca-Cola and Diet Coke cost more to make than they produce in revenue. Would The Coca-Cola Company keep producing these brands if they lost more than they made year after year? Unlikely.

The Coca-Cola Company's objective is to maximize profits for its shareholders. It also has no governing body forcing it to produce a minimum number of products. Those two facts alone make it completely unlike a college athletic department.

When we think about college athletics, we think about big-time football programs and the millions they make. Rarely, however, do we pull back the curtain and take a look at where those millions are going. We hear about coaching salaries (a large portion of which may be funded by third parties like apparel companies, as discussed previously) or recruiting expenses, but not what it takes to run all the non-revenue producing sports in the athletic department.

Postseason Play

Another area of FBS football finances that is highly scrutinized is the money lost from football teams' participation in bowl games. Although bowl games all have payouts for the participants, most also have a minimum ticket purchase required by the schools. Factor in payouts going to the conference to be split amongst all member schools, and the end result is that many institutions lose money on the experience.

Following the 2011 season, San Diego State University played in the New Orleans Bowl. The Aztecs payout for the bowl was $500,000, which went to the Mountain West Conference. Although SDSU only received $248,000 in bowl revenue from the conference, additional income from travel reimbursements from the conference and ticket sales produced total revenue of $898,380.

That sounds pretty good considering the bowl payout was only $500,000, right?

That's only because we haven't talked about the expenses yet. SDSU failed to sell $71,420 of its ticket allotment, eating into its profit. When you factor in travel costs, bonuses earned by coaches and other expenses associated with the bowl, SDSU lost over $260,000. See the table below for a full list of all revenue and expenses.

SDSU bowl expenses

- Transportation: $565,792

- Staff bonuses: $192,000

- Meals and lodging: $185,850

- Entertainment: $7,635

- Promotion: $25,580

- Awards: $42,250

- Equipment: $70,607

- Tickets absorbed: $71,420

- Total: $1.16 million

SDSU bowl revenue

- League expense reimbursement:$596,800

- League bowl distribution: $248,000

- Tickets sold: $53,580

- Total: $898,380

"Clearly we don't want to lose the money," associate athletic director for business operations at SDSU, Chuck Lang, told the *San Diego Union-Tribune* after the Aztecs' trip to the New Orleans Bowl, "but I think it's worth it."[3]

As you'll see in Chapter 10, bowl appearances can have a positive indirect benefit for a university. The increased exposure in newspapers, not to mention the national television appearance during the bowl game itself, can improve recruiting, both for athletes and non-athletes. Schools have also experienced increases in other areas as well, such as licensing.

When viewing these numbers, perhaps the correct question is whether SDSU could have mounted a national advertising campaign that would have reached the same number of people for the $260,000 it lost on its New Orleans Bowl appearance.

Other bowl appearances have produced far larger losses on paper. On January 1, 2009, Virginia Tech beat Cincinnati in the Orange Bowl. Unfortunately, the financial picture doesn't make the Hokies look like a winner.

As a BCS bowl game, the Orange Bowl had one of the largest payouts in 2009 at approximately $17 million. However, it also required participating schools to buy 17,500 tickets at $125 each. Virginia Tech sold just 3,342 of those tickets, amounting to a $1.77 million loss.

A simple internet search returns a number of articles referencing the Hokies' $1.77 million loss for the 2009 Orange Bowl. However, what isn't reported by most is that the ACC absorbed $1.34 million of the unsold tickets. That's in addition to the $1.6 million allowance from the conference.

In the end, Virginia Tech had a net loss of $875,154. That loss was more than covered by the ACC's distribution of all conference bowl revenue, which totaled over $1.5 million.

Entire books have been written on the bowl system, which expand far beyond what is covered here. What hasn't been written about are the costs associated with postseason competition for other sports. For most sports, it's a given that postseason competition will be a losing venture financially.

To illustrate, let's take a look at the postseason financials of every sport at University of Florida. Keep in mind, with the exception of football, men's and women's basketball and baseball, the only revenue generated is from hosting postseason events.

As you'll see, the expenses often outweigh the income.

	Revenue	Expense	Profit
Football			
SEC Championship	$1,272,586	$7,624	$1,264,962
Bowl Game	$2,607,362	$1,364,079	$1,243,283
		Profit/Loss	**$2,508,245**
Men's Basketball			
SEC Tournament	$444,734	$145,804	$298,930
NCAA Tournament	$2,093,099	$195,814	$1,897,285
		Profit/Loss	**$2,196,215**
Baseball			
SEC Tournament	**$18,034**	**$25,331**	**($7,297)**
NCAA Regionals (host)	$91,660	$101,547	($9,887)
NCAA Super Regionals (host)	$68,009	$71,427	($3,418)
NCAA Championships	$0	$226,976	($226,976)
		Profit/Loss	**($247,578)**
Men's and Women's Tennis			
Men's SEC Championship (host)	$8,282	$19,630	($11,348)
Women's SEC Championship	$0	$17,771	($17,771)
Men's and Women's NCAA Regionals (host)	$9,301	$3,171	$6,130
Men's NCAA Championship	$0	$29,454	($29,454)
Women's NCAA Championship	$0	$36,431	($36,431)
		Profit/Loss	**($88,874)**
Men's Golf			
SEC Championship	$0	$6,355	($6,355)
NCAA Regionals (host)	$16,667	$18,936	($2,269)
NCAA Championship	$0	$7,520	($7,520)
		Profit/Loss	**($16,144)**
Men's and Women's Swimming			
SEC Championship (host)	$73,735	$153,959	($80,224)
NCAA Championship	$0	$67,291	($67,291)
		Profit/Loss	**($147,515)**
Men's and Women's Track			
SEC Championship	$0	$183,929	($183,929)
NCAA Championship	$0	$255,026	($255,026)
		Profit/Loss	**($438,955)**

Women's Golf

SEC Championship	$0	$3,695	($3,695)
NCAA Championship	$0	$8,032	($8,032)
		Profit/Loss	**($11,727)**

Women's Basketball

SEC Tournament	$0	$71,735	($71,735)
NIT - 1st Round (host)	$1,054	$68,525	($67,471)
		Profit/Loss	**($139,206)**

Women's Soccer

SEC Championship	$0	$37,336	($37,336)
NCAA - 1st/2nd Rounds (host)	$5,361	$8,888	($3,527)
NCAA Championship	$0	($747)	$747
		Profit/Loss	**($40,116)**

Women's Volleyball

NCAA - 1st/2nd Rounds (host)	$15,378	$27,506	($12,128)
NCAA Regionals (host)	$0	$241	($241)
NCAA Championship	$0	$25,834	($25,834)
		Profit/Loss	**($38,203)**

Softball

SEC Championship	$0	$25,652	($25,652)
NCAA Regionals (host)	$17,105	$23,661	($6,556)
NCAA Super Regionals (host)	$14,708	$17,531	($2,823)
NCAA Championships	$0	$102,664	($102,664)
		Profit/Loss	**($137,695)**

Women's Gymnastics

SEC Tournament	$0	$29,995	($29,995)
NCAA Regionals	$0	$0	$0
NCAA Championship	$0	$64,733	($64,733)
		Profit/Loss	**($94,728)**

Women's Lacrosse

NCAA - 1st Round (host)	$2,037	$6,956	($4,919)
NCAA - 2nd Round (host)	$2,192	$4,227	($2,035)
ALC Championship		$36,458	($36,458)
NCAA Championship		($1,877)	$1,877
		Profit/Loss	**($41,535)**

The reported expenses shown above are expenses incurred above and beyond any NCAA expense reimbursement.

Taking football and men's basketball out of the equation, which both showed a net profit from postseason play for Florida in 2010-2011, the average postseason net loss per sport was over $120,000. Total losses, not including football and men's basketball, were over $1.4 million. However, once you factor in the revenue from football and men's basketball postseason distributions, Florida had a net profit of $3.3 million on postseason participation.

There are a couple of things to note with respect to Florida's postseason financial picture. First, Florida hosted quite a few postseason contests. As mentioned previously, this is virtually the only way sports outside of football, men's and women's basketball and baseball produce revenue. With that in mind, Florida isn't necessarily representative of the average FBS school. It is a school, however, which produces very detailed audited financials, available to the public, that we can use for analysis.

Second, being in an AQ conference, Florida receives a much larger bowl distribution than a non-AQ school, which goes a long way toward allowing the athletic department to show a net profit for postseason play. Accordingly, it's not hard to imagine how many non-AQ schools lose money on postseason participation across all sports.

If most sports lose money in postseason competition, why is all the focus always on the money schools lose playing postseason football? Again, it all comes back to television. Just as the highly publicized television deals discussed in the first chapter lead to assumptions about the ability of athletic departments to be self-sustainable, the figures attached to bowl television contracts set the stage for high expectations in terms of the profitability of bowl games.

As of 2012, ESPN paid a reported $125 million per year for the national championship, Fiesta, Orange and Sugar Bowls. ESPN/ABC had a separate contract with the Rose Bowl for $30 million per year. Together, the BCS bowl games brought in $155 million per year.

However, BCS payouts alone total more than is brought in by television revenue. Here's a look at the payouts for the 2011-2012 season, straight from the BCS Media Guide:

- The share for an automatic qualifier from one of the five non-AQ conferences (i.e., a conference without annual automatic qualification) will be approximately $26.4 million—18 percent of the net revenue. (Those conferences have elected to divide the revenue among themselves according to a formula they have devised.)

- If no team from the non-AQ conferences participates, those conferences would receive approximately $13.2 million—9 percent of the net BCS revenue.

- The net share for the automatic-qualifying team from each AQ conference will be approximately $22.3 million.

- The share for each team selected at-large by one of the bowls will be $6.1 million.

- Notre Dame will receive $6.1 million if it participates in a BCS game; its share will be approximately $1.8 million if it does not—1/66th of the net BCS revenue.

- Each FCS conference will receive $250,000.

- If Army, Navy or BYU becomes an automatic qualifier or is selected at-large, it will receive $6.1 million; if not selected, each will receive $100,000.

Let's take a look at how it played out for the 2011-2012 season:

National Championship: LSU vs. Alabama

Rose Bowl: Wisconsin vs. Oregon

Orange Bowl: West Virginia vs. Clemson

Fiesta Bowl: Stanford vs. Oklahoma State

Sugar Bowl: Michigan vs. Virginia Tech

The AQ conferences alone took home $133.8 million right off the top, $22.3 million each for their automatic-qualifiers: LSU, Wisconsin, Oklahoma State, West Virginia, Clemson and Stanford.

Although Alabama is from an AQ conference, LSU was the automatic-qualifier from the SEC because they were the conference champion. Alabama was considered an at-large selection, and the SEC received $6.1 million for their participation in the national championship.

The same is true for Oregon, Michigan and Virginia Tech. Each is from an AQ conference, but was considered at-large bids because there can only be one automatic-qualifier from each conference. Therefore, each brought $6.1 million in for their conference.

No non-AQ was selected for a BCS bowl, so those conferences split $13.2 million. Notre Dame received $1.8 million and BYU, Army and Navy each received $100,000. Additionally, each of the 13 FCS conferences received $250,000 for a total of $3.25 million.

The grand total for 2011-2012 is $176.75 million, well above the television revenue of $155 million. Although the television money sounds huge, you can see how quickly it goes. Of course, this doesn't take into consideration any revenue from ticket sales, sponsorships, contributions and other sources of revenue for the BCS bowls.

Going back to the San Diego State example discussed earlier in the chapter, not all bowl games produce that kind of revenue. Audited financials filed by the New Orleans Bowl, Inc. for the year ending December 31, 2010 show television and radio revenue of $144,000. Total revenue from all sources was $2.5 million.

Payouts alone accounted for $650,000 of the bowl's expenses. After factoring in operating costs and other expenses, the bowl showed net assets of $610,000 at the end of the year.

San Diego State lost over $260,000 on their New Orleans Bowl appearance, but chances are most of its sports lost money on their postseason appearances. Few, if any, of those competitions would have received television time and certainly not on national television.

Another sport that offers national television coverage of its postseason is baseball. In 2011, the College World Series drew over 3,000 more fans per session than March Madness. The real difference between the two postseason tournaments is television viewership. March Madness averaged 10.2 million viewers in 2011. Although every game of the College World Series airs on ESPN or ESPN2, viewers averaged just 1.3 million per game on ESPN and 999,000 per game on ESPN2.

Due to obvious viewership differences, revenue from the College World Series television deal pales in comparison to March Madness, which brings in an average of $771 million per year. The baseball tournament is part of a three-year deal with 20 other NCAA championships worth $55 million total.

Unlike March Madness, schools that participated in the College World Series took home no share of the revenue produced by the event, save travel reimbursements. Those reimbursements are not always enough to cover expenses. For example, Florida was left with expenses of over $226,000 not covered by the NCAA following its second-place finish in the 2011 tournament. That's only slightly less than San Diego State lost playing in the New Orleans Bowl.

Although over 321,000 fans attended games during the 2011 tournament, no money from ticket sales or other revenue was distributed to the participating teams. The NCAA divides the money with the host in Omaha and uses the remainder to cover various organization expenses.

The NCAA's treatment of the College World Series is not unlike its procedure for postseason competitions in every sport except football and basketball. As shown earlier in the chapter, Florida experienced losses for participating in the postseason in those other sports, as most schools do. This is the uniqueness of college athletics. Activities are not always about profit. Schools do not send their teams to postseason play in volleyball or soccer because it earns them money. In fact, more often it costs the schools money. They do it for the student athletes, to give them a goal during the season and a reward at the end.

NOTES

[1] Jones, Jonathan, "Butch Davis' firing will deliver major financial blow to UNC," *SI.com* (July 28, 2011). Retrieved November 24, 2011, from http://sportsillustrated.cnn.com/2011/football/ncaa/07/28/butch-davis-unc/index.html.

[2] Yost, Mark, *Varsity Green* (Stanford, CA: Stanford University Press, 2010), 115.

[3] Schrotenboer, Matt,"SDSU lost money on bowl game," *San Diego Union-Tribune* (April 4, 2012). Retrieved February 24, 2012, from http://www.utsandiego.com/news/2012/apr/04/sdsu-takes-money-loss-bowl-game/.

WHY STUDENT ATHLETES CAN NEVER BE PAID

One of the greatest paradoxes of college sports fandom is simultaneously wanting athletic departments to be self-sustaining and wanting greater compensation for student athletes.

With a playoff on the horizon, the most hotly debated topic left for college football fans to debate is whether college athletes should be paid. When it comes to paying college athletes, let's be clear. Fans only care about football, and to a smaller degree men's basketball, players. We'll get to why that's an issue later on in the chapter.

Proponents of paying college football players point to the millions of dollars in net revenue some football program post. As was discussed in the previous chapter, the top programs make tens of millions of dollars on football. However, contrary to popular belief, it does not sit in a vault marked "Football Only" waiting to enrich the football program. At some schools, it funds the operating expenses of every other sport. When it doesn't, the athletic department is forced to turn to other sources such as student fees.

Paying players isn't as simple as proponents would have you believe. It's not just about athletic departments finding the money in their budget or the NCAA changing its notion of amateurism. In fact, it's such a Pandora's box that even if the NCAA decided players *should* be paid that doesn't mean they *could* be paid.

Pay-For-Play, Meet Title IX

Let me introduce you to one of the largest, if not insurmountable, roadblocks to paying players: Title IX. Before we go any further, I should clarify that Title IX is not an NCAA regulation that can simply be revised if the NCAA modified its regulations to allow college athletes to be compensated. Title IX is a federal law, and there's no reason to believe it's going anywhere. In fact, its 40th anniversary was celebrated with much fanfare in 2012.

Most fans know Title IX requires comparable treatment of female student athletes when it comes to collegiate athletics, and a great many also know about the so-called three-prong test for compliance, which looks at proportionality, history of the program or full accommodation of interests. What many don't seem to not know, however, is that the three-prong test only covers one of three requirements for Title IX compliance.

The three requirement areas are: Participation, Athletic Financial Assistance and Treatment of Athletes.

First, there's the three-prong test many of you know, which falls under Participation. This area basically measures the opportunities for female vs. male athletes. Institutions can show they comply with this area by meeting one of the following prongs:

- Proportionality: the institution can show that it offers opportunities for females and males based on their respective enrollment numbers at the university.

- History and Program Expansion: the institution can show that it has continued to offer new and additional opportunities as the needs of the underrepresented sex have risen.

- Full accommodation of interests and abilities: the institution can show that the current offerings fully meet the interest level of the underrepresented sex.

Fans believe this three-prong test that is part of the first requirement of Title IX is the only test for compliance because it is the portion of the test most often focused on by the media. Generally, when reports surface that a school is in danger of not complying with Title IX, it is because they're being accused of not meeting one of these three prongs.

If the three-prong test of the first requirement was all there was to Title IX, it's easy to see why fans don't understand how paying only football players would create an issue. The problems become more apparent when you look at the second and third requirements of Title IX.

The second requirement for compliance is entitled Athletic Financial Assistance. The only express requirement under this section is that scholarships be allocated proportionately in accordance with the number of female vs. male athletes.

Here's how the math is calculated under this section. The total amount of aid awarded to male athletes is divided by the total amount of aid awarded to all athletes. The same is then done for female athletes.

For example, in 2010-2011 Virginia Tech had total aid of $9,027,685. Of that, $5,591,672 was awarded to male athletes and $3,436,013 to female athletes. The percentages come out at 61.94 percent and 38.06 percent, respectively.

Now you look at the unduplicated count of male athletes versus the total number of unduplicated athletes and then do the same for the female athletes. For example, if an athlete competes on both the football and baseball teams he only counts once for this calculation.

At Virginia Tech in 2010-2011, the unduplicated count of male athletes was 358 and female was 204, registering at 63.07 percent and 36.30 percent, respectively.

The test for Athletic Financial Assistance is whether financial assistance is provided in a substantially proportionate manner. There is no set percentage deemed appropriate, instead it is reviewed on a case-by-case basis.

In our example at Virginia Tech, male athletes account for 63.70 percent of all athletes and receive 61.94 percent of all aid. Female athletes account for 36.30 percent of all athletes and receive 38.06 percent of all aid. There would seem to be an argument to be made there that it's substantially proportionate.

Now that you know what the math looks like, here are two different discussions to be had based on what the proposed pay-for-play plan looks like: (i) cost-of-attendance increases for scholarships, and (ii) other types of payment.

During the summer of 2011, Big Ten Commissioner Jim Delaney and SEC Commissioner Mike Slive, commissioners of arguably the two most powerful conferences in college football, made statements supporting the increase of scholarships to cover cost of attendance. Currently, athletes on full scholarship receive free tuition, room and board. Cost of attendance is often described as the amount necessary to cover all of a full-time student's reasonable expenses for the year. It would cover things like gas or other transportation costs and laundry money.

Each school individually determines its cost of attendance. Some use figures from the federal government and some use student surveys to determine the amount. There's also variance for expenses like health insurance or a computer, if the school requires students to have a computer. The number is much higher at a school located in an expensive city like Los Angeles than one in Bowling Green, Kentucky.

The potential for artificially inflating the figure aside, cost of attendance increases would be considered a part of the athlete's scholarship. Largely, the proposals for cost of attendance increases have been advocated for all student athletes, not just those in revenue sports. If the increase was the same for every scholarship athlete in proportion to their scholarship, the percentages under the Athletic Financial Assistance section would remain unchanged.

If, however, a school decided (and the NCAA allowed it) to award the extra cost of attendance money only to football and basketball players, schools might have problems with Title IX compliance. Let's take a look at what happens to Virginia Tech's numbers if only football and men's basketball players received the increase.

According to a study by *USA Today*, Virginia Tech's added costs to go to cost of attendance would be $3,891 per student athlete.[1] NCAA limits football scholarships to 85 student athletes and men's basketball to 13. If those 98 scholarship athletes received the additional cost of attendance figure of $3,891 each, it would add $381,318 to the male financial aid used in the calculations for compliance detailed earlier in the chapter.

Using those figures, male financial aid would represent 63.48 percent of all aid and female financial aid would amount to 36.52 percent. Based on Virginia Tech's unduplicated participation numbers, males represent 63.70 percent and females 36.30 percent. On the surface, it would seem Virginia Tech would remain in compliance. However, other schools might come out on the wrong end of that equation.

Many Title IX scholars believe courts would step in, even if the mathematics work out like the Virginia Tech example. Much of Title IX has been shaped by courts' interpretation of the law, not simply the black and white letter of the law. Add that to the vague nature of the "substantially proportionate" language, and courts have a lot of leeway in these cases. Previous courts have emphasized that the spirit of the law stands for male and female athletes being awarded the same *opportunities*. Few believe compensating only those athletes in revenue sports would pass muster in a court of law, and as you'll see later in the chapter, Title IX investigations and lawsuits are extremely easy to initiate.

If a pay-for-play plan could survive the courtroom, the next question is whether schools could afford to implement the plan. At SEC Media Days in July 2011, Commissioner Mike Slive noted the difficulty some institutions would have if scholarships were increased to cover cost of attendance: "We recognize that this proposal may be a financial hardship on some, yet at the same time economics cannot always be the reason to avoid doing what is in the best interests of our student athletes."

Only five of the SEC's twelve member institutions are self-sustaining by NCAA definition, meaning student fees, institutional support or government support are necessary to balance the budget. Right off the bat over half of Slive's members have no net revenue to pay increased scholarship costs.

The cost to each school in the SEC would vary widely because cost of attendance is school-specific and takes into account a number of variables at each institution. According to a *USA Today* study, the average cost (found by averaging the cost for an in-state and out-of-state student) at Kentucky would be the lowest at $2,610 per scholarship athlete for a grand total of $664,405. The price would be much higher at South Carolina at $6,844 per scholarship athlete for a total of $1,678,080 in additional expenses.[2] Neither school was self-sustaining in

2010-2011. According to financial statements for Kentucky's athletic department, $440,819 of the total $819,124 in student fees it received was necessary to balance the budget for the 2010-2011 school year. South Carolina needed $1,584,163 of the $2,146,393 it received in student fees in 2010-2011 to balance its athletic department budget.

There are schools in other conferences that rely on as much as $18.8 million in student fees to balance their budget (see Chart 3.1 for the top 25 athletic departments in terms of the dollar amount received from student fees). What will athletic departments do if there is a conference mandate to increase scholarships to cover cost of attendance, or even simply pressure to do so to stay competitive in recruiting?

Chart 3.1
Top 25 Student Fee Recipients at Public FBS Institutions (2010-2011)

	School	Amount	% of Total Revenue Received
1	Central Florida	$18,818,806.00	44%
2	Akron	$17,698,300.00	69%
3	Florida International	$16,931,986.00	71%
4	South Florida	$15,231,708.00	36%
5	Miami Ohio	$14,172,373.00	53%
6	Virginia	$12,973,298.00	17%
7	Kent State	$12,151,130.00	57%
8	East Carolina.	$11,187,866.00	33%
9	Bowling Green	$10,676,975.00	53%
10	Florida Atlantic	$10,425,354.00	54%
11	Toledo	$10,125,436.00	52%
12	San Diego St	$9,729,474.00	22%
13	Maryland	$9,508,278.00	15%
14	Ball State.	$9,157,741.00	45%
15	Rutgers	$9,032,350.00	15%
16	N. Illinois.	$8,769,232.00	36%
17	Memphis	$8,757,769.00	22%
18	Connecticut	$8,744,642.00	14%
19	Mid. Tenn. State	$8,342,547.00	31%
20	Buffalo	$7,874,074.00	30%
21	Florida State	$7,528,006.00	10%
22	Virginia Tech	$7,237,091.00	11%
23	North Carolina	$7,006,090.00	9%
24	Western Kentucky	$6,521,111.00	29%
25	Southern Miss.	$6,056,608.00	29%

Data obtained from individual school NCAA financial statements.

Another wrinkle with increasing scholarships to cover cost of attendance is that it could *disadvantage* the student athlete financially. A compliance department official at an FBS school explained the situation like this:

> If you look at the federal guidelines for financial aid, schools are not allowed to award a student beyond their cost of attendance.
>
> But currently, a full scholarship student athlete with a cost of attendance of say $20,000 and a full athletic grant-in-aid of $17,000 would be able to receive an additional $5,500 in Pell Grant (if eligible) bringing his/her total scholarship/financial aid package to $22,500 without being in violation of federal law. Pell Grants are excluded and can allow a student to go over cost of attendance. Now if schools offered a 100% cost of attendance athletic scholarship, the same student would only be able to receive $20,000. They would have a shortfall of $2,500. In order to maximize this for the "good of the student athlete" you would have to reduce the 100% scholarship in order to award the student his/her entitled Pell Grant.

For those who aren't familiar with Pell Grants, they do not have to be repaid by the recipient and are based on financial need. However, you can only apply for a Pell Grant if your award package is below cost of attendance. If you're eligible, you receive a flat $5,500, which in many cases can take you over cost of attendance. Thus, student athletes with demonstrated financial need could actually lose money if scholarships covered cost of attendance.

We've covered increasing scholarships to cover cost of attendance, but what if players are paid in some other fashion outside of their scholarship? Maybe University of South Carolina football players receive $300 each from the pocket of Steve Spurrier (his idea at the SEC's Spring Meetings in June 2011). Or perhaps boosters donate to a fund to pay student athletes.

In the eyes of Title IX, it's all the same. The Office of Civil Rights has previously offered this interpretation with regards to boosters or other donors who donate funds for specified sports: "a school cannot use earmarked funds as an economic justification for discrimination."

In other words, the school can honor the sport-specific designation for such donated funds, but it still must comply with the proportionality requirement. It cannot dedicate those funds to football, throwing the proportionality out of whack, and then say they had to do so because the funds were earmarked. The excess funds that cannot be applied simply have to be put aside for the future, or they can be applied and revenue from other sources can be moved out of football in order to maintain compliance.

Similarly, funds of any type cannot be used to provide greater benefits to male athletes than female athletes under the third and final requirement: Other Program Areas.

Other Program Areas basically looks at how athletes of both sexes are treated in terms of facilities, support and benefits. The following 11 criteria are looked at in their totality for each sex:

- Locker Rooms, Practice and Competitive Facilities: this is self-explanatory. It looks at the facilities provided for both practice and competition from the locker room to the playing surface to practice facilities.

- Equipment and Supplies: again, self-explanatory. The quality, amount, availability, etc. of equipment and supplies will be reviewed.

- Scheduling of Games and Practice Times: this factor looks at everything from opportunities provided for practice, competition, preseason and postseason to the time of day practices and competitions are held.

- Publicity: this covers everything from the publications produced for each sport to the resources devoted to promoting each sport.

- Coaching: this covers the number of coaches for each sport, the expertise of those coaches, their compensation, etc. When compensation is considered, they look to a number of factors, so don't get carried away with the fact that football and men's basketball coaches tend to make more. Not only are there a number of things considered under just this factor, but this factor is only one of 11 that are viewed in their totality.

- Travel and Daily Allowance: not only are the monetary figures considered, but also the length of stay before and after a game or competition. One area becoming more highly scrutinized is whether opportunities to stay in a hotel before a home contest are provided equitably.

- Academic Tutoring: the availability of tutors for men's and women's programs, the qualifications of those tutors, the compensation provided to them, the number of athletes tutored per session, etc.

- Provision of Medical Training Facilities and Services: everyone from medical personnel to athletic trainers are encompassed. Also included is weight training and conditioning facilities. Expenses and the qualifications of such personnel are all reviewed.

- Provision of Housing and Dining Facilities and Service: this one is self-explanatory but covers everything from the type of housing provided, the number of people per room, the laundry services available, parking spaces allotted and housekeeping services.

- Recruitment of Student Athletes: there must be equal opportunities to recruit for coaches of both male and female athletes. Monetary expenditures are reviewed as well as the overall treatment of athletes in the recruiting process.

- Support Services: reviews the administrative-type services provided to each men's and women's sport.

When reviewing these factors, a disparity in the money spent on female versus male athletes can trigger an investigation into the entire athletic department for Title IX compliance. Thus, there's no room to increase expenditures on travel or daily allowance, equipment and supplies or anywhere else in order to increase the benefits athletes are receiving unless you do it on both sides of the gender aisle.

The bottom line is that Title IX doesn't distinguish among sports based on profit. Even though football and men's basketball make the money, it can't all be spent on them per federal law.

Athletic departments must monitor compliance with Title IX very carefully and can't afford for there to be any perceived biases toward one sex over the other. Title IX doesn't require notice or standing, which means anyone can bring a case any time. The absence of the notice requirement means the person with a grievance can go straight to court without any mention to the athletic department or any opportunity for the department to correct the problem or explain why the perceived inequity is just that: perceived. The absence of a standing requirement means it doesn't have to be the aggrieved person who brings the suit. It can literally be anyone: a parent watching their child play on a field that doesn't seem equitable or a fan who simply thinks one sex is being treated differently from the other.

A perceived inequity in one area can quickly lead to a full-fledged investigation of the entire athletic department for compliance with each and every portion of Title IX. In addition, there is no requirement that the person bringing the case show the athletic department intended to treat the two sexes differently. In Title IX cases the intent is assumed. There's also no cap on damages, opening up the athletic department and the university to incalculable harm.

It is for these reasons any pay-for-play plan that treats the sexes differently must be carefully scrutinized before being implemented. Due to the high risks, not the least of which is the ability of a perceived inequity to easily become a lawsuit and full-blown investigation, athletic departments are unlikely to approve a plan that benefits one sex any more than the other, which also means greater costs to implement the plan.

Goodbye Nonprofit Status

Let's assume the NCAA lifted its regulations against paying athletes and athletic departments came up with the cash to pay athletes. Staying within Title IX compliance, let's say these athletic departments chose to pay athletes above and beyond cost of attendance. Many pay-for-play plans propose paying athletes far greater amounts than the cost of attendance difference. Many believe college athletes deserve outright compensation.

Paying college athletes presents more than one way athletic departments, and possibly even universities, could lose their tax-exempt status. Most universities are 501(c)(3) tax-exempt organizations under the exemption for educational purposes, and most athletic departments either operate under the university's tax-exemption or have formed their own 501(c)(3) that is tax-exempt.

One issue that could arise from paying student athletes is revocation of tax-exemption because of private benefit. Rules against private benefit are meant to ensure charitable assets are preserved for the benefit of the public. In the case of universities, assets are supposed to be used for educational purposes.

In the case of student athletes being paid, a court might ask: is the compensation the student athlete is receiving (including tuition, room and board and additional compensation) conferring an excess benefit that doesn't relate to the university's exempt purpose?

Under the exemption for educational purposes, expenditures should further an educational purpose. Money spent on tuition, room and board furthers an educational purpose. But would outright pay-for-play? There has been debate over whether high-paid coaches further an educational purpose, but the debate would surely be hotter if it were the student athletes being paid.

The penalty is steep if an organization is found to have conferred a private benefit: loss of tax-exemption. There are no other less severe penalties available. In many cases, it wouldn't only be the athletic department losing its exemption—it would be the entire university if the athletic department isn't a separate 501(c)(3).

How much money are we talking? It would vary from school to school based on a number of factors from the amount of revenue produced to the effective tax rate at both the federal and state level. As an example, University of Florida reported $1.5 billion in operating revenue for fiscal year 2011. It's difficult to say what sort of deductions would be available to lower the university's taxable income, but with a federal corporate tax rate of 35 percent and state corporate tax rates ranging from a high of 12 percent in Iowa to a low of 4.63 percent in Colorado, a university could be looking at tens of millions, if not hundreds of millions, in taxes. That doesn't take into consideration the lost revenue from gifts, which would no longer be tax deductible for the donor (and possibly subject to gift taxes), the loss of grants earmarked for nonprofits or how state appropriations might be impacted. Needless to say, it would alter the landscape of higher education nationwide.

Which is probably why the odds of universities being found to be conferring an impermissible private benefit if they paid players aren't all that high according to most who are knowledgeable in this area. Universities pay employees every day, including students who serve as residence assistants, graduate assistants and in other positions around campus. The only difference in the case of student athletes would be whether athletics would continue to be considered part of the educational experience if student athletes were treated like employees.

In addition, the test for excess benefit is whether the person is being paid above and beyond market rate, looking to both the nonprofit and for-profit world. Coaching salaries have long been thought to be immune from challenge because they are less than professional coaching salaries. The same logic would likely apply to student athletes, who would surely be paid far less than professional athletes.

Although private benefit is all or nothing in terms of penalty, intermediate sanctions are another way the IRS could attack a pay-for-play plan. Intermediate sanctions provide for return of any excess benefit, plus interest and two-tiered excise taxes. A student athlete would have to make $115,000 before intermediate sanctions could apply, and it's unclear whether the IRS would consider the value of the athlete's tuition, room and board along with any additional compensation or only the additional compensation alone.

Intermediate sanctions were created by the IRS to avoid the all-or-nothing result seen under the private benefit rules. It requires a return of the excess plus 25 percent of the excess benefit. If not immediately repaid, there is a 200 percent penalty.

In addition to levying intermediate sanctions on the individual who received the excess benefit, the IRS can also assess penalties on any executives or board members who approved the excess benefit. It's unchartered territory for the IRS, and therefore, a risky proposition for the NCAA and universities without coordination with the IRS or federal government.

The real danger in paying college athletes according to experts on nonprofit organizations is in student athletes being deemed employees. The definition of "employee" varies according to various federal acts and also state legislation.[3] It's unlikely a court, Congress or the National Labor Relations Board would find a student athlete is an employee based on a scholarship that covers cost of attendance, as many academic scholarships and other financial aid cover up to cost of attendance. However, any amount paid over that amount could surely be used to make a strong case that a college athlete is an employee.

The National Labor Relations Board has previously found graduate research assistants to be employees based on a broad interpretation that an employer/employee relationship exists where one performs services for another, under the control or right of control of the other person, in return for payment. However, just four years after making that ruling in 2000, the NLRB reversed its decision and found graduate assistants were not employees because their relationship with the university was primarily educational, not economical. In that opinion, the NLRB emphasized the graduate research assistants' roles as researchers and teachers.

Scary fact number one if you're going to look into implementing a pay-for-play plan is that the definition of employee can change. At the time of this writing, the NLRB is considering two cases regarding whether graduate research assistants are employees entitled to unionization at private universities (public universities are subject to state laws). Why reconsider the issue so many times in the course of just a little over a decade? Because it's all political.

Generally speaking, Democrats support union rights and Republicans do not. Three Democrats serving on the NLRB in 2012 granted review to the cases, seeking to overturn the 2004 decision that graduate research assistants are not employees. The lone Republican on the committee did not vote in favor of review.

The scope of political involvement in the issue goes far beyond the NLRB. In September of 2012, after the NLRB granted review of the cases, the House Committee on Education and the Workforce with the subcommittees on labor and higher education called a hearing on the matter. The title of the hearing underscores the adversarial nature of the issue: "Expanding the

Power of Big Labor: the NLRB's Growing Intrusion into Higher Education". As expected, Democrats supported the NLRB's power to review the cases, while Republicans did not.

The facts become scarier for athletic departments thinking about paying athletes and trying to determine where they'd stand legally speaking. It turns out the definition of "employee" isn't necessarily consistent among the NLRB, the IRS, courts, federal laws and state laws. For example, in some states graduate research assistants are considered employees and can unionize. In others they are not employees and cannot unionize, the basis for the NLRB reexamining whether graduate research assistants are employees anew in two cases in 2012.

The final scary fact for athletic departments and universities is that graduate research assistants have a much closer tie to the educational mission than student athletes being paid above and beyond cost of attendance. The former are researching and teaching classes in return for payment, while presumably the student athlete is being paid to play a sport.

Not only is there no clear answer as to whether student athletes would be considered employees, but there's the distinct possibility the rules can change. You can't stuff the genie back into the bottle, which is why you have to be darn sure before you go rubbing on it.

If student athletes are deemed employees, a host of new issues arise, as do costs. In addition to the compensation provided to athletes, as an employer the athletic department would have to pay for Social Security/Medicare at a rate of 7.65 percent of each athlete's compensation, federal unemployment tax at a minimum of .008 on the first $7,000 of compensation and state unemployment and worker's compensation insurance, which varies in expense.

Let's use University of Florida as an example, and let's assume the new model had the athletic department offering scholarships up to the cost of attendance and an additional $5,000 per student athlete per year in compensation. According to the USA Today study, it would cost University of Florida $826,119 per year to increase athletic scholarships to cover cost of attendance.

Compensating each of its 514 total athletes at $5,000 each would cost the department $2,570,000 in base pay. Social security taxes would add another 6.2 percent per year, Medicare 1.45 percent and federal and state unemployment taxes and worker's compensation insurance another 2-3 percent (we'll use an average of 2.5 percent since it varies by state). That raises the cost of additional compensation to over $2.8 million.

If athletes were considered full-time employees, there would also be additional costs for 401(k) plans, vacation time and health insurance. Athletic departments would likely also be bound by minimum wage requirements, but as you'll see later in this chapter, the value of the scholarship received by the athlete would bring compensation high enough to meet that threshold.

On top of taxes that would have to be paid on wages, there's still the matter of whether the athletic department continues to serve a tax-exempt charitable purpose if student athletes become employees.

If paying athletes is deemed to change the athletic department into more of an entertainment enterprise than a part of the educational experience, athletic department revenue could become subject to the unrelated business income tax ("UBIT"). Under this scenario, the university would be subject to the corporate income tax (at a rate varying from 15-35 percent) for any revenue deemed to be outside the normal realm of education. The application could take a few different incarnations, from a ruling that all athletic department revenue is subject to the UBIT to a ruling that only revenue from the so-called revenue sports, football and basketball, is subject to the UBIT.

Thus far, the IRS (sometimes at the behest of Congress) has always treated athletics as sufficiently related to education for its revenues to escape this tax. However, rising media rights deals, amongst other things, have begun to bring into question how closely related education and athletics are within a university.

The most recent inquiry into the NCAA's tax-exempt status was in 2006 when Rep. Bill Thomas, via his position as chair of the House Ways and Means Committee, sent a letter to then-NCAA president Myles Brand asking him to defend the organization's tax-exempt status. In the letter, the NCAA is asked to explain what differentiates college athletics from professional athletics, citing examples like rising television deals and coaching salaries in excess of $1 million annually.

As explained previously, there doesn't seem to a foundation for using coaching salaries (along the same lines, any potential student-athlete compensation) as a basis for declaring either the revenue sports or the athletic department subject to taxation. Producing revenue alone also isn't enough, as the Treasury has long held that paid-admission performances by arts programs are sufficiently related to education. But could a line be drawn when the commercial activities of athletics dwarf any commercial activities carried on by other educational units?

In 1977, the IRS issued a surprising ruling that the sale of broadcast rights to the Cotton Bowl would be subject to the UBIT. It was the first time the UBIT was ever applied to college athletics and the estimated back taxes owed came to a whopping $150 million. By 1978, Southern Methodist University, Texas Christian University and the University of Kansas had successfully fought to get the decision reversed. Had they not been successful, the trajectory of college athletics would have dramatically changed given the important role television rights began to play in the 1980s.

However, experts believe there is still an argument to be made that a number of factors have transformed college athletics into an entertainment enterprise no longer aligned with an educational purpose, and that compensating student athletes above and beyond cost of attendance could be a deciding factor.

The ruling in 1979 in favor of the universities was a "private letter ruling" by the IRS, meaning it set no precedent and was only binding between those particular entities and the IRS. Several other universities filed requests for similar private letter rulings thereafter and received them. In 1980, the IRS issued a public revenue ruling that an athletic conference is not taxable on its sale of broadcast rights. Although that ruling does hold precedential value, and has been relied upon since, it's not beyond overruling or amendment. Public revenue rulings are a tier below other authority like legislation, the Internal Revenue Code and court rulings.

It's not only athletic departments and universities whose fundamental business models would change if athletics-related activities were taxed. Many bowl games use an exemption for promotion of amateur athletics in order to be tax-exempt. If student athletes become employees there's certainly an argument to be made they are no longer amateurs, leaving bowl games open to taxation.

In addition to the taxes each athletic department would have to pay on any income, there's also the possibility donor contributions would no longer be tax deductible. How would that impact athletic departments, which rely heavily on donor contributions to survive?

The Chief Financial Officer of a large FBS athletic department says a "very conservative estimate" would be athletic departments losing 50 percent of their current donations. Others estimate it at closer to 30 percent, saying many would still be willing to make ticket-related contributions. It would obviously vary from school to school.

Not only would donors no longer be receiving a tax deduction for their donation (including an 80 percent deduction enjoyed for ticket-related contributions), but they could be paying for the pleasure of donating to the university because their donation would now be a gift.

The Internal Revenue Code proscribes a gift tax on any transfer of property (including money) for which something of equal value is not received in return. Ticket-related contributions might be immune to the gift tax, at least partially up to the fair market value of the ticket, but they would still cease to be tax deductible. Other donations for which nothing is received in return would be subject to the gift tax, payable by the donor.

The Internal Revenue Code allows for an annual exclusion of $13,000 per recipient (according to 2012 rates)[4]. This means each taxpayer can make a donation to an athletic department of up to $13,000 before they incur the gift tax. With the possible exception of athletic departments formed as separate corporate entities, the gift threshold would apply to gifts from a donor to the athletic department and university in the aggregate. Donations larger than $13,000 are often the backbone of large facilities fundraising campaigns, and minimum contribution levels for the best season tickets are often upwards of $13,000.

For an idea of the impact a reduction in contributions would make because of loss of tax-deductibility, first consider that contributions are generally a larger source of revenue than conference distributions (which include payouts from billion dollar television contracts and football bowl games) and NCAA March Madness combined (see Chart 3.2).

Chart 3.2
Contributions vs. NCAA & Conference Distributions at the 2010 BCS Top 25

	School	Contributions	NCAA/Conference Distributions	Difference
1	Auburn	$29,731,122.00	$19,646,038.00	$10,085,084.00
2	Oregon	$73,809,775.00	$12,756,603.00	$61,053,172.00
3	TCU*			
4	Stanford*			
5	Wisconsin	$19,247,563.00	$21,521,927.00	($2,274,364.00)
6	Ohio State	$27,327,347.00	$23,943,397.00	$3,383,950.00
7	Oklahoma	$26,601,241.00	$13,548,733.00	$13,052,508.00
8	Arkansas	$13,124,745.00	$20,556,381.00	($7,431,636.00)
9	Michigan State	$21,292,589.00	$22,578,159.00	($1,285,570.00)
10	Boise State	$6,553,812.00	$6,242,864.00	$310,948.00
11	LSU	$38,255,521.00	$19,883,259.00	$18,372,262.00
12	Missouri	$13,454,020.00	$10,681,242.00	$2,772,778.00
13	Virginia Tech	$16,138,765.00	$12,081,194.00	$4,057,571.00
14	Oklahoma State	$51,877,388.00	$12,570,471.00	$39,306,917.00
15	Nevada	$4,686,526.00	$2,368,894.00	$2,317,632.00
16	Alabama	$33,739,056.00	$21,288,565.00	$12,450,491.00
17	Texas A&M	$20,512,889.00	$11,900,472.00	$8,612,417.00
18	Nebraska	$6,103,706.00	$10,978,295.00	($4,874,589.00)
19	Utah	$5,750,835.00	$4,175,348.00	$1,575,487.00
20	South Carolina	$23,987,283.00	$19,549,286.00	$4,437,997.00
21	Mississippi State	$0.00	$18,234,538.00	($18,234,538.00)
22	West Virginia	$15,729,528.00	$10,416,908.00	$5,312,620.00
23	Florida State	$23,245,513.00	$13,323,332.00	$9,922,181.00
24	Hawaii	$13,323,332.00	$2,284,893.00	$11,038,439.00
25	UCF	$5,308,200.00	$3,337,076.00	$1,971,124.00

Data obtained from individual school financial statements. No data was available for private institutions.

The direct impact is best understood by looking at an example. During fiscal year 2010 (which encompasses the 2009-2010 school year), according to audited financials for the University Athletic Association, Inc., the separate legal entity that operates athletics at University of Florida, $34,676,729 was taken in from the Gator Boosters, Inc. Another $3,588,562 was donated from Gator Boosters, Inc. for capital costs.

In the University of Florida's case, as is the case for many athletic departments, contributions flow through an athletic foundation or booster club, which is a separate 501(c)(3) organization from the athletic department. If athletic departments were found stripped of their tax exempt status, the same would follow for the athletic foundations and booster clubs.

Using the 50 percent estimate for declining contributions, a loss of tax-exempt status at University of Florida would have meant $19.7 million less in donations for the 2010 fiscal year. According to its NCAA financial disclosure, Florida's athletic department had a surplus of $11,280,031 in 2010-2011, an enviable position for most athletic departments. However, cutting donations in half would leave the department with a shortfall of $8.4 million. That's before adding in the additional cost of the actual compensation paid to athletes and the accompanying taxes and insurance.

In addition to contributions being impacted by the lack of a tax deduction, another area that could be affected is corporate naming rights deals for athletic facilities. A major source of revenue for many new facilities, Congress overruled the IRS in the late '90s to allow a tax deduction for these type of transactions.

Naming rights deals are becoming an important component to many new building projects. University of Minnesota inked a deal with TCF Bank worth $35 million for naming rights to the new football stadium it opened in 2009. When the University of Central Florida built an on-campus stadium in 2007, it sold the naming rights to Bright House Networks for $15 million.

Surely these naming rights deals would become less attractive to companies without the tax deduction.

Speaking of facilities, another area where expenses would be affected by a loss of tax exemptions in the athletic department would be capital costs. Currently, most athletic departments use tax-exempt bonds to finance renovation and construction costs. The interest on tax-exempt bonds is exempt from federal tax, and sometimes from state and local tax. In addition, the interest rates are generally lower than commercial lending rates.

Sticking with University of Florida, the athletic department had over $83.9 million in outstanding bonds at the end of the 2010 fiscal year. Interest rates on those bonds varied from 3.50-4.39 percent, with two bonds accumulating interest at a variable rate.

Here's how University of Florida's monthly payments on its debt would change if it were paying back commercial loans at 6.00 percent (a conservative average of interest rates at the time the bonds were issued) instead of its current tax-exempt bond rates:

Series	Outstanding Amount	Term	Interest Rate	Bond Monthly Payment	Commercial Loan Monthly Payment
1990	$10,000,000.00	09/01/05-10/01/10	3.50%	$181,917.45	$193,328.02
2001	$14,235,000.00	10/01/06-10/01/11	3.80%	$260,876.37	$275,202.43
2007	$9,000,000.00	10/31/07-10/01/11	3.75%	$202,206.20	$211,365.26
1990	$5,600,000.00	12/17/09-10/01/14	4.39%	$104,121.04	$108,263.69
2001	$22,130,000.00	12/17/09-10/01/24	4.39%	$168,051.56	$186,745.52
2005	$7,000,000.00	12/17/09-10/01/20	4.39%	$72,176.29	$77,714.35
2001	$10,970,000.00	Daily Rate	Variable		
2001	$4,980,000.00	Weekly Rate	Variable		
Totals	$83,915,000.00			$989,348.91	$1,052,619.27

The total monthly difference in payments would be $63,270.36 on the fixed-rate debt, for a grand total of $759,244.32 per year in additional expenses.

If the university were a tax-exempt entity (as most are), it could issue the bonds, or be the beneficiary of an issue, and build athletic facilities. However, that could impact a university's ability to build academic facilities. There is a limit to the amount of bonds that can be issued, based on revenue stream, before the university's rating is impacted. Several FBS athletic departments already live under restrictions on bond financing even though the athletic department is a separate legal entity, because it is a subsidiary of the university and its bonds still impact the debt rating.

Combining the added cost of obtaining commercial loans for facilities and no longer being able to solicit tax-exempt donations could cost an athletic department tens of millions of dollars each year, on top of the cost of compensating student athletes.

Sticking with our University of Florida example and taking into consideration only the expenses detailed above for compensation and associated taxes and insurance, if the additional cost of commercial loan debt and the loss of contributions is added, the grand total is over $23.6 million. Deduct University of Florida's $4.8 million in cash and cash equivalents that still leaves $18.8 million in additional expenses to cover.

The debate isn't simply over whether college athletes *deserve* to be paid or not. There's also a debate about if and how it could be done. There's no certainty that any of the scenarios I've detailed here would come into play if college athletes were paid. However, there's also no certainty they wouldn't, and that's the real danger.

If you follow Major League Baseball, you might know baseball has an antitrust exemption that allows it to engage in what might otherwise be considered anticompetitive behavior. This exemption was created through case law, not statute. It has been used over the years to allow Congress to assert a certain degree of influence over Major League Baseball, even in matters unrelated to the exemption, such as steroids.

College athletics has enjoyed support from Congress over the years in terms of favorable treatment under the tax code. Several times the IRS has been swatted on its collective hand by Congress for interfering, such as when it attempted to rule naming rights deals or ticket-related contributions were not tax deductible.

That's where the real danger is. Any of the things I mentioned in this section *could* apply to college athletics, if Congress wanted it to: rules against private benefit, intermediate sanctions, unrelated business income tax and changes in tax-exempt status. Congress could back up a court ruling on any one of those matters or could simply create new laws regarding tax exemption.

The bottom line is that this isn't just about what a school or conference or the NCAA wants. It's also about what Congress wants. Even if it wanted to (which it seemingly does not), the NCAA could not move forward with any plans to pay players above cost of attendance unless it was 100 percent sure Congress was on board and schools were protected going forward. Losing tax-exempt status is just too risky of a game to play. Couple that with the fact that the NCAA has been steadfast about not paying players and it seems unlikely that day will ever come.

Collective Bargaining, Lockouts and Strikes, Oh My . . .

Suppose student athletes became employees and did receive compensation. The school wouldn't be the only one with new expenses. With compensation could come increased expenses for student athletes.

Student athletes would certainly be taxed on anything above tuition (the $5,000 in our example, plus any amount needed to bring the scholarship to cost of attendance), as scholarship monies toward room and board and anything other than tuition are already taxable income under the current tax code. If student athletes are deemed employees they could also now be taxed on the full value of their scholarship.

What type of expenses would our athlete with the cost of attendance scholarship and $5,000 yearly compensation looking at? In our University of Florida example, an in-state student would be taxed on his $19,830 cost of attendance scholarship and his $5,000 in additional compensation. The athlete would pay 6.2 percent for Social Security and 1.45 percent for Medicare. According to the IRS, if the athlete is single he would fall in the 15 percent tax bracket, which would leave him owing the federal government $3,724.50 in income taxes before any exemptions or deductions for which he might be eligible.

In most states he'd also owe state income taxes, but that is not the case in Florida (which might give schools in states without state income tax a recruiting advantage they don't currently have). Without exemptions or deductions, he'd owe almost half of what he gained in the scenario ($3,290 in cost of attendance increase and $5,000 in additional compensation).

For an out-of-state student at University of Florida the cost of attendance figure is an additional $22,236, which makes his bill to the federal government even higher. An out-of-state student would be taxed at a higher rate of 25 percent and would owe $11,766.50 before exemptions or deductions, which means he'd owe more than twice as much as he was receiving from the cost of attendance increase and additional compensation!

But, there's always collective bargaining to assist the players in getting a better deal. If college athletes became employees, there's every reason to believe they would form a players' association and collectively bargain. Some might argue their career is too short to move to the collective bargaining system we see in the professional leagues. However, keep in mind the average career for an NFL player is just 3.5 years.

In fact, a players' association of sorts has already formed: the National Collegiate Players Association ("NCPA"). As of October 2012, the NCPA claimed over 14,000 former and current college athletes as members. The group has taken on the NCAA several times seeking changes to the way student athletes are treated. The group lists as its accomplishments: establishing a fund to assist former athletes who want to complete their undergraduate degrees or attend a graduate program; elimination of limits on health care for student athletes; getting the NCAA death benefit increased from $10,000 to $25,000; expansion of the NCAA's insurance policy to allow home health care for student athletes who suffer permanent, debilitating injuries; and elimination of the $2,000 salary cap on money earned by student athletes from part-time jobs.

The NCPA also recently lobbied in California for the Student Athlete Bill of Rights, which increases the ability of a student athlete at a California school receiving $10 million or more per year from media rights deals to complete his degree if he's injured or if he fails to graduate before he exhausts his eligibility and his team's graduation success rate is lower than 60 percent (which, generally speaking, would only apply to some football and men's basketball programs). It also requires financial skills workshops for first- and third-year student athletes, medical insurance for needy athletes, timely responses to transfer requests from student athletes and concussion-related guidelines. The law will go into effect for the 2013-2014 school year. Currently, the schools in California that receive more than $10 million annually from media rights deals are the University of Southern California, Stanford University, University of California at Los Angeles and Berkeley.

At the time of this printing, Connecticut has similar legislation under consideration. The threshold in Connecticut would be $5 million in media rights revenue, which means the law would only apply to UConn. The Connecticut legislation would require institutions to provide scholarships for student athletes whose athletic scholarships aren't renewed following an injury or illness that resulted from participation in their sport or those who have exhausted their eligibility but are still in good academic standing and want to continue to pursue their degree. The portion of the Connecticut legislation dealing with student athletes who have exhausted their eligibility does not include the qualifying language of the California law limiting it to sports with graduation success rates under 60 percent.

If student athletes were classified as employees, there's every reason to believe the NCPA, or another similar organization, would move for a collective bargaining agreement between the employees and the NCAA. They would have every right to do so as employees. But can you imagine the impact of a strike or lockout in college football? It would make lockouts in professional sports look like child's play.

Over the course of the 2011 regular season, 35.6 million fans attended FBS football games. Compare that to 17.1 million who filled NFL stadiums. Add in the economic impact to 120 cities on game day (as compared to 32 in the NFL), which for top programs is in the tens of millions of dollars, and the numbers are staggering.

Lisa Horne of FOX Sports wrote on the issue in July 2011. She noted that State College, Pennsylvania, where Penn State is located, is home to 42,034 residents, according to the 2010 census. However, on gameday, Beaver Stadium, home to Penn State's football team, "can swell to over 107,000 fans." Jose Felix, an employee at Marriott's Residence Inn State College interviewed by Horne, said half of the hotel's yearly profit comes from college football season, which is six to eight weekends a year.[5]

How does the economic calamity of a lockout or strike happen in college football?

Let's say college athletes are being paid some amount, any amount, over cost of attendance. One or more players decide schools, conferences and/or the NCAA are violating antitrust laws. Essentially, antitrust laws disallow business practices that discourage competition or restrict an employee's ability to make a living. So, for example, players could sue over the NCAA requirement that they sit out one year when transferring. Similar issues in professional sports have been considered by courts such as the franchise tag in the NFL and the reserve clause in Major League Baseball.

Restraints such as not allowing a player to reach free agency for a specified number of years are only allowed in professional sports because they've been collectively bargained. The product of collective bargaining between an employer and unionized employees is protected by the non-statutory labor exemption.

Back to our scenario. One or more players files suit against a conference or the NCAA for a restraint like the rule regarding transfers. If players were classified as employees (which could be determined in a suit like this), it's highly likely the court would find this to be a violation of antitrust laws. Much like we've seen in the history of each professional sport, the players would form a players association and collectively bargain these issues with the NCAA, assuming the NCAA was still the governing body for collegiate athletics. If not the NCAA, it would be what-ever governing body we have for collegiate athletics at that time.

What would collegiate athletics look like then? Maybe there would be a salary cap for each athletic department or even each football program. Players would likely get a share of licensing revenue. Health insurance and maybe even post-career benefits might be covered by schools or the governing body. The more expensive the venture becomes for the athletic department, the bigger the question of the source of the money becomes. Donations from boosters, which by way of example accounts for approximately 25 percent of University of Florida's athletic department's revenue, have likely been slashed following the athletic department's loss of its 501(c)(3) status. Expenses are higher with cost of attendance scholarships, compensation and loss of tax-exempt bonds for construction. Who pays? Non-athlete students by way of student fees? Taxpayers?

Other areas that could be collectively bargained concern the rules on recruiting or transfer-ring. Mechanisms from professional athletics like a draft and trading players wouldn't fit in collegiate athletics. Players have an opinion about where they want to attend school. One that's much stronger than say a prospect in the MLB draft who wants to play for his hometown team. Brett Hundley, a freshman quarterback at UCLA in 2011, is said to have chosen UCLA for its pre-med program. Because many of these athletes are taking advantage of the academic opportunities afforded to them, it doesn't make sense to have a draft or allow trades. What if a player ended up at a school that didn't have his preferred major?

Coming to an agreement on an initial collective bargaining agreement would take a great deal of time and negotiation and could introduce a number of new governing principles to col-lege sports. In the end, collegiate athletics can never be treated exactly like professional athlet-ics. The "owner" of a college football team, the athletic department, also happens to run a multitude of other sports programs, all of which feed off the same revenue stream. Add in NCAA regulations and federal laws like Title IX and college football cannot be run like the NFL. College football players will never be paid like professional athletes.

A Pretty Sweet Deal Already

Even putting aside the expense of paying players, as detailed in this chapter, there's a strong case to be made against paying college athletes above and beyond what they already receive.

One of the most frequent arguments from those who are proponents of paying college ath-letes is that college athletes can't get jobs like other college students. Formerly, the NCAA lim-ited part-time work to summer and other school breaks and capped the amount a student athlete could earn. However, the NCAA currently allows student athletes to work during the school year, and there are no longer limitations on the amount of money that can be earned, provided the wage is fair market value.

Even not taking into consideration what a student athlete can earn off the field (and the discussion of whether they have the time), there's an argument to be made that they already have the best paid internships of anyone on campus. Many students forgo paying jobs in college in order to intern in their chosen field. Most do internships for little or no pay and perhaps school credit. In the latter situation not only is the student not getting paid, he is paying the school tuition for the credits he's earning.

Jay Paterno, formerly an assistant coach at Penn State, wrote an article for StateCollege.com in June 2011 on the value each Penn State student athlete on full scholarship was receiving. First he broke down NCAA regulations on the number of hours a student athlete can spend on his sport. The NCAA does not allow a student athlete to work more than 20 hours a week for 21 weeks, with at least one mandatory day off every week. The other 23 weeks of the year, the student athlete can only work 8 hours a week. All student athletes get 8 weeks off a year. That's 604 hours a year worked.

In return for those 604 hours, an in-state student at Penn State receives an education, room and board valued at $33,976, while an out-of-state student receives a package valued at $50,286.[6] These amounts do not include several hundreds of dollars included in each scholarship for books and other supplies.

Based on those rates and the maximum number of hours a student athlete can work each year, an in-state student is being paid $56.25 per hour and an out-of-state student $83.25 per hour.

Critics point out that student athletes spend additional hours watching tape and working out beyond the NCAA limitations. They also reference that the student athletes are spending hours as a student as well.

Perhaps those numbers don't account for that, but they also don't account for the value of the degree the student can earn and their future earning power—$2.8 million in average lifetime earnings per a recent study by Georgetown University, 84 percent more than someone without a bachelor's degree[7]. The numbers also don't account for the value of the world-class strength and conditioning training and equipment, state-of-the-art stadiums and other facilities, medical treatment and academic tutoring they receive.

Scott Charland, Director of Strength and Conditioning at Saint Louis University, says he would charge at least $60 per hour if he were training in a private gym. In a group situation it would be $30/hour for each person, at the absolute minimum. He says the minimum number of hours per year a football player would spend training is 124 hours, with 145 being a likely average. That would make the range of value a student athlete receives in strength and conditioning training anywhere from $3,720 (124 hours x $30 discount rate) to $8,700 (145 hours x $60 rate). And that's if each workout is only an hour. Double those numbers for two-hour workouts, which Charland says are also common.

Putting aside what a student athlete would spend in the private sector for his training, let's look at what University of Florida actually spends on average for each athlete above and beyond scholarship, room and board:

Meals over break, postseason and training table meals	$1,652
Training Room	$5,703
Office of Student Life (career and academic counseling and support for athletes)	$3,847
Strength & Conditioning and Equipment Rooms	$2,616
TOTAL	**$13,818**

That's nearly $14,000 per student athlete, and over $7 million total for all 514 of University of Florida's athletes, the athletic department writes checks for each year in addition to the $8.2 million in tuition, room and board. Not included in these numbers are expenses like team travel, coaching salaries, compliance staff salaries, facilities (construction, improvement and maintenance), marketing or administrative expenses and salaries, all of which are necessary in order for the athletic department to operate so each student athlete can compete in his/her sport.

The numbers above also don't include the world-class medical treatment received when a student athlete sustains an injury. For example, world-renowned orthopedist James Andrews is a team doctor for both Alabama and Auburn. Dr. Andrews has performed surgery on famous professional athletes like Drew Brees, Michael Jordan and Roger Clemens. Care is given at no cost to the student athlete, which would otherwise cost the average person tens of thousands of dollars, if they could even get on Dr. Andrews's schedule.

If you take all of Florida's athletic department expenses for 2010-2011 (with the exception of the $6,521,019 the athletic department gave to the university above and beyond its obligations) and divide it evenly among the 514 student athletes, the grand total is $193,197 per student athlete. Sure, portions of that go to unexciting things like administrative staff salaries, electricity and medical tape, but it takes a lot to put on hundreds of sporting events a year involving hundreds of student athletes who have to be cared for in every way from tutoring to being given medical attention.

That's why it's ludicrous to compare the so-called plight of student athletes to slavery. A scathing piece in *The Atlantic* in 2011 entitled *The Shame of College Sports* by Taylor Branch starts out by saying, "slavery examples should be used carefully" and then goes on to include five analogies to slavery throughout the piece.[8] How many slaves lived in multimillion dollar facilities and received world-class medical care? How many were offered education and the chance to earn millions over their lifetime with a college degree? Add in private charters, training tables and eight weeks off a year, and it's tough to see the similarities.

Branch's piece, along with many others, reference the number of poor African American males playing big-time college football and basketball. They use it to subtly make the slavery analogy, but how many of those young men would have gone to college at all without an athletic scholarship? Given what's been shown in this chapter about the money spent and services provided per student athlete, and the incredible 84 percent increase in lifetime earning potential with a college degree, it's clear student athletes are far from slaves.

There are some valid points made in Branch's piece, particularly with regard to the lack of due process student athletes find in some situations with the NCAA, but overall the piece is decidedly one-sided.

Early on in his piece, Branch mentions how football programs at schools like Texas, Florida, Georgia, Michigan and Penn State show net revenue of $40 million to $80 million per year. There's a quick reference afterwards to multimillion-dollar coaching salaries. Where's the rest of the story? There's no mention of the fact that all five of the schools mentioned field more varsity sports than the NCAA minimum and provide more than the minimum in grants-in-aid to student athletes. For example, Texas fielded 20 varsity sports in 2010-2011, four more than required. Texas awarded the equivalent of 261 grants-in-aid, for a grand total of $9.0 million. The NCAA minimum for FBS is 200 grants-in-aid or $4 million.

Where's the explanation by Branch of how those net profits from football fund the other sports? The fact of the matter is that the federal government is not repealing Title IX, so you're never going to have a situation in college sports where a school can choose to only sponsor football. Branch's accusation that universities are, "enriching themselves on the backs of uncompensated young men," serves as an attention-grabbing statement, but it's not an accurate depiction of student athlete life.

I don't mean to pick on Branch; his opinions on the matter are far from unique. As a Pulitzer-Prize–winning author, his piece received a great deal of media attention, but the arguments are ones that have existed in the media for years. They're unfortunately one-sided and do little to educate fans about the regulations college athletic departments have to live within and the realities of implementing any pay-for-play plan.

The debate over pay-for-play also creates a bit of a paradox for some. In one breath, student athletes aren't compensated enough, but in the next breath it's deplorable that athletic departments are spending more per student athlete than for other students. A study by the Knight Commission was released in January 2013 showing SEC schools spent $164,000 per student athlete on average in 2010. However, throughout the rest of the student body just $13,390 was spent per student for academic spending. It wasn't exactly an apples-to-apples comparison, as the athletic spending included tuition, room and board and spending on other students for tuition and related fees was not. It's also tough to compare the two categories of students when you take into consideration the equipment, facilities and staff needed at even a base level for athletics. Nonetheless, it made headlines across the country.

So why is public sentiment so strong that college athletes deserve to be paid above and beyond what they're already receiving? The problem is the amount of money proponents of paying athletes believe each athlete is bringing into the school. Unfortunately, at least for their argument, it is a lot of indirect correlation that can't be measured. There might be one football player on a team who gets the most media attention, but no one football player gets a team to a bowl game or convinces Nike to sign a multimillion-dollar contract with the school. It's actually much easier to trace those things to a coach, as was shown with the Bobby Petrino example at Arkansas.

However, one area of revenue that can presumably be traced to a specific student athlete is the sale of jerseys with a specific player's number. Universities never sell jerseys with players' names, but they do choose to produce jerseys with certain numbers. For Florida, #15 formerly worn by Tim Tebow is popular. For Texas A&M in 2011 it was #40 worn by Von Miller.

Jersey sales aren't making athletic departments millions. Collegiate Licensing Company, which represents over 150 universities, says jerseys account for an average of 1.1 percent of total licensing revenue for the schools it represents. For Texas A&M's 2013 fiscal year, during which quarterback Johnny Manziel won the Heisman trophy, jersey sales totaled just $59,690, which accounted for 1.53 percent of total licensing revenue.

When it comes to jerseys and video games with players' likenesses there are interesting potential legal issues (currently being taken up in the O'Bannon court case[9]), and even Title IX questions if compensation were provided for those licenses, but the focus of this chapter is on the challenges with compensating student athletes like employees, a separate issue.

In the end, college athletes play for one of three reasons: (i) experience and exposure for a future career in the sport, (ii) a free education or (iii) because they love to play. If it's the first reason, they're essentially doing an internship, like many other college students do each year. Many internships are unpaid, regardless of how much money the company makes. Athletes on full scholarship are receiving tuition, room and board on top of access to superb facilities, strength and conditioning staff, medical treatment, academic support and sometimes better lodging and dining than other students. Sounds like college athletics might be the best paying internship around.

Why then has the debate over paying college athletes reached an undeniable roar? Likely because proponents of pay-for-play hear University of Florida football turns a $44.3 million profit. Fans see those numbers and find it shocking that athletic departments are banking that kind of cash while the athletes go unpaid.

Let's not forget that football or basketball or any other revenue-producing sport represents only one unit of an athletic department largely made up of sports operating at a net loss. At University of Florida the $44.3 million football profit covers less than half the $96.9 million in operating expenses for the athletic department.

Deciding to pay players is not a simple decision. You've seen how it would impact University of Florida, one of only 23 self-sustaining athletic departments in 2011-2012 by NCAA standards. Now imagine how it would impact a school like University of Virginia who already takes in over $12 million in student fees to balance its athletic department budget.

Paying college athletes would cripple collegiate athletics as we know it if events unfolded as described in this chapter. At a minimum, sports outside of football and men's basketball would be on the chopping block. Student fees could soar. Lockouts or strikes could cost cities, and the businesses within them, tens of millions of dollars with each game that is lost. While proponents of paying players might say that economic realities shouldn't govern what they consider is fair and right, it's how the business world works. And college athletics is at heart a business, even if it is a nonprofit one.

NOTES

[1]   Berkowitz, S., Silcox, C. & Upton, J., "NCAA cost-of-attendance puzzle: many schools, many methods", *USA Today*, July 29, 2011. Retrieved August 7, 2011, from http://www.usatoday.com/sports/college/2011-07-29-athletic-departments-cost-of-attendance_n.htm?csp=34sports .

[2]   *Ibid.*

[3]   For a detailed account of the many definitions of "employee" in American labor law, see: Kenneth G. Dau-Schmidt, J.D., Ph.D. and Michael D. Ray, B.A., "The Definition of Employee in American Labor and Employment Law." Retrieved August 8, 2011, from http://www.jil.go.jp/english/events_and_information/documents/clls04_dauschmidt2.pdf.

[4]   The Internal Revenue Code also allows a person to make gifts that exceed the limit for a lifetime total of $1 million in overages. It's not unreasonable to assume that anyone making a gift of this size is making gifts elsewhere, so it's unclear how much of their $1 million lifetime overage they'd be willing to use on athletic department gifts.

[5]   Horne, Lisa (July 25, 2011). "Pay for play could be disastrous," FoxSports.com. Retrieved August 9, 2011, from http://msn.foxsports.com/collegefootball/story/Paying-student-athletes-could-open-door-to-a-union-and-a-strike-072411.

[6]   Based on data from the 2010-2011 school year.

[7]   Anthony P. Carnevale, Stephen J. Rose and Ban Cheah, "The College Payoff," The Georgetown University Center on Education and the Workforce. Last accessed at: http://www9.georgetown.edu/grad/gppi/hpi/cew/pdfs/collegepayoff-complete.pdf.

[8]   Branch, Taylor, "The Shame of College Sports," *The Atlantic*. October 2011. Retrieved November 2, 2011, from http://www.theatlantic.com/magazine/archive/2011/10/the-shame-of-college-sports/308643/.

[9]   O'Bannon v. NCAA, No. CV 09-3329 (N.D. Cal. July 21, 2009)

CONFERENCE REALIGNMENT

Since the early 1990s, conference realignment has been a force of nature in college football. Just when movement settles down with order restored, here it comes again.

Two primary factors drive conference realignment: power and television revenue. Keep those factors in mind as this chapter leads you through the major events in conference realignment history.

When West Virginia joined the Big 12 in 2012 and Missouri and Texas A&M made their move to the SEC, fans waxed nostalgic about the days when geography and rivalry meant more than dollars. The problem is those days haven't existed for a very long time.

Those fans might not remember, but when Penn State joined the Big Ten in 1989 the commentary was similar. It's tempting to say Penn State kicked off modern day conference realignment when it gave up independence for the security of the Big Ten. It's easy to forget years later that Arkansas and South Carolina didn't always seem like a natural fit in the SEC. That's why this chapter is going to trace the history of conference realignment and illustrate how the motives for realignment have always been the same. Perhaps that'll help us more accurately predict the future.

I think it was the 1984 Supreme Court decision in NCAA v. Board of Regents of University of Oklahoma, et al.[1] that started the ball rolling. More simply, it was television.

In 1939, the first college football game was commercially televised by the University of Pennsylvania. For the next decade, all of the University's home games were televised. This led the NCAA to commission a study on the impact of televising games and the institution of controls through the NCAA's Football Television Committee. The District Court found controls commenced in 1953, but the Supreme Court found they began in 1951, prior to the study.

The initial rules stated that only one football game could be televised each Saturday, with three of the ten Saturdays during the season blacked out. In addition, no team could appear on television more than twice per season. The NCAA negotiated the television contract, and revenue was shared among the teams that were televised and the NCAA.

1970s

The major powers in college football began to grow unhappy with the way the NCAA was handling television rights. In the late 1970s, a new broadcasting phenomenon began: the super regional. The super regionals broadcast the biggest games to virtually the entire nation while showing a much smaller game to two to three markets. Despite the disparity of each game's reach, all participants were compensated equally by the NCAA.

On top of that, the NCAA was airing games that weren't exactly ratings drivers. Smaller conferences like the Mid-American and the Ivy League were guaranteed appearances by the NCAA. It began to impact ratings, which declined from an average audience of 10.04 million in 1976 to 8.7 million in 1979.

In 1976, a group of major football programs took matters into their own hands and formed the College Football Association. Although the NCAA had finally split into Division I, II and III in 1973, there still existed a large gulf among programs within Division I, and the major college football programs numbered a minority when it came time to vote on rules and regulations. The major college football programs didn't initially form the CFA to compete with the NCAA, only to have a forum to discuss matters pertinent to them in order to reach a consensus and stand united before the NCAA.

In 1978, the NCAA proposed a split within Division I to Division I-A and I-AA. The CFA supported the plan, but the Big Ten and Pac-10 had a different idea about the composition of the new subdivisions than the rest of the group. Those conferences supported including the Ivy League, along with several other smaller programs that could qualify simply by sponsoring at least 12 sports.

It has been suggested the Big Ten and Pac-10 supported the inclusion of those schools in order to increase their voting power within the new subdivision. Without those additional schools the Big Ten and Pac-10 might have been outnumbered, but having supported their inclusion the Big Ten and Pac-10 believed they would have the support of those additional schools when it came time to vote on matters where the Big Ten and Pac-10 might not agree with the rest of the CFA.

1980s

In the end, the Big Ten and Pac-10 never joined the CFA. Some believe it was because they didn't want to share power with the other conferences and knew they could go at it alone with their Rose Bowl affiliation. Others surmise it was because the commissioners, Wayne Duke and Tom Hansen, formerly worked under NCAA executive director Walter Byers and supported him.

Regardless, the end result was that the Big Ten and Pac-10 separated themselves from the CFA, and the latter continued to separate itself from the NCAA. Fed up with the way the NCAA was handling television rights, the CFA began negotiating its own contract with NBC. At the same time, the NCAA was in negotiations with both ABC and CBS. Upon learning of the CFA's negotiations with NBC, the NCAA issued an "Official Interpretation" stating that the NCAA controlled all television rights for all schools.

The CFA continued its negotiations and reached a deal with NBC on August 8, 1981. Meanwhile, the NCAA had reached an agreement with ABC and CBS that covered the 1982-1985 seasons.[2] Despite the fact that individual schools controlled their own rights for basketball, the NCAA was laying claim to football rights. The governing body threatened to sanction any school that participated in the CFA contract (which would have had ramifications for the schools' other sports).

ABC, fearful of what its television deal would look like minus CFA members, urged NCAA executive director Walter Byers to come to an agreement with the CFA. Byers, however, refused to change his position, leading two CFA schools, the University of Georgia and the University of Oklahoma, to file suit in federal court for an injunction against the NCAA.[3] NBC, aware of the value it was getting under its deal with the CFA, offered to cover half the court fees.

Unfortunately for the CFA, it was unable to convince enough members to ratify the NBC deal. Many simply wanted to wait out the lawsuit to find out what, if any, rights they really had.

At the NCAA's convention in January 1982, the NCAA pushed through legislation stating it could promulgate bylaws covering the televising of all college football games. The measure was voted on by all NCAA members, with a final vote of 631-178. Although all 61 of the CFA members voted against it, they simply didn't have enough members to defeat the legislation.

In the background, the federal court case against the NCAA continued. In June 1982, the case was finally heard by Judge Juan Burciaga of New Mexico after Judge Luther Eubanks, an Oklahoma grad, recused himself.

Instead of making a property rights claim, the schools decided to attack the NCAA's actions on antitrust grounds. One claim was that the NCAA was engaging in price fixing, which violated antitrust laws.

The NCAA's new television deals contained both "appearance requirements" and "appearance limitations" for each two-year period during the term of the contract. Each network was required to schedule appearances for at least 82 different schools during each two-year period. No school could appear more than four times nationally and six times total during a two-year period, nor could any school negotiate separately to televise games not picked up under the contract. The NCAA's contract with both networks also set a maximum number of games per season that could be televised.

The NCAA first argued that it was a voluntary membership organization and any school could choose to leave. Next, it argued the rules regarding television were necessary to protect attendance and foster competitive balance. The District Court judge found the evidence insufficient to prove attendance was suffering and that other NCAA regulations, such as rules on recruiting practices, achieved competitive balance on their own.

The District Court judge found the NCAA engaged in both price fixing and that it limited production by restricting the number of games that could be televised. An example of price fixing noted by the judge was the fact that in 1981 Oklahoma and University of Southern California (which were both ranked in the top 5) received the same amount of money for a regional broadcast on 200 stations as Citadel and Appalachian State, which both appeared on just four stations.

Additionally, the District Court judge found the NCAA's threats to sanction the CFA schools constituted a group boycott. Based on all of those antitrust violations, the judge issued a judgment for the CFA schools, declared the NCAA's contracts with ABC and CBS null and void, and issued a permanent injunction against the NCAA to prohibit it from interfering with the CFA's contract with NBC.

The NCAA appealed to the Tenth Circuit Court of Appeals. Unfortunately for the NCAA, its arguments were again dismissed and the lower court's ruling was upheld. The NCAA appealed, and the United States Supreme Court agreed to hear the case.

There was little doubt the NCAA's televisions policies were a restraint of free trade. However, U.S. law does not prohibit all restraints, only those that are unreasonable. The burden was on the NCAA to justify its decision to deviate from a free market concept.

The NCAA had to find an argument to counterbalance the District Court's finding that in a free market many more games would be available on television, prices paid by networks would be lower and viewer demand would be better met. In addition, the television plan had been found to exclude networks that didn't have the capacity to cover the entire NCAA. Unresponsiveness to consumer demand in terms of price and supply is the crux of many antitrust violations, making it an uphill battle for the NCAA.

The NCAA decided to argue it had no market power—basically that it had no ability to control the supply. The NCAA contended it could not demand higher prices from networks because advertisers and broadcasters could choose other content to air.

The Supreme Court summarily rejected this argument, because the District Court had found college football attracts a unique audience. An audience that is in fact more appealing to advertisers than most because of its demographics and can therefore demand a higher premium. Essentially, the Supreme Court ruled college football has market power in spades.

The NCAA then turned to an argument that the television plan was a joint venture among schools that allowed for greater efficiency than each could find individually. Ultimately, this was found not to be the case. The District Court had found broadcast rights could be marketed by schools as effectively without the NCAA's television plan, making the plan unjustifiable. In addition, college football's market power was found to be so strong, there was no reason to pool rights together in order to compete against other programming.

Next the NCAA argued the television plan was necessary in order to protect attendance at games. It was a tough position to defend given that games were already being shown on television at the same time as the live event. Furthermore, the Supreme Court found the NCAA could not limit television output because of a base concern that live games weren't compelling enough to draw their own audience. That strategy was found to be inconsistent with the policy of antitrust laws.

Lastly, the NCAA renewed its argument that its television plan improved competitive balance, a position it was unable to successfully defend in the District Court. The Supreme Court acknowledged that many NCAA rules regarding participation and rules of the game itself, although restraints, are necessary to foster competition. However, it did not find the television plan to be a reasonable restraint or even a necessary one.[4]

That decision, more than anything else in college football's history, has defined the sport's course. It would take almost a decade for the tremors to travel from Washington, D.C. to places like State College, Pennsylvania and Fayetteville, Arkansas.

Following the 1984 Supreme Court decision, the Big Ten and Pac-10, still not a part of the CFA, sponsored NCAA legislation that would allow the NCAA to continue negotiating television deals, but without the restrictions that had been deemed to be in violation of antitrust law. Under their plan, the major football programs would have more appearances and could even enter non-competing regional deals by conference.

The us-versus-them mentality between the Big Ten and Pac-10 on the one side and CFA members on the other continued. CFA members were convinced they could land a better deal on their own, which led the Big Ten and Pac-10 to negotiate their regular season television deals jointly, along with the Rose Bowl deal.

The Big Ten and Pac-10 combined to sign for a $10 million deal with CBS, while the CFA received only a slightly larger $13 million contract with ABC. Both paled in comparison to the $73.6 million the NCAA deal would have generated in 1984 or the $50 million the CFA/NBC deal would have brought in that same year.

With more college football on television than ever before, demand had decreased. Revenue plummeted for schools that first year. For example, the SEC saw its revenue decrease from $11.2 million to $7.5 million the first year of the CFA contract. CBS made a deal to air the Army-Navy game and placed it in the same timeslot as ABC's Alabama-Auburn coverage to disastrous results: all-time low ratings.

It wasn't long before the CFA realized it needed to do something to promote ratings and revenue while still offering maximum exposure for schools. The answer was the syndication window, which allowed for conferences and independents to sell off any games that weren't picked up by the primary rights holders. The ACC partnered with Jefferson-Pilot, the Southwest Conference with Raycom, Notre Dame with WGN, and the SEC with WTBS.

It still wasn't enough to move college football back to the kind of television revenue it was producing under NCAA control. In his book, *The Fifty-Year Seduction: How Television Manipulated*

College Football, for the Birth of the Modern NCAA to the Creation of the BCS, Keith Dunnavant estimates college football made $200 million less in the ten years following the Supreme Court decision than it would have made under the NCAA deal and subsequent deals at the same growth rates.

Some schools had the opportunity to break away from the CFA and make more money individually—most notably Notre Dame and the SEC, both of which were courted by networks. Neither left, both remaining convinced there was power in unity.

At the time of the Supreme Court decision, conferences were largely aligned based on geography. Although the free market for television rights hadn't increased revenue for schools yet, there remained a strong belief that one day it would. Coupled with the power struggle going on between the Big Ten/Pac-10 and the CFA, the atmosphere was ripe for a power grab.

In December 1989, the Big Ten shocked the world when it announced Penn State would be the first team added to the conference since Michigan State in 1949. Commissioner Jim Delany had been quietly meeting with university presidents about the addition, meaning the announcement was a shock to not only fans but also athletic directors and coaches around the conference.

Bo Schembechler, Michigan's athletic director at the time, said, "[Y]ou don't add someone to the conference and not consult the people in athletics. That was the most ridiculous thing I've ever seen done.

"I, and most of the other athletic directors in our conference, resent the way it was done, and if I offend some presidents, that's too damn bad."[5]

Schembechler went on to say:

> They (the presidents) did it because of the friendship they have with each other. One president probably said, 'Hey, I'd like to play in your league,' and the other president said, 'Come on over and do it.' That's about how much research went into that decision.

Schembechler wasn't the only one displeased. Athletic directors and coaches around the conference spoke out against the addition. So much so that Delany was forced to form a committee to study the viability of Penn State joining the conference, giving that committee the power to retract the invitation.

Everyone seemed perplexed by the decision. Those involved in athletics around the Big Ten couldn't fathom what Penn State brought to the table. Instead, they worried about what would be left for them after Penn State took its share.

Minnesota athletic director at the time, Rick Bay, said "For the presidents to make that decision in a vacuum presents some problems to athletic directors in that there was some competitive and financial ramifications that haven't been discussed on the directors' level."

The *Chicago Tribune* nailed it though: it was a move about power and television money.

An article in the *Chicago Tribune* on December 15, 1989 described the invitation from the Big Ten to Penn State as follows:

> From the Big Ten's point of view, Penn State is an attractive addition in helping the conference build on its nationwide reform agenda. The league is trying to marshal its forces to push through legislation that would eliminate freshmen eligibility and call for tighter academic standards.[6]

The article also said "[g]eographically, Penn State might pose some problems for the Big Ten," noting Ohio State as the closest school some 325 miles away and Minnesota the furthest at 1,500 miles. What would people have thought back then about San Diego State announcing its intention to join the Big East in 2011?

It was months later before the *Chicago Tribune* covered the increasingly important television angle:

> Conference insiders say Penn State`s only plus from that standpoint would be in televised football. Having the state of Pennsylvania would add an additional 5.3 million homes to the Big Ten`s base, which now numbers 17.4 million.
>
> That`s a significant jump, but will the additional revenue be enough to offset dividing those funds with an 11th and possibly a 12th school?[7]

Indiana's president at the time, Thomas Ehrlich, also emphasized the academic reputation Penn State brought to the conference:

"When I look at some institutions across the country, too many, I have to be worried. Players never graduate; there is just no concern about progress toward a degree. Within the conference, we have higher standards than the average, and we can control those standards."

Ehrlich also noted the increased television revenue for the conference, but insisted it was a "secondary" factor.[8]

For Penn State the move meant stability. It had been competing in the Atlantic 10 in every sport except football. The football program had thrived up through 1986 when it won the national championship over Miami. Only two seasons later it faced its first losing season in 49 years. In addition, coach Joe Paterno was saying he planned to retire at age 65, which was only a few years away.

At the time, Penn State's basketball program was struggling to keep up financially. The Big East had formed in 1979 and then–athletic director Joe Paterno had declined the new conference's advances. Paterno was hoping to create an eastern all-sports conference with schools like Pitt and Syracuse, but his plan hit a roadblock when it came to revenue sharing. The others joined the Big East, and it wasn't long before Big East basketball made Penn State's program look financially deficient.

Against this backdrop, it was Penn State that came knocking on the Big Ten's door. Former Penn State President John Oswald had approached the Big Ten after Penn State played Ohio State in the 1980 Fiesta Bowl. It had been discussed over the years that proceeded, but nothing ever came of it.

Then, in the spring of 1989 as Big Ten Commissioner Wayne Duke was retiring, Penn State athletic director Jim Tarman contacted the conference again. With Duke on the way out, it would be up to Delany to take the reigns. In the end, it was then–Illinois President Stanley Ikenberry, who was chairman of the Council of Ten (which consisted of the presidents from each Big Ten school), who began meeting with Penn State officials secretively and helped pave their way into the conference.[9]

1990s

Even after the presidents voted 7-3 to admit Penn State—with Indiana, Michigan and Michigan State the rumored dissenters[10]—the Nittany Lions weren't exactly welcomed with open arms. Penn State's sports joined the Big Ten in stages from 1991 to 1993, when football finally joined.

Following an Atlantic 10 conference tournament title in 1991, Penn State basketball found itself without a conference for a season. Only two Big Ten schools would agree to play them that year, forcing the rest of the schedule to be filled with small eastern schools.

Then-Penn State basketball coach Bruce Parkhill said in 1991, "I'm disappointed more Big Ten people didn't help out. It's not that they couldn't. They wouldn't."

On top of Big Ten athletic directors feeling as though Penn State was forced upon them without any opportunity for input, they also felt Penn State basketball was beneath them. Then-Penn State athletic director Jim Tarman told his board of trustees Big Ten schools were threatening not to play in State College because of poor facilities.[11]

Football didn't have an easy time integrating into the Big Ten either. In 1993, Penn State went 10-2, losing only to perennial conference heavyweights Ohio State and Michigan. However, the following year the Nittany Lions were undefeated and finished the season No. 2 in the nation.

Penn State historian Lou Prato explained the situation in the early 1990s to the *Daily Nebraskan*, saying, "You have to understand Big Ten football and Big Ten football fans: They look down their nose at Eastern football. They have no respect. They say, 'We play real football out here.' So when Penn State won in '94, they weren't too happy."

The relationship between the Big Ten for Penn State improved when the football program went 11 years before winning another conference title. Prato says it wasn't until 2005, when the Nittany Lions had an 11-1 season following a string of losing seasons, that Penn State was fully accepted into the Big Ten.[12]

The addition of Penn State meant the Big Ten and Pac-10 were no longer equal, at least in terms of members. In 1992, the two conferences reached an extension with ABC through 2000 for regular season games. ABC already held the rights to the Rose Bowl through the 1997 game.

Prior to the 1992 extension the two conferences had split revenue 50/50, but the addition of Penn State meant the Big Ten had one more mouth to feed—albeit a mouth that brought a lot to the table in terms of national stature. The *LA Times* reported at the time that the Pac-10 agreed to a split that gave the Big Ten 52.4 percent of the revenue and the Pac-10 47.6 percent:

> [The Pac-10] recognizes the value of an 11th Big Ten institution such as Penn State. The agreement is also an acknowledgement of the power of the Central and Eastern time zone television audiences.[13]

While the Big Ten was adjusting to the idea of admitting Penn State and working out a new television deal along with the Pac-10, other schools and conferences were starting to realize the growing importance of television revenue. In 1990, Notre Dame introduced the notion that certain schools were more valuable than others, at least from a television perspective.

Since the beginning, the Fighting Irish had brought more value to the CFA package than they received. In fact, following the 1984 Supreme Court decision, WTBS had attempted to acquire exclusive rights to Notre Dame's home games, and other networks came calling in the years that followed. Notre Dame was committed to making the CFA work back then, but times had changed.

The CFA was negotiating a new contract that would cover 1991-1995. The group had been with CBS, but after a disappointing offer from the network the CFA decided to speak with ABC and NBC. Because ABC already had the Big Ten/Pac-10 deal, signing on with the CFA would mean eliminating competition, which might allow for higher ad rates and better ratings.

ABC came in with a contract worth $210 million over five years, well above CBS' $110 million, five-year offer. However, because ABC's deal with the Big Ten/Pac-10 guaranteed at least one game each Saturday broadcast to at least 50 percent of the nation, the CFA deal would be built around a regional approach.

Notre Dame had long enjoyed its status as a national brand. The Fighting Irish had established a national radio presence decades previously. Prior to the 1984 Supreme Court decision, Notre Dame appeared on television 78 times, the most of any program. Six of the twelve highest-rated games in college football history featured the Fighting Irish. The exposure was great for Notre Dame, especially when it came to recruiting.

Although Notre Dame had been loyal to the CFA, and the new CFA deal would for the first time surpass revenue levels under the NCAA television plan, the Fighting Irish simply refused to watch their national brand shrink. For the first time it started seriously listening to an offer from a network who wanted to broadcast it individually.

Notre Dame ended up negotiating its own deal with NBC in February 1990. This caused the CFA's new deals with ABC and ESPN to be renegotiated, resulting in a combined $45 million reduction. The CFA estimated Notre Dame would have received $20 million a under the new CFA contract if it had "maximized its appearances."[14]

The Fighting Irish reportedly received $38 million over five years with NBC.[15] On top of that, Notre Dame was able to maximize its appearances by having all six home games a year on national television, in addition to away games being broadcast on other networks. Under the CFA's new deal with ABC, they would have been subject to a new broadcasting strategy that would see less national games and more regional exposure.

Notre Dame's value was in its success, both on the field and in the ratings game on television. As you can see from Chart 4.1, Notre Dame consistently out-rated every other college football game it was up against during the 1989 season, the last before signing with NBC.

Chart 4.1

SEPTEMBER 16	ABC	Notre Dame-Michigan	10.5
	CBS	Illinois-Colorado	2.8
SEPTEMBER 23	ABC	Ohio State-USC	4.4
	CBS	Michigan State-Notre Dame	7.3
SEPTEMBER 30	ABC	Notre Dame-Purdue	4.4
	CBS	Auburn-Tennessee	4.0
OCTOBER 21	ABC	Michigan-Iowa, UCLA-Oregon State	2.8
	CBS	USC-Notre Dame	10.9
NOVEMBER 18	ABC	UCLA-USC, Indiana-Illinois	4.1
	CBS	Notre Dame-Penn State	9.1
NOVEMBER 25	CBS	Notre Dame-Miami	14.9*
	NBC	227	12.5
		Amen	16.1
		The Golden Girls	20.4
		Empty Nest	20.0
	ABC	Mr. Belvedere	8.0
		Living Dolls	7.3
		Columbo	10.0

As noted by *Sports Illustrated* at the time, Notre Dame had, "eight national championship teams and seven Heisman Trophy winners, not to mention the Four Horsemen, the Gipper and various other heroes, all of which have produced a national following that is unique in sports."[16]

The Fighting Irish took plenty of criticism for their move, perhaps even overshadowing Penn State's move, which was equally driven by financial stability.

Penn State coach Joe Paterno was quoted in a 1990 *Sports Illustrated* article as saying, "It's been a fun year for all of us.

"We got to see Notre Dame go from an academic institute to a banking institute."

Arkansas athletic director, Frank Broyles, who would move his school from the Southwest Conference to the SEC two years later, said, "To me, Notre Dame has vacated its leadership role. This is greed."

The sentiment was echoed by Georgia athletic director Vince Dooley, whose school would be part of the SEC's new television deal just a few short years later. "Surprise, shock, greed and ultimate greed. That's the reaction I'm getting from people."[17]

The CFA could have fallen apart right then and there had the SEC not opted to turn down its suitors and stay with the collective. CBS, TBS and others were courting the SEC, and Notre Dame had planted the seed that in the end everyone had to look out for themselves. Given assurances their conference would receive at least 22 percent of the appearances under the new deal, the SEC stuck with the CFA. For the time being.

The moves by Penn State and Notre Dame put the writing on the wall. Although Penn State's addition to the Big Ten was partially at the university's behest, it was also perceived as a power move by other conferences. Coupled with Notre Dame's decision shortly thereafter to leave the CFA for its own deal with NBC, and a subsequent investigation by the Federal Trade Commission into the CFA's television contract on antitrust grounds, others began planning for a suddenly uncertain future. It became obvious television was moving away from the collective and toward the power of individual schools and conferences to command coverage.

Harvey Schiller, SEC commissioner until 1990, began quietly discussing expansion within his conference in the late 1980s. He developed a partnership program that would later be copied by other conferences, but he kept running into roadblocks when it came to the markets his conference reached. He felt that if he could expand westward into Arkansas or Texas, eastward into South Carolina or even further into Florida with Florida State or Miami, he could open up new opportunities for the SEC with marketers who wanted to blanket the South.

Schiller left the SEC in January 1990, only a month after the Big Ten announced its invitation to Penn State and shortly before Notre Dame signed its new television deal. The atmosphere was ripe for the SEC to act on its previous discussions, and new commissioner Roy Kramer picked up where Schiller left off.

On May 31, 1990, the SEC voted to authorize expansion. Ole Miss President Gerald Turner cited the CFA's inevitable decline as the primary reasoning, saying the SEC must prepare to negotiate its own contracts in the future. The "first step in that direction is minimizing the force of competing conferences in our geographic area," Turner told the *Washington Post*.

Years later, Vince Dooley would tell author Keith Dunnavant, "The Notre Dame decision and Penn State's moving to the Big Ten sent us a signal. The train was leaving the station. If we were going to be prepared to negotiate our own television contracts in the future, and hold a championship game as we'd talked about, we needed to move to strengthen our television base."[18]

Targets for SEC expansion included Texas, Texas A&M, Arkansas, Florida State, Miami and South Carolina. To achieve his goal, Kramer favored moving into Arkansas, South Carolina and Texas. This move was very different than the Big Ten's expansion, as some targets (Texas, Texas A&M and Arkansas) were members of a conference for football, whereas Penn State had been independent. At this point in history, raiding another conference was unprecedented.

Arkansas ended up being the first domino to fall to the SEC, which, as it would turn out, prevented Texas or Texas A&M from becoming members. Losing Arkansas had a huge impact on the Southwest Conference. At the time, Arkansas represented a quarter of the Southwest Conference's revenue. Had either, or both, of the Texas schools followed Arkansas, it would have been a fatal blow to the conference. Texas legislators, many of whom had attended Southwest Conference schools, effectively prevented either Texas school from joining the SEC.

The move made sense for Arkansas, which stood to make $1 million more per year, according to then–athletic director Frank Broyles.[19]

"Once, TV was a novelty," said Broyles following the announcement in 1990 that Arkansas joining the SEC, "But as the dollars kept accelerating, and we started to depend on it, I guess we sealed our own fate."[20]

There are varying accounts on why Florida State didn't become the 12th member of the SEC. Some believe Florida State didn't think it could compete on the field in the SEC. Others believed Florida State didn't want to be in the same conference as Florida or that the Seminoles preferred to be associated with the academic programs in the ACC.

As it turned out, both the SEC and ACC were simultaneously pursuing Florida State. The ACC's first vote on expansion in September 1990 received only three votes in favor of expanding at all. While ACC commissioner Gene Corrigan worked to secure the other three votes he would need, the SEC's talks with Florida State broke down over scheduling issues. Corrigan found the votes and the Seminoles agreed to become the 9th member of the ACC.

The SEC was down to Miami and South Carolina. The latter had already held a vote of the trustees approving SEC membership. Miami, however, was eyeing the Big East, which covered a geographic area mimicking that of the school's enrollment. In addition, the Big East offered an opportunity to improve the Hurricanes basketball program.

The Big East had been watching realignment with growing concern. Boston College, Pittsburgh and Syracuse were independent in football but placed other sports in the Big East. Should one of them be lured into another conference for football, they would leave the Big East for all sports. The Big East couldn't afford that.

After South Carolina was invited to join the SEC in September 1990, Miami officially joined the Big East, solidifying the league. Virginia Tech, Temple, West Virginia and Rutgers also signed on to play football in the Big East, joining Pittsburgh, Syracuse and Boston College to form an eight-team football conference.

The SEC might not have been the first to make a move, although it did establish a significant first: create a conference championship game in football. At the time, an NCAA rule allowing a conference with 12 members to split into two divisions and play a conference championship game had never been used in Division I-A (now FBS). Kramer and the SEC believed the additional game would make them more attractive to television networks.

And, of course, they were right. The conference championship garnered the SEC an extra $4.5 million per year initially, which quickly totaled nearly $40 million in the first five years.[21] No longer ignorant of their broadcast value, the SEC effectively destroyed the CFA in 1994 when it announced it had negotiated its own contract with CBS worth $85 million over five years, beginning in 1996. It would represent more than double what the SEC had earned under the last CFA contract and was the first contract after the 1984 Supreme Court decision that really allowed schools to experience the benefit of the free market approach.

In a way, the SEC signed the Southwest Conference's death warrant. Taking away Arkansas left the Southwest Conference with only Texas schools. While the SEC covered 9 states and 19 percent of the nation's television sets, the Southwest Conference was left with 6.7 percent and was unable to land its own television contract when the CFA dissolved.[22]

The Southwest Conference wanted to join the Big Eight to form a 16-team conference, but the Big Eight was only interested in Texas, Texas A&M, Texas Tech and Baylor (although the latter was included thanks to political maneuvering). It was becoming clear to conferences that schools should be added only when they brought more to the table than they consumed.

Although the remaining Southwest Conference members (Rice, SMU, TCU and Houston) were located in large television markets of Dallas and Houston, the Big Eight felt it already had those markets covered with the additions of Texas, Texas A&M, Texas Tech and Baylor. In addition, the schools left behind had suffered attendance declines after professional sports increasingly moved into their cities and a series of football-related scandals that rocked the Southwest Conference in the 1980s. The fan bases remaining at Rice, SMU, TCU and Houston were simply too small to justify dividing revenue with them.

Rice, SMU and TCU went to join the WAC, which expanded to 16 members, and Houston went to Conference USA. The newly formed Big 12 signed a five-year, $100 million with ABC and Liberty Sports shortly thereafter.

Two years later, in 1997, the deal among the Rose Bowl, ABC, the Big Ten and Pac-10 was over, although the deal that covered the regular season ran through 2001. Since the last regular season deal had been signed, college football's value in the eyes of the networks had increased. Year after year new contracts being signed were growing longer in length as networks fought to hold onto what they had.

The Pac-10 agreed to extend with ABC through 2006, which meant a huge increase in revenue. Under the previous contract it would have received approximately $10 million over the next four seasons; the new deal started at $13.75 million and increased each year until it reached $19 million in the final season.

ABC and ESPN had recently joined under the same corporate roof, and the Big Ten's contract called for airtime on each. The new deal ran through the 2006-2007 season and included men's and women's basketball and women's volleyball.[23]

The next big moment in conference realignment history arrived in 1999 when eight members of the WAC formed a new conference: the Mountain West Conference. BYU, Utah, San Diego State, Colorado State, Air Force, New Mexico, UNLV and Wyoming made up the new Mountain West, while UTEP, Rice, SMU, Tulsa, Hawaii, Fresno State, San Jose State and TCU remained in the WAC.

The WAC had been large, which made both scheduling and traveling difficult. In addition, none of the schools carried enough weight to merit a television deal that could feed all the hungry mouths adequately. Years later, as you'll learn in Chapter 9, the Mountain West would become the first conference to start its own television network.

2000s

Conference realignment is more closely related to El Nino than a yearly season like fall. It doesn't come through annually, and when it does it leaves a wake in its path. The next storm arrived in 2003.

In May 2003, it became public knowledge that the ACC was looking to expand by three and had its eyes set on Big East targets—Miami, Syracuse, Boston College and Virginia Tech. Rumors had been spreading that the football members of the Big East were contemplating forming a new conference, which made the ACC want to move fast. A 7-2 vote of the ACC members during the conference's annual spring meetings approved expansion, although there was debate regarding which would receive invites.

A month later, UConn, joined by Pittsburgh, Rutgers, Virginia Tech and West Virginia, filed suit against Miami, Boston College and the ACC, a preemptive move meant to stop the ACC's advances before official invitations were extended. The suit alleged a number of violations of law, including breach of fiduciary duty, unjust enrichment and violation of the Connecticut Unfair Trade Practices Act. It noted assurances given by the schools to the Big East in the past, which plaintiffs now believed constituted false and misleading statements.

"This lawsuit reveals a backroom conspiracy, born in secret, founded on greed, and carried out through calculated deceit," Connecticut Attorney General Richard Blumenthal said in a press release announcing the lawsuit. "Our legal action seeks to stop ongoing fraud and other illegal misconduct and recover millions of dollars that may be lost as a result of repeated false and misleading statements—reassurances that these schools were committed to the Big East, while they were secretly negotiating to defect and break their agreements. Their assurances and promises were explicit and unequivocal, made with clear knowledge that we would rely on them."

The concern for UConn and other members that would stay behind in the Big East was a significant loss in revenue. The belief was that the loss of schools would force the Big East out of BCS automatic-qualifying status. The previous year BCS participants received $13.5-16.5 million, compared to payments under $1 million for teams in non-BCS bowls. The lawsuit also surmised the remaining Big East members would lose millions of dollars in "broadcasting fees, season ticket sales, away-game revenues, and game day revenues."

In addition, several schools had recently invested millions in facilities presumably on the assumption conference revenue would stay on the same trajectory. Virginia Tech had expanded its football stadium to the tune of $37 million, Pittsburgh had negotiated a long-term lease to play at Heinz Field, and Connecticut had completed a $90 million construction project on a football stadium.

Shortly after the lawsuit was filed, a surprise announcement was made: the ACC had voted to invite Miami and Virginia Tech, not Boston College or Syracuse. The vote to approve a package that included Miami, Boston College and Syracuse had not garnered the necessary seven of nine votes, falling one short. Instead, Virginia Tech, a plaintiff in the lawsuit, was being invited at the insistence of Virginia, which would not vote for expansion otherwise.

Duke, North Carolina and North Carolina State, the dissenting votes for Miami and Virginia Tech, would vote several months later in October 2003 to make Boston College the conference's 12th member. Having seen the SEC's success with a championship game, the ACC was interested in staging its own, which was believed to be capable of producing $10-12 million a year in revenue. The ACC applied for an NCAA waiver that would allow it to hold a championship with 11 members, and it was denied in September, no doubt reopening the expansion conversation.

President of Boston College, William P. Leahy, listed a number of reasons for his school's move in an interview days after accepting the ACC invitation. In addition to a list of academic benefits, he also commented on the stability of the ACC and the added financial benefits, which he said would benefit female sports.

In the meantime, a Connecticut superior court had dropped the lawsuit against the ACC for jurisdictional reasons, leaving Miami as the only defendant. UConn, Pittsburgh, West Virginia and Rutgers promptly filed suit against Boston College, which the plaintiffs had named in the first lawsuit and then dropped after invites were extended to only Miami and Virginia Tech initially. The second suit also included four ACC officials individually, hoping to overcome the jurisdictional issues faced when the group sued the conference as a whole.

A court in Massachusetts eventually entered a declaratory judgment in favor of Boston College and an out-of-court settlement was reached by all parties in the spring of 2005. The settlement was worth a reported $5 million and a public records request showed UConn deposited $1 million. In addition, the settlement provided for several home-and-home series between Big East and ACC schools: Florida State and West Virginia (a series West Virginia would cancel when it left the Big East for the Big 12 nearly 10 years later), North Carolina and Rutgers, North Carolina State and Pittsburgh, and Virginia and Connecticut.

It wouldn't take long for the ACC to collect on its new investment. At the time the conference had a television deal with ABC and ESPN through the 2005 season, choosing to invoke a clause that allowed for renegotiation if the membership composition changed following the 2003 season.

Prior to renegotiating, the ACC was receiving $25 million per year from ABC and ESPN. The new deal would extend the relationship through 2010, starting at $28 million a year and increase to $42 million by 2010. Add in the additional income from a championship game and each ACC member was expected to see a 59 percent revenue increase.

The new deal brought the ACC closer to the SEC, which had already been bringing in approximately $40 million a year. It also increased the ACC's exposure. Thursday night appearances would double to six and the conference would receive a primetime game on Labor Day and games during Thanksgiving weekend.

As Miami and Virginia Tech prepared to join the ACC in 2004, and Boston College in 2006, the Big East found itself searching for new members in order to maintain its total at eight. UConn had planned to move its football program into the Big East (it had been playing football in Division I-AA) in 2005 but moved the date up to 2004.

Although the defections impacted the conference most in terms of football, the support of the basketball schools would be necessary when it came time to replace the departed. Cincinnati and Louisville emerged immediately as favorites, as both schools were attractive additions in football and basketball. Memphis and South Florida were also considered, the latter because of the fertile recruiting ground in Florida.

UConn basketball coach Jim Calhoun was outspokenly in favor of the additions of Louisville and Cincinnati.

"If we were to replace (Miami and Virginia Tech) with Louisville and Cincinnati, our league would be as good as anybody's in the country," Calhoun said.

"Just imagine us adding [Cincinnati coach Bob] Huggins and (Louisville coach Rick) Pitino. That would make for one heck of a league schedule. I say let's not wallow in what's already happened. There's only one way to get back at the ACC—and that's to become a better conference than the ACC."[24]

The football-playing members of the Big East had considered splitting off and forming their own conference even before losing members and would revisit the idea as they considered Cincinnati and Louisville's addition. The fear was that scheduling would become an issue in Olympic sports as the conference grew and it made sense to some members to split football schools apart into a new conference. That idea would eventually be pushed aside with the Cardinals and Bearcats being added to the Big East, in addition to DePaul and Marquette as non-football members.

UConn President Philip E. Austin noted the final decision to stick together as a conference was heavily influenced by television's role.

"To have a conference—and you're negotiating TV contracts—that reaches just shy of 25 percent of the television sets in the country, that's something that's very strong," said Austin.

Louisville was an easy choice for the Big East. Not only was it strong enough in both basketball and football, it had injected millions into facilities since Tom Jurich's arrival in 1997. The university's sports dominated the town, which lacked any professional sports.

Cincinnati was a tougher decision. Nippert Stadium, where the Bearcats play football, seated only 35,000 and fewer than 29,000 had attended the 2003 home opener. With a solid basketball program and the chance to move into the Cincinnati market, the Big East decided to add them in the hopes being part of a BCS conference would increase the Bearcats attendance.

When Boston College was announced as an ACC addition, the Big East was forced back to the drawing board for another member. South Florida immediately emerged as a favorite, both from a recruiting and television standpoint. In early November 2003, the Big East announced its five new additions, approved unanimously by all members: Louisville, Cincinnati, DePaul, Marquette and South Florida.

Figures released by the conference at the time showed the newly configured conference would reach nearly 24 million households, more than 22 percent of the nation. However, there was debate over whether it made up for the loss of the other schools. Miami and Virginia Tech had accounted for 70 percent of the Big East's football games on ESPN and ABS over the previous several years.

Prior to the conference's reorganization, the Big East was receiving approximately $15 million a year under its football deal with ESPN and, including basketball, $22 million total. There were reports the network wanted to reduce the contract by almost half.

Len DeLuca, who was a programming executive at ESPN at the time, characterized the situation as a difficult one.

"What happened in 2004 was that the [Big East] football rights diminished incredibly. At that point, there were some very difficult negotiations that ESPN had, but ESPN also recognized the value of Big Monday," DeLuca said, referring to college basketball doubleheaders it featured on Monday nights. "The new deal was crafted so that the Big East could save face, but obviously they were of diminished importance in football."

In 2007, the Big East would receive a new deal worth approximately $33 million a year.

The conference would do well in another area, thanks to the new basketball members: sponsorships. Shortly after the addition of the new members, the Big East signed new deals with Verizon Wireless and Discovery Channel, for three years each, both of which had the conference basketball tournament as a major focus.

Virginia Tech had similar success in landing new sponsorships as a result of its move to the ACC, signing two new partners shortly after announcing the move: Sheetz and SunTrust. These deals were made possible presumably because of the new geographic reach of the Hokies.

Individual schools joining the Big East would also see positive financial benefits in the years that followed. Average revenue growth for all public FBS universities from the 2004-2005 school year to 2010-2011 was 58 percent. Each of the schools that joined the Big East eclipsed that mark. Louisville saw the largest growth at 113 percent, followed by South Florida at 104 percent and Cincinnati at 63 percent.

The ACC and Big East moves would trickle down into the non-AQ football conferences. All five of the schools added to the Big East came from Conference USA. Instead of filing suit or forcing high exit fees for those schools, Conference USA reached agreements with the schools for scheduling over the next five years.

In addition to the losses to the Big East, Conference USA was further depleted by other moves. Charlotte and Saint Louis left for the Atlantic 10, TCU joined the Mountain West and Army opted to become independent. These teams were replaced with Central Florida and Marshall from the MAC, Rice, SMU, Tulsa and UTEP from the WAC. In the end, Conference USA was able to split into two divisions of six schools each and host a football conference championship game.

The reconfigured Conference USA wouldn't lose television money, although it wouldn't gain any either. In January 2005, the conference signed new deals with ESPN and CSTV for football and men's and women's basketball, replacing an eight-year ESPN deal signed in 2001. The two new contracts together would equal the previous contract, which would mean a 68 percent drop in ESPN's deal. The conference would maintain exposure, with at least ten regular-season football games on ESPN or ESPN2, at least six men's basketball game and three women's basketball games.

2010s

Conference Realignment Since 2010

2010

June 10, 2010
Colorado to Pac-10
Colorado announces move from the Big-12 to Pac-10.

June 11, 2010
Boise State to MWC
Boise State announces move from WAC to MWC as MWC attempts to assemble AQ-worthy membership.

June 12, 2010
Big Ten Adds Nebraska
Nebraska leaves Big-12 for the Big Ten, leaving the Big-12 with only 10 teams

June 17, 2010
Utah Joins the Pac-10
The Mountain West doesn't get to celebrate Boise State's addition for long before Utah departs for the Pac-10.

Aug 18, 2010
Mountain West Adds and Subtracts
Amidst reports BYU is going independent in football and joining the WAC in other sports the Mountain West lures Fresno State and Nevada from the WAC.

Aug 31, 2010
BYU Goes Independent
BYU announces it will be an independent in football and place all other sports in the WAC.

Nov 11, 2010
WAC Adds Two from Texas
Texas-San Antonio and Texas State decide to move up from FCS and join WAC, but Montana turns down invite.

Nov 29, 2010
TCU to Big East
TCU to move from Mountain West to Big East.

Dec 10, 2010
WAC Loses Another
Hawaii, the oldest-running member of the WAC, announces it's leaving for Mountain West.

2011

Sept 18, 2011
ACC First to 14
Sensing realignment is not yet over, the ACC scoops up Syracuse and Pittsburgh.

Sept 25, 2011
Big 12 in Danger Again
Texas A&M announces it's heading to the SEC.

Oct 10, 2011
TCU on the Move Again
Last year TCU was leaving the Mountain West for the Big East, but now the Horned Frogs are headed to the Big 12.

Oct 14, 2011
The First Mega-Conference is Born?
Mountain West and Conference USA announce they will merge for the 2013 season and have 20-24 teams.

Oct 28, 2011
WVU to Big 12
WVU leaves Big East for Big 12 and helps replace SEC-bound Missouri

Nov 6, 2011
SEC Goes to 14
The SEC announces it will round out its ranks with Missouri. Dec 7, 2011
Big East Adds Five
Boise State, San Diego State, Houston, SMU and Central Florida are announced to be the Big East's newest members, effective 2013.

Conference Realignment Since 2010

2012

January 24, 2012

Navy Jumps on Board with Big East

Navy opted to end its independence and join the Big East as a football-only member.

Feb 8, 2012

Memphis on the Move

The Big East takes a fourth member from C-USA when it adds Memphis.

March 7, 2012

Temple is Back

Temple will move back to the Big East, this time in all sports.

April 9, 2012

Georgia State Moves Up from FCS

The Sun Belt announces Georgia State will move up from FCS in 2013.

May 2, 2012

Sun Belt Adds Another

Texas State announces it will move to the Sun Belt from the WAC.

May 4, 2012

Two More Say Goodbye to WAC

The Mountain West Conference announces it will add San Jose State and Utah State from the WAC.

May 4, 2012

C-USA Grows by Five

After being depleted by the Big East, C-USA announces it will add five: Florida International and North Texas from Sun Belt, Louisiana Tech and University of Texas – San Antonio from the WAC and UNC-Charlotte from FCS.

May 17, 2012

Old Dominion Moves Up from FCS

C-USA announces Old Dominion will move up from FCS to join the conference.

May 24, 2012

Sun Belt Moves Another Up from FCS

The Sun Belt announces UT-Arlington will be moving up from FCS in 2013.

July 25, 2012

C-USA/MWC Mega-Conference Dead

MWC commissioner Craig Thompson says the merger unlikely to happen.

August 20, 2012

WAC Will No Longer Sanction Football

WAC commissioner Jeff Hurd announces the conference will no longer sanction football due to the defections of members.

September 12, 2012

Notre Dame's Big News

The Fighting Irish join the ACC for all sports, except football. However, they agree to play five football games per season against ACC opponents.

November 19, 2012

The Big Ten Goes to Fourteen

The Big Ten just got bigger, adding Maryland and Rutgers to its stable.

November 27, 2012

Big East Continues to Fill Vacancies

Tulane announces it will join the Big East in all sports, and East Carolina will join as a football-only member.

November 28, 2012

Louisville Jumps Ship

Louisville beats out UConn and Cincinnati to replace Maryland in the ACC.

November 29, 2012

C-USA Grows Again

Florida Atlantic and Middle Tennessee announce moves from the Sun Belt.

December 15, 2012

Catholic 7 Announce Split

The basketball members of the Big East announce they've unanimously voted to leave conference.

December 31, 2012

Boise State and San Diego Do About-Face

With the Big East of the future looking more like a reunion of C-USA, Boise State and San Diego decide they're not going to leave the Mountain West after all.

2013

March 27, 2013
Sun Belt Adds Four
The Sun Belt announces it will add four to fill vacancies: Georgia Southern and Appalachian State from FCS and Idaho and New Mexico State from the WAC. The latter two will play as independents in 2013 before joining in 2014 as football-only members.

April 1, 2013
C-USA Adds One More
Western Kentucky announces it will join C-USA from Sun Belt.

April 2, 2013
Another C-USA School Moves to Big East
Tulsa announces it will join the Big East in all sports in 2014.

As soon as fans started becoming used to the new-look ACC, Big East and the rest, a conference left out of the last round of realignment tipped a domino that would set off a new series of shifts. To keep track at home, you might find Figure 1 handy.

In June 2010, the Pac-10 invited Colorado to become its 11th member. The addition was, not surprisingly, about revenue generation. The Pac-10 had hired Larry Scott, former Women's World Tennis Association chief executive, as commissioner the previous summer and tasked him with improving revenue. The easiest place to do that? Television.

Adding Colorado meant adding the nation's 17th largest television market in Denver, which gave the Pac-10 eight of the top 30 markets. The addition was also timely, as the Pac-10 was preparing to enter an exclusive negotiating window with Fox for its media rights.

It was widely reported that the Pac-10's original plan was to move to 16 teams with the addition of Colorado, Texas, Texas A&M, Oklahoma, Oklahoma State and Texas Tech. That plan would fall apart just five days after the Colorado announcement. In those five days, the Big 12 would secure an extension to its contract with Fox and assurances from its other media partner, ESPN, that it would not reduce its payouts as a result of the conference losing Colorado and Nebraska, the latter announcing it would be moving to the Big Ten two days after the former.

Meanwhile, the Mountain West wasn't sitting back and waiting for realignment to trickle down this time. Instead, it announced it would be adding Boise State on June 11th, 2010, the day between the Colorado and Nebraska announcements. The Mountain West's motivation was also money, but it wasn't simply looking for a better television deal down the road, it wanted to become an AQ conference. The BCS would consider adding a seventh AQ based on football results from 2008-2011, and adding Boise State whose 2006 and 2009 seasons had culminated with Fiesta Bowl appearances gave the Mountain West its best shot at inclusion.

Increased television rights fees would be icing on the cake, of course. The Mountain West had contracts with Versus and CSTV/CBS Sports, both of which allowed for renegotiation if a member was added or subtracted. The contracts were worth $12 million annually for the conference through 2015-2016, which was $8 million more per year than Boise State's former conference, the WAC.

AQ status seemed to be within reach for the Mountain West after adding Boise State—for about six days.

Thanks to Texas' last-minute demands to keep its local television rights and the Pac-10's plans to start a conference network in the future, the rumored 16-team Pac-10 made up of Big 12 additions quickly fell apart. Some sources reported Texas had also asked for unequal revenue distribution, which had been instituted for years in both the Big 12 and Pac-10. The Pac-10 was steadfast in moving to equal sharing under Scott's leadership. Those issues sealed the Longhorns' decision to stay in the Big 12, and combined with a new Fox deal and ESPN assurances, the rest of the Big 12 remained intact for the time being.

The Pac-10 found itself at 11 members, one short of what it would need for a lucrative conference championship game. It next turned to another school with a major television market, University of Utah. The move made sense for Utah, which was receiving only $1.2 million per year from television revenue in the Mountain West. With Salt Lake City's 32nd-ranked television market, the Pac-10 had arguably locked up the top available markets.

Heading into its exclusive window with Fox, the Pac-10 (which would later be renamed the Pac-12) was distributing $8-9 million in revenue per school. Meanwhile, Big Ten and SEC television deals averaged $17-22 million per year and the ACC had recently signed a new deal that would bring its schools an average of $13 million per year.

Adding Colorado and Utah meant the Pac-12 would be able to host a conference championship game, another opportunity to boost revenue. The SEC had been holding its conference championship game since 1992, and the Big 12 and ACC followed suit in 1996 and 2005, respectively.

The SEC Championship Game remains the most lucrative of the bunch, accounting for $15.3 million in 2011. The ACC game tried multiple host cities before settling in Charlotte in 2010 and reporting revenue of $5.4 million. The Big 12's championship game in 2009 produced $6 million in ticket revenue alone.

Reports had the Pac-12 seeking $300 million annually from Fox during the exclusive negotiating window, more than either the SEC or Big Ten received. Some speculated that number might have included what it would take to keep the Pac-12 from starting its own network, but it became clear once the rights were on the free market that the Pac-12 wanted its own network.

The Pac-12 rights hit the market at an opportune time, right after Comcast bought NBC and merged the networks. Hoping to find a toehold in the college football market, Comcast told the Pac-12 it would pay $225 million annual for the rights to put games on Versus and NBC. That's when something historical happened: ESPN and Fox partnered to obtain the rights.

Neither ESPN nor Fox could outbid NBC/Comcast and find the timeslots the Pac-12 wanted for its games. Together the picture was different. The Pac-12's media consultant, Evolution Media's Chris Bevilacqua, brought the idea to ESPN's then–executive vice president of content John Skipper.

Skipper was receptive to the idea and called Fox Sports' co-president Randy Freer. The two networks owned the rights to all the major conferences, with the exception of CBS' deal with the SEC, and found a combined effort made sense, especially given the conference's urging the two to see if they could provide more value to the conference.

In the end, the Pac-12 would end up with a deal worth $3 billion over 12 years, averaging out to $250 per year or $20.8 million per school. The two networks would split regular season football games and rotate the basketball tournament and football championship and the conference would receive one of college football's most lucrative contracts while still retaining rights to enough games and digital rights to form its own network, which is covered more extensively in Chapter 9.

Meanwhile, the Big Ten would hold at 12 after adding Nebraska. The conference had hired a Chicago-based company to evaluate expansion, which had looked at adding schools such as Pittsburgh, Notre Dame, Missouri, Syracuse and Rutgers. Results of the report were not made public, but it's safe to assume the conclusion was that not enough additional revenue would be generated to make the additions worthwhile at that time.

Nebraska, however, did make sense for the Big Ten. The Cornhuskers gave the conference its 12th member, allowing it to host a conference championship game. Although the Omaha media market ranked 76th, Nebraska had other advantages, including a large fan base and membership in the American Association of Universities, a credential all Big Ten schools held. Unfortunately, Nebraska was stripped of its membership the following year.

Nonetheless, the addition allowed the Big Ten to sign a six-year deal with Fox for the conference championship game reportedly worth $145 million, or $24 million per year.

Back to the Mountain West, which was left reeling after the loss of Utah to the Pac-10 on June 17th. The very next day, the conference was hit with the news BYU was exploring becoming a football independent and joining the WAC for all other sports. Not wanting to wait around, the conference quickly issued invites to Fresno State and Nevada from the WAC.

The additions allowed the conference's network, The Mtn., to add two new markets to its repertoire. The Mountain West also believed it would assist in its bid to become an AQ. By the end of the month, however, the BYU move to independence would become final and any hopes of the Mountain West achieving AQ status were dashed.

It would take until November of 2010 for the WAC to shore up its membership with the addition of Texas-San Antonio and Texas State, which was moving up from FCS. However, it would lose Hawaii, its oldest member, to the Mountain West in December after the latter lost TCU to the Big East.

The dust had hardly settled from these moves when rumors began to surface in August 2011 that Texas A&M wanted to join the SEC. Talk of the Aggies fleeing the Big 12 for the SEC was nothing new. In June 2010, *Sports Illustrated* reported the SEC had initiated contact with Texas A&M months earlier, a fact that would become a hotly debated topic in 2011 when the Aggies were officially invited to join.

It appeared the Aggies had been weighing their options: go in the proposed six-team deal to the Pac-10 or strike out on its own for the SEC. While the Pac-10 deal fell through, Texas A&M didn't quit looking and talks progressed with the SEC.

In January 2011, Texas announced a 20-year, $300 million partnership with ESPN to form its own network: the Longhorn Network. Many would speculate the Aggies wanted to leave the Big 12 because of the network, but reality is probably that it was just one reason on a list of many. A reason that created several related issues. On top of the revenue disparity it would create between Texas and the rest of the Big 12—a big gulf already—there was concern the network would show high school football games, which might create a recruiting advantage for Texas, and that one conference game a year could end up on the network.

While Texas A&M was considering its options, the ACC decided it would not sit idly by and watch conference realignment unfold. On September 18, 2011, the ACC would surprise everyone by announcing it was adding Pittsburgh and Syracuse a mere 24 hours after news broke that the two schools had applied for membership. The ACC attributed its swift action to the fact that the conference had been studying the potential impact of expansion for the previous 18 months. The two-team expansion would make the ACC the first 14-team AQ conference.

The additions would not only strengthen the conference from both a football and basketball perspective, they would open up additional media markets to the ACC. Syracuse was the 82nd-largest media market at the time, while also drawing from New York, the nation's top media market. Pittsburgh was the 24th largest. The additions allowed the ACC to essentially extend its recruiting base and media coverage across the entire East Coast.

North Carolina's then–athletic director Dick Baddour had this to say:

> "From our position, if you think about this nationally, it's obvious that the world is turning upside down, and you want the ACC —I want the University of North Carolina—to be in a position where we are strong, that we are strong in all areas, that all of our sports are strong, that our television packages are strong as well."

The conference was indeed able to strengthen its television contract. Although its rights weren't out on the free market, a provision in its deal with ESPN allowed renegotiation with a change in membership. The final result was a $3.6 billion agreement reached in May 2012, which would increase each member's average yearly revenue from television from $12.9 million to $17.1 million.

The ACC's expansion also ushered in a shift in the way the entire process of realignment played out. The first news of the expansion wasn't about the ACC *inviting* Pittsburgh and Syracuse, it was about the schools *applying* for admission. This was perhaps an attempt by the ACC to insulate itself from the lawsuits it faced in the last round of realignment, and those rumored to be brewing in response to the Texas A&M to SEC rumblings. This time the ACC said it received applications for membership that numbered in the double-digits as schools sought stability for the future and that the conference essentially had the pick of the litter.

Whatever the case may have been, the expansion moves that would follow would also be the result of applications, not invitations.

On the same day as the ACC's expansion announcement, reports began to swirl that the Pac-12 was again courting Texas, Texas Tech, Oklahoma and Oklahoma State.

One week after the ACC made its move, the SEC would expand West by making Texas A&M its 13th member. After the SEC announced Texas A&M's addition, it would become clear Texas A&M was fed up with the unequal revenue sharing in the Big 12, Texas' dominance of the league's governance and the general lack of an all-for-one, one-for-all attitude in the conference.

Unfortunately, the announcement would kick off months of accusations that the SEC had interfered with the Big 12's conference agreements by inviting Texas A&M and claims by an economist that the entire state of Texas would suffer economically because of the move. Legal terms including "tortious interference" were thrown around, suggesting the SEC had intentionally damaged the Big 12's contractual relationship with Texas A&M. Legal action was considered by several schools, prompted more by the possibility that Texas, Oklahoma and company would bolt to the Pac-12 than by the loss of Texas A&M alone. Once it became clear the Big 12 would survive everyone moved on.

For the SEC, Texas A&M made sense because it opened up the Texas market for both recruiting and television. Although not the same impact as University of Texas, A&M still delivered portions of the Dallas, Houston and San Antonio markets, which rank 5th, 10th and 37th amongst national media markets. Schools such as Florida State and Miami had been mentioned as possible SEC targets, with most believing they were passed up because they represented markets the SEC already had cornered.

In addition, Texas A&M would improve the academic profile of the SEC. It would become the third SEC school with membership in the prestigious Association of American Universities (AAU), a group of recognized research institutions. It also brought a student body that topped 47,000, meaning a large fan base of both current students and alumni.

With the loss of Texas A&M, the Big 12 had fallen to nine members in the course of barely more than a year's time. After Texas and Oklahoma recommitted to the conference, including agreeing to share all television revenue equally amongst all members, the Big 12 turned its sights on expansion.

TCU, which had announced its move from the Mountain West to the Big East just eleven months prior, would be invited to fill one of those slots. As it would turn out, the Horned Frogs would never play a single game as a member of the Big East. Although TCU brought no new market to the table, given Texas already effectively delivered the Dallas market, it did bring a strong football program.

The Big 12 had signed a new television deal with Fox worth $1.17 billion in April of 2011 based upon a membership of ten. TCU would slide into Texas A&M's slot to maintain the necessary number, but the conference still feared Missouri would follow to the SEC.

A little more than two weeks later the Big 12 would announce its next addition: West Virginia. Publicly reports were surfacing that Missouri would become the SEC's 14th member, and it seemed that behind closed doors the deal was done save an agreement over exit fees. Again, West Virginia wouldn't move the needle much in terms of television market, although it did expand the conference's reach eastward and add another program with a strong football tradition.

The Big 12 would remain at 11 for only a week before Missouri announced its move to the SEC, as expected. With it the SEC would gain access to the 21st and 30th largest television markets in St. Louis and Kansas City. Missouri also gave the SEC another of the prestigious AAU schools, bringing its total to four.

In the midst of the SEC and Big 12 moves, the Mountain West and C-USA were contemplating how to best position themselves amidst reports they'd be losing schools to the Big East. In mid-October they would announce a merger of the two conferences to form a 20-24 member conference. At the time of the announcement, the leagues had yet to determine how the partnership would work in terms of scheduling, media rights, championship games and other logistics.

In December of 2011, the Big East would make its additions from the Mountain West and C-USA official with formal invitations to Houston, SMU, Central Florida, Boise State and San Diego State. The latter two would be joining as football-only members of the conference.

In the coming months, the Big East would add two more full members, Memphis and Temple, bringing its ranks to the magic 12 necessary for a conference championship game.

In May of 2012, the Mountain West and C-USA would announce more additions, with the Mountain West adding San Jose State and Utah State and C-USA adding Charlotte, Florida International, Louisiana Tech, North Texas and Texas-San Antonio.

As the calendar turned to 2012, the Big East continued to shore up its membership. First, Navy announced in January that it would no longer be independent in football, but would instead join the Big East as a football-only member. Navy's tradition as an independent in football dates back to 1879, but the administration felt the conference landscape had changed so much as to make it difficult to continue on independently. From scheduling games to negotiating television contracts and being invited to bowl games, being an independent had become more and more difficult over the years.

Soon after the Navy announcement, in early February, Memphis announced it would move all of its sports from C-USA to the Big East. Many believed the Big East added Memphis in order to please the non-football members of the conference, generally referred to as the "basketball schools," or later the "Catholic 7"—DePaul, Georgetown, Marquette, Providence, Seton Hall, St. John's and Villanova. At the time of the announcement, Memphis had made 23 appearances in March Madness, having reached the Final Four three times and the championship game once in 2008. Memphis also brought the Big East the 49th-largest media market.

In March, the Big East accepted an old friend back into the fold: Temple. After being unceremoniously forced out of the conference as a football-only member in 2004, the Owls played two seasons as an independent before joining the MAC for football (its other sports played in the Atlantic 10). This time around, the Big East announced all Temple sports would play in the conference.

All of the Big East moves had a trickledown effect, causing the Sun Belt and C-USA to scramble to replace departing members. On April 9, 2012, Georgia State announced it would up from FCS to the Sun Belt in 2013 after having played just three seasons of football. Over the next six weeks, the Sun Belt grabbed Texas State from the WAC and invited University of Texas-Arlington to move up from FCS.

C-USA, which had been depleted by the Big East, added five schools in early May 2012: Florida International and North Texas from the Sun Belt, Louisiana Tech and University of Texas-San Antonio from the WAC and UNC-Charlotte from FCS. Two weeks later, C-USA announced another school would be moving up from FCS to join the conference: Old Dominion.

By the time conference media days rolled around in July, it became clear the C-USA/Mountain West mega-conference wasn't going to happen. Essentially, the scheduling and administrative details were just too complicated. That and both conferences were too busy trying to stabilize their own membership. Meanwhile, the WAC had been so decimated by the departure of the majority of its membership it was forced to announce on August 20, 2012 it would no longer sanction football.

Just as it seemed conference realignment would end, with everyone having shored up their membership and the WAC folding, another round kicked up in the fall of 2012. It began with Notre Dame announcing it would take all of its sports except football and hockey to the ACC. Football would remain independent, but the Irish would agree to play five football games a year against ACC opponents.

Not only does the agreement allow for ACC football programs to have a storied program as an opponent, but ACC Commissioner John Swofford revealed at the 2013 ACC Kickoff that the agreement requires Notre Dame to join the ACC if it decides to join a conference during the term of the agreement. In addition, Notre Dame fit well with ACC members in terms of academic prestige and basketball history. For the Irish the move means better bowl tie-ins through the ACC than it had in previous years with the Big East for the football program and games against the traditional powerhouses like UNC and Duke for the basketball program.

Unfortunately, for the Big East it meant more water to bail out of an already sinking ship. It was no secret schools like UConn, Cincinnati and Louisville were trying to leave. There'd also been rumblings about the increasing unhappiness of the so-called Catholic 7, the conference's basketball schools.

The bad news piled on for the Big East when the Big Ten announced on November 19th it was adding Rutgers. To continue the somewhat surprising turn of events, Maryland would leave the ACC to join Rutgers in the Big Ten.

Big Ten commissioner Jim Delaney said the conference looked to contiguous states with institutions that were members of the AAU, which led the conference to Rutgers and Maryland. It didn't hurt that the schools were in the New York and D.C. television markets, although many were skeptical about the ability of the schools to actually deliver those markets for the Big Ten.

Meanwhile, a new hole in the ACC meant the Big East had to prepare for yet another departure, as the ACC would no doubt turn to UConn, Cincinnati or Louisville to replace Maryland. On November 27th, the Big East would announce the addition of Tulane in all sports and East Carolina as a football-only member. The very next day Louisville would announce it was exiting for the ACC.

The story of how Louisville beat out UConn and Cincinnati for a spot in the ACC is interesting. General sentiment when Maryland's announcement was made was that UConn was the easy choice. With a better academic profile and a larger television market, most already had UConn slotted into the ACC.

"They already had UConn, not penciled in, but penned in," said Louisville athletic director Tom Jurich.[25]

Jurich and university president James Ramsey went to work quickly, attempting to overcome the academic and television issues and make the case it should be Louisville and not UConn. Jurich spoke with television executives and looked for information about the Cardinals' television performance in an attempt to turn the conversation away from television market size. Ramsey approached the academic issue, focusing on the university's fast rise from a commuter school just a decade ago and its future trajectory.

Then Jurich called in every favor he'd ever been owed and cashed in on the good will he'd been building with folks around college athletics during his 29-year tenure in the industry.

"I pulled in every marker I had in the United States. I really did," said Jurich. "Every marker I had in 29 years as an AD, I pulled in, from TV people to other league commissioners to professional sports. Anyone who could vouch for us, I asked them. You've got to sell yourself."[26]

Jurich had relationships with the athletic directors at Florida State, Clemson and Syracuse, and Ramsey had a relationship with UNC's chancellor, who'd been an associate professor there when Ramsey served as UNC's vice chancellor years before. Duke's athletic director, Kevin White, had previously been at Notre Dame and an integral part of Louisville getting into the Big East in 2006. In the end, Louisville proved sometimes it really is all about who you know. The ACC announced Louisville as a member on November 28, 2012.

The beginning of the end for the Big East as we knew it became official on December 15, 2012 when the Catholic 7 presidents announced they had voted to split from the other members of the Big East. In a statement released by the Catholic 7 presidents, they explained:

> "Earlier today we voted unanimously to pursue an orderly evolution to a foundation of basketball schools that honors the history and tradition on which the Big East was established. Under the current context of conference realignment, we believe pursuing a new basketball framework that builds on this tradition of excellence and competition is the best way forward."

As it turned out, the defection of the Catholic 7 was the last straw for Boise State and San Diego State, both of which had developed cold feet about joining the Big East after watching the changing makeup over the previous two years. On December 31, 2012, both schools announced they would not be leaving the Mountain West to join the Big East.

It would take several more months for the picture to come into focus, but in March of 2013 the Catholic 7 announced they had reached an agreement to take the Big East name with them, leaving behind a collection of football-playing schools that looked nothing like the membership just two years prior and without so much as a name for their conference. In April 2013, those schools would announce they had become the American Athletic Conference.

In the meantime, C-USA would add Florida Atlantic and Middle Tennessee in November 2012 to replace the departing Tulane and East Carolina. In April, the conference would also add Western Kentucky to replace a departing Tulsa, which announced it would be moving all of its sports to the soon-to-be-renamed American Athletic Conference.

Each of these teams left the Sun Belt, which led the Sun Belt to add Georgia Southern and Appalachian State from FCS and Idaho and New Mexico from WAC, the last two WAC football programs without conference homes after the WAC announced it wouldn't sponsor football any longer.

Is it safe to say this round of conference realignment, which stretched nearly three years, is over? Not so fast. Conference USA commissioner Britton Banowsky has already gone public with his thoughts on adding two more schools to get to sixteen members:

"We've modeled it at 16, and it does kind of create some divisions that are a little more geographically connected," Banowsky said. "We haven't acted on it. I think personally a larger conference is better because you get some efficiencies, you get the benefit of a bigger group. We don't want to lose our identity in the process. We're just kind of moderating the growth at a pace where people are comfortable. It could be folks are just comfortable [at 14]."

Which football program would C-USA add? Speculation surrounds Arkansas State or Louisiana-Lafayette. Both are currently in the Sun Belt, which could cause the Sun Belt to look to the FCS for more members, which reports have them already actively pursuing even without C-USA poaching more members.

The good news is everything seems settled at the top amongst college football's five power conferences. With the exception of the SEC, members of those conferences have each agreed to a "grant of rights" with the conference. In essence, each school is pledging its television rights to its conference for a given duration, usually the length of the conference's current television contract. If a school left one of these conferences, its television rights would stay behind. Pretty unlikely scenario, because why would another conference want that school if it couldn't cash in on its television rights?

That leaves the only moves to be made involving schools from outside the five major conferences. For the time being, it doesn't seem as though any of them will be moving up to the power conferences, although there does still seem to be some room for addition in conferences like C-USA and the Sun Belt.

NOTES

1 *National Collegiate Athletic Association v. Board of Regents of the University of Oklahoma, et al.*, 468 U.S. 85 (1984).

2 The NCAA reached another deal with cable superstation WTBS in 1982 for a period of two years.

3 The University of Texas sued the NCAA the same day in state court. It served one of its own employees, law professor Charles Alan Wright, with the lawsuit because he chaired the NCAA's Committee on Infractions.

4 What the Supreme Court did do was allude to some restraints that might pass muster: proscribing how much a school could spend on football or how revenue from television rights could be used. Those have never been implemented, but it is interesting to hear those ideas coming from the Supreme Court.

[5] Woolford, Dave (December 30, 1989). "Rose Bowl coaches not in favor of grid playoffs," *Toledo Blade*, p. 9.

[6] Myslenski, S. and Sherman, Ed, "Big Ten Asks Penn State to Join Conference," *Chicago Tribune*, December 15, 1989. Retrieved July 7, 2012, from http://articles.chicagotribune.com/1989-12-15/news/8903180229_1_penn-state-commissioner-james-delany-12th-team.

[7] Sherman, Ed. "Opposition to Penn St. Still Strong in Big Ten," *Chicago Tribune*, April 15, 1990. Retrieved July 7, 2012, from http://articles.chicagotribune.com/1990-04-15/sports/9002010891_1_penn-state-commissioner-jim-delany-presidents.

[8] Associated Press (June 3, 1990), "Big Ten likely to go with expansion," *The Vindicator*, D10.

[9] Asmussen, Bob, "Believe it or not, Penn State's inclusion had Illinois influence," IlliniHQ.com, October 2, 2009. Retrieved July 7, 2012, from http://www.illinihq.com/sports/illini-sports/football/2009-10-02/believe-it-or-not-penn-states-inclusion-had-illinois-influe.

[10] Olson, Max. "Penn State's transition to Big Ten proves much more tumultuous than Nebraska's," *Daily Nebraskan*, April 24, 2011. Retrieved July 9, 2012, from http://www.dailynebraskan.com/news/penn-state-s-transition-to-big-ten-proves-much-more-tumultuous-than-nebraska-s-1.2551167?pagereq=1#.T_SWYBejuf4.

[11] Associated Press (November 10, 1990), "Big Ten warns Penn State on basketball arena," *Pittsburgh Post-Gazette*, C1.

[12] Olson, op.cit.

[13] Wojciechowski, Gene (November 3, 1992), "Rose Bowl Deal Favors the Big Ten: College Football: New ABC contract would be adjusted if Pac-10 adds a team," *Los Angeles Times*. Retrieved July 12, 2012, from http://articles.latimes.com/1992-11-03/sports/sp-1277_1_big-ten-total.

[14] Sherman, Ed (February 10, 1990), "Cfa Loses $30 Million In New Tv deal," *Chicago Tribune*. Retrieved July 12, 2012, from http://articles.chicagotribune.com/1990-02-10/sports/9001120908_1_cfa-notre-dame-neinas.

[15] Sandomir, Richard (August 25, 1991), "Notre Dame Scored a $38 Million Touchdown on its TV Deal," *New York Times*. Retrieved July 12, 2012, from http://www.nytimes.com/1991/08/25/sports/college-football-notre-dame-scored-a-38-million-touchdown-on-its-tv-deal.html?pagewanted=all&src=pm.

[16] Reed, William (February 19, 1990), "We're Notre Dame And You're Not," *Sports Illustrated*. Retrieved July 11, 2012, from http://sportsillustrated.cnn.com/vault/article/magazine/MAG1135990/index.htm.

[17] Reed, op.cit.

[18] Dunnavant, Keith, *"The Fifty-Year Seduction: How Television Manipulated College Football, from the Birth of the Modern NCAA to the Creation of the BCS"* (New York: St. Martin's Press, 2004), 225.

[19] Dunnavant, op.cit.

[20] Dunnavant, Keith (1990), "College football's new era is a click of the dial away," *The National*. Retrieved July 11, 2012, from http://keithdunnavant.com/byline_college_footballs_new_era_a_click_of_the_dial_away.php.

[21] Barnhart, Tony, "Conference Realignment: A History Lesson," *Athlon Sports College Football Annual* (1998); Dunnavant, *"The Fifty-Year Seduction."*

[22] Blair, Sam, "A Look Back at the Southwest Conference," *Texas Almanac* (1998-1999).

[23] Hirsley, Michael (July 30, 1997), "Big Ten Extends Tv Package with Abc, Espn for 10 Years," *Chicago Tribune*. Retrieved July 12, 2012, from http://articles.chicagotribune.com/1997-07-30/sports/9707300018_1_abc-sports-espn-over-the-air-network.

[24] Carter, Al (July 27, 2003), "Cincinnati, Louisville could be realignment's keys," *Houston Chronicle*, Sports, Page 1. Retrieved July 11, 2012, from http://www.chron.com/CDA/archives/archive.mpl/2003_3675346/cincinnati-louisville-could-be-realignment-s-keys.html.

[25] Crawford, Eric (November 29, 2012). "How U of L changed its conference fate in 11 days," WDRB.com. Retrieved May 11, 2013, from http://www.wdrb.com/story/20216639/crawford-how-u-of-l-changed-its-conference-fate-in-11-days.

[26] Crawford, op.cit.

WHY AQS SHOULD FORM THEIR OWN DIVISION

A frequent discussion in the BCS era has been with regards to the distribution of revenue by the BCS. The AQ conferences have always taken home the lion's share of the payouts (an issue that wasn't necessarily resolved with the new College Football Playoff, as you'll see in Chapter 6). Under the 2011-2012 BCS model, detailed in Chapter 2, non-AQ conferences were entitled to 9-18 percent of the revenue, depending on whether a non-AQ team was invited to a BCS bowl. The majority of the 82-91 percent remaining went to AQ conferences.

Based on BCS bowl participation in 2011-2012, AQs ended up taking home 89.5 percent of all money paid out by the BCS. On the face of it, that might seem disproportionate, but is it really?

First, it makes sense to take a look at what it takes to be eligible to compete at the FBS level of college football. Per NCAA rules, the school must sponsor a minimum of 16 varsity sports, including football. A minimum of six sports must be all male or mixed teams and a minimum of eight must be all female. At least 60 percent of football contests must be against FBS schools, including at least five regular season home games against FBS opponents.

In addition, the school must average at least 15,000 in actual or paid attendance for all home football games over a rolling two-year period. It must also provide at least 90 percent of the permissible maximum of football grants-in-aid per year over a rolling two-year period, and offer a minimum of 200 athletics grants-in-aid or spend at least $4 million on grants-in-aid for student athletes.

A school doesn't have to have a specified winning percentage before moving up to FBS. It doesn't even have to have been playing football for long. There's no competitive approval process. You simply meet these requirements and you're in.

Once you're part of the FBS, you're now a part of the BCS. The BCS doesn't require you to meet attendance benchmarks or draw minimum ratings or even perform well on the field in order to be included. If you field a team at the FBS level, you're included in the BCS system.

Now it's helpful to take a look back at how the non-AQs came to find themselves included, but not equal partners, in the BCS. Prior to 1992, bowls and conferences didn't coordinate much as a whole. Sure, there were deals between individual bowls and individual conferences, but the industry didn't act in a cohesive manner. There was no overarching governance or organization.

Bowls were born in Pasadena, Miami, New Orleans and Dallas primarily as tourist attractions. The first bowl game was the 1902 Rose Bowl, which has been hosted continually since 1916. It wasn't until 1946 that the Rose Bowl signed contracts with the Big Ten and Pacific Coast Conference. Thereafter, the Orange Bowl had an on-again-off-again relationship with the Big Eight through the 1950s and 1960s before severing all ties and remaining independent until 1975 and then going back to the Big Eight. Likewise, the Sugar Bowl had a stable, if not annual, relationship with the SEC from its inception in 1935, and the Cotton Bowl featured the Southwest Conference champion following its inception in 1937.

Other bowls came and went through the 1930s, 1940s and 1950s. The Sun Bowl, which began in El Paso in 1936, and the Gator Bowl, which hosted its first game in Jacksonville in 1946 were the first of the second-tier bowls to truly establish themselves. By the early 1970s, the Liberty Bowl in Memphis, Bluebonnet Bowl in Houston, Peach Bowl in Atlanta, Tangerine Bowl in Orlando and Fiesta Bowl in Tempe had joined them.

In those early years, teams were invited because of conference ties or geographic proximity and willingness of the fan base to travel, so the bowls made the majority of money from ticket sales. However, television changed all that in the early 1970s, with rights fees more than doubling for the top bowl games from the early 1970s to early 1980s. That's when it became less important to fill the seats and more important to garner good ratings, which would in turn mean a larger paycheck during the next round of negotiations with the networks.

During the 1974 offseason, seeing the money they were leaving on the table, the Big Ten and Pac-10 decided to end their ban on participating in bowls outside of the Rose Bowl. The top team from each conference would still meet one another in the Rose Bowl, but other teams from the conferences would vie for spots in other bowls. Perhaps most illustrative of the climate at that time is the fact that Wayne Duke, then–commissioner of the Big Ten, carried around a map depicting the television households his conference could command when he went to visit bowls to lobby for his conference's inclusion.

As bowls saw increasing success on television, others wanted to get into the mix. The Fiesta Bowl would be established during this time period, and would usher in a few changes to the system over the years. The WAC became the first of the non-major conferences to get a conference tie-in in 1971. Arizona State was in the WAC at the time and had won five consecutive league championships. The university also happened to be the location of the brand new Fiesta Bowl. Arizona State would go on to play in the first three Fiesta Bowls before joining what became the Pac-10 in 1978.

However, Arizona State would be one of the few from outside the Big Eight, Big Ten, SEC, Pac-8, Southwest Conference, Penn State and Notre Dame to play in a bowl game. WAC and ACC teams, along with lower-level independents like Miami and Florida State, were largely relegated to the second-tier bowls. Teams from outside those groups, including those in the MAC, Southern and Southland, rarely played in bowl games and were absent from television after the NCAA lost control of television rights.

The Rose, Orange, Sugar and Cotton bowls continued to dominate the postseason landscape into the 1980s, hosting their games on New Year's Day and maintaining relationships with the top conferences. The Rose Bowl had the Big Ten and Pac-10 champions, the Orange Bowl had the Big Eight champion, the Sugar Bowl had the SEC champion and the Cotton Bowl had the Southwest Conference champion. They had created the bowl system and no one challenged their New Year's Day schedule or their ties with the top conferences.

No one until the Fiesta Bowl. In 1981, with the backing of NBC, the Fiesta Bowl asked the NCAA postseason football committee to allow it to host its event on New Year's Day. Despite an outcry from the four bowls already on New Year's Day, the NCAA approved the move, perhaps fearing overstepping legal boundaries if the request was denied. The Fiesta Bowl moved to New Year's Day in 1982 and received a series of increasing contracts from NBC, but it still remained behind the other four bowls in the pecking order. Until 1986, that is.

In 1986, independents Miami and Penn State finished the season ranked #1 and #2, making it impossible for the Rose, Orange, Sugar or Cotton bowls to host a matchup because of their contractual relationships with the conferences. The Fiesta, Citrus and Gator bowls all sought to bid for the chance to host the national championship showdown.

The Fiesta Bowl won the hosting opportunity thanks in part to an extra $1 million contributed by Sunkist, the new title sponsor of the Fiesta Bowl. The extra money allowed the Fiesta Bowl to offer a payout second only to the Rose Bowl. In addition, NBC offered to move the game to prime-time on January 2nd so there would be no competition with the Cotton and Citrus bowls.

When Penn State upset Miami 14-0 on January 2nd, the largest audience in college football history tuned into watch. It remains the highest-rated college football game of all time. It also signaled a new era for the bowl system. One in which any bowl felt like it could compete.

In the new age, competition became fierce. The NCAA required 75 percent of a bowl's revenue to go to the participating schools and also set a minimum payout, which it increased every year or two. As the payouts became an important determining factor in which schools a bowl could attract, the bowl's ability to generate revenue was declining thanks to the 1984 Supreme Court decision. As regular season football flooded the airwaves, advertisers had many options outside the bowls. As more bowls crowded into a small number of dates, and saturated New Year's Day, ratings plummeted, quickly followed by television rights fees.

Against the backdrop of decreased ratings and an unstable market for the bowls, there was the rising issue of bowls extending bids prior to the NCAA-regulated date. The NCAA rule stated bowls could not extend bids until the conclusion of a team's game on the Saturday following the third Tuesday of November. However, the rule wasn't enforced and was routinely broken. As a result, bowls extended invitations earlier and earlier in the season trying to snag the best teams first. Sometimes this was to a bowl's detriment when a team it picked had a late-season collapse. By the late 1980s, both the major conferences and the bowls knew they had a problem on their hands with the issues in college football and the increased clamor for a playoff.

As college football entered the 1990s, the same conferences that were finding it more advantageous to negotiate television deals individually during the regular season realized they wielded a bigger stick collectively when it came to the postseason. In 1992 they formed the Bowl Coalition, the first time in history conferences and bowls agreed to work together to control the postseason. On the bowl side, the Cotton, Sugar, Orange and Fiesta Bowls joined, and on the conference side the SEC, ACC, Big Eight, Big East, Southwest Conference and Notre Dame rounded out the group.

Conspicuously absent were the Big Ten and Pac-10, both of which continued to operate separately with the Rose Bowl as they had since the split following the 1984 Supreme Court decision over television rights. This made it impossible to stage a true national championship game, which combined with issues over the use of the Associated Press poll and bowls continuing to select lower-ranked teams in favor of teams that would draw higher ratings did little to improve fans' perception of the postseason.

Playoff proposals began to make the rounds, but the most powerful conferences resisted the lure because it would be administered by the NCAA and force them to share revenue with the so-called have-nots. In a system of equal revenue distribution, like that under the NCAA's previous television plan, the have-nots outnumbered the power conferences and would actually take home a larger slice of the pie. No way was that happening.

It was back to the drawing board and in 1994 the SEC, ACC, Big East and Big 12[1] came up with a new idea to maximize revenue: only allow three bowls into the highest level of postseason competition and force them to bid for their spot at the table. Participating bowls would have to abandon any agreements with conferences, the plan being there would be a #1 vs. #2, #3 vs. #5 and #4 vs. #6. However, the Big Ten and Pac-10 were still out. This left the champions of the SEC, ACC, Big East and Big 12 to have automatic bids, leaving two at-large spots. Notre Dame would qualify automatically if it met certain conditions under a predetermined formula.

In addition to the opportunity to host one of the top bowl games, the three bowls would also rotate hosting the national championship. Although submission to this system would mean some bowls would be giving up a measure of their power, the atmosphere was ripe for compromise given the growing cry for a playoff and years of unstable television and advertising money.

But which three bowls would be chosen? CBS offered $300 million over six years if the Orange, Fiesta and Gator bowls were chosen. In the end, however, the Sugar, Orange and Fiesta bowls emerged as winners, thanks in no small part to their corporate sponsor and network partners. The Fiesta Bowl, along with CBS and corporate partners, bid $106 million over six years. Another CBS bowl, the Orange Bowl, offered $101 million over the same time period, and the Sugar Bowl, which partnered with ABC, bid $104 million.[2]

What followed was a series of deals where the bowls who were left attempted to lock in long-term relationships with the top conferences. The SEC, Big Ten, Big XII, Pac-10 and ACC entered deals, while other conferences found themselves relegated to lower-level bowls who continued to pop up and saturate the postseason.

The Bowl Alliance's first official season in 1995 ended with unsatisfactory results. Nebraska and Penn State were the top-ranked teams, but Penn State was committed to the Rose Bowl. The Big Ten and Pac-10 had declined to be a part of the Bowl Alliance, preferring to maintain their Rose Bowl tradition. This meant non-consensus national champion was possible. The same situation would arise in 1997 with Michigan and Nebraska.

What did happen, however, was that the Bowl Alliance delivered on its promises. When Nebraska met Florida in the Fiesta Bowl following the 1995 season, the bowl paid out the largest sum in history: $12 million per school. That got the attention of the Big Ten and Pac-10.

The Rose Bowl had continued to be a highly rated affair, but the Big Ten and Pac-10 acknowledged there were disadvantages to being separated from the other conferences. The Bowl Alliance was producing increasing revenue and attention, and Big Ten teams were missing out on the chance to compete for the national championship. In the end, it would be ABC that would help grease the wheels for the Big Ten and Pac-10 to join the other conferences, including outbidding CBS for rights to all four bowl games to allow payouts to reach $12 million (just $1 million less than the Big Ten and Pac-10 had been enjoying in their Rose Bowl deal).

Beginning with the 1998 season, the Rose Bowl agreed to release a Big Ten or Pac-10 team that qualified for the national championship in exchange for becoming the fourth bowl in the national championship rotation, which also meant giving up its Big Ten vs. Pac-10 matchup once every four years when it hosted the championship. For the first time since the 1984 Supreme Court decision on television rights, all of college football's major conferences would be united.

Although the BCS replaced the controversial method of relying on the Associated Press poll, it still allowed for teams from the top conferences to automatically qualify for the top bowl games. It wasn't anything new, it was simply an extension of the historical trend.

The Rose Bowl maintained itself as the home of the Big Ten and Pac-10 champions, the Sugar Bowl hosted the SEC champion, the Orange Bowl hosted the ACC champion and the Big 12 champion went to the Fiesta Bowl. If any of those conference champions played for the national title, the second place team would go in its place. The Big East had no official tie, but was guaranteed a spot. That left three at-large spots, one of which could be automatically claimed by Notre Dame if it met certain conditions. Essentially, a non-AQ was only guaranteed a spot if a team finished in the top six.

Lower-level bowls also maintained deals with the top conferences, but the market was flooded with bowls willing to take on members of the other conferences. Of course, those bowls weren't nearly as lucrative.

"[T]he BCS was devised outside the structure of the NCAA. It was a creation not just of the big six leagues but of the free market, of television," said Keith Dunnavant in his book *The Fifty Year Seduction*, "and while the marketplace had lobbied long and hard for the inclusion of the Big Ten and Pac-10, the marketplace could live without the WAC, MAC, C-USA, Mountain West and Sunbelt, who had traditionally been shunned by the big bowls anyway."[3]

The have-nots were essentially included by lack of exclusion. When the NCAA divided into Division I-A and I-AA, any school that met the baseline requirements set by the NCAA became part of the Division I-A, now called the FBS. While conferences like the MAC and C-USA have always been a part of the highest level of football competition, they've never been sought-after by the premiere bowls or television. They're quick to blame the BCS, because they receive less access and financial reward than the so-called power conferences, which they say puts them at a disadvantage at everything from recruiting to facilities, but the BCS merely continued a historical pattern. The market had never demanded those conferences be a part of football's highest tier—the NCAA simply placed them there.

In the end, it's still not market demand that keeps the non-AQ conferences at football's highest level, it's antitrust law—or, as you'll see in Chapter 6, the threat of an antitrust lawsuit.

Individually, none of the five non-AQ conferences carried any weight when it came to negotiating the framework of the BCS. However, together they represented almost half of the BCS, and technically they competed at the same level as the other conferences in the eyes of the NCAA. It was against this backdrop the Coalition for Athletics Reform was born, a joint effort of the have-nots, led by Tulane president Scott Cowen.

In 1998, the first year of the BCS, Tulane went 11-0 and was not chosen for a BCS bowl game. In addition to rankings, the new BCS formula also considered strength of schedule, which put non-AQs at an immediate disadvantage because their inter-conference games would be scored as being weaker than those played within an AQ conference. Instead of competing in a BCS bowl with a payout of $11.5 million, Tulane played in the Liberty Bowl for a $1.1 million payout.

Although there had always been a gulf between the major conferences and the rest of Division I-A/FBS, the gulf had narrowed over the years. Despite not being a major television draw, conferences like the MAC eventually earned television deals in the late 1990s and early 2000s, because the advent of cable meant more networks had time to fill and live sports were a hot commodity.

In addition, NCAA legislation from the late 1970s was finally starting to level out the playing field for recruiting student athletes as signing limits prevented the top programs from bloating their rosters, allowing more talented players to trickle down into the lower-level conferences. This meant that it was no longer impossible for a team from a conference like the MAC to beat a team from one of the power conferences on occasion. This began to make the non-AQs feel empowered to enact change.

By 2003, Cowen and his counterparts at other non-AQ schools were fed up with the BCS, which had never once chosen one of their teams to compete in a BCS bowl. They formed the Coalition for Athletics Reform, which considered antitrust litigation and then convinced both Congress and the House of Representatives to hold committee hearings on the legality of the BCS system.

The issue of whether the BCS could survive antitrust litigation in taken up in Chapter 6, but as is often the case in sports, the threat of litigation and the negative PR related to the congressional hearings was enough to get the AQ presidents to settle with the non-AQ presidents. The BCS agreed to add a fifth bowl game, which would improve access by adding two additional at-large spots. No new bowl was chosen as a host, instead the host of the national championship would now also host a separate BCS bowl game the week previous. Both the bowl games and ABC, the BCS's television partner, feared the presidents had committed the BCS to a system that couldn't be as profitable.

ABC had the television rights to all the BCS games from 1998 through 2006. It's last deal, which covered the four seasons from 2003-2006 was worth approximately $305 million over four years. Dissatisfied with the addition of a fifth game, ABC withdrew from bidding before a network was selected, leaving the door open for Fox. A four-year deal from 2007-2010 from Fox garnered the BCS slightly more than the last deal at $320 million.

Four years later, the BCS would cash in when ESPN outbid Fox and offered $125 million a year for four years from 2011-2014. While it's tempting to say that contract proves the five-BCS bowl format and greater inclusion of non-AQs was a winner with consumers, it doesn't tell the whole story. ESPN doesn't have to rely solely on advertising to produce revenue like the broadcast networks. As a cable channel it receives the bulk of its revenue from carriage fees, which were $4.40 per subscriber per month in 2010 and estimated to total over $5.27 billion that year.

Adding the BCS games gave ESPN 33 of the 35 bowl games in 2010, leverage it could use to increase its carriage fee in future negotiations.

"Content always wins the war and major sporting events are the most powerful weapons," RBC Capital Markets analyst David Bank told AdWeek in December 2010. "They can point to these investments and say, 'Why not cut an early deal and avoid all the drama . . . and we won't hit you with as big of an increase.'"[4]

Not only did additional money pour into the BCS as a result of ESPN's television contract, but the new distribution methods decided upon after the Coalition for Athletics Reform allowed for non-AQs to receive a greater share. Prior to the BCS restructuring in 2004 (which was put into place for the 2006 season), the six AQ conferences took home 93.6 percent of BCS bowl revenue, leaving just 6.4 percent for the non-AQs and Division I-AA (now called FCS) conferences. If you'll remember, the 2011-2012 BCS model resulted in 89.5 percent going to AQ conferences.

In addition, access was indeed improved under the revised BCS. Following the 2006 season, Boise State, the WAC champion, faced Oklahoma in the Fiesta Bowl and pulled off a 43-42 overtime win. Hawaii, a member of the WAC, played in the Sugar Bowl the next year and lost to Georgia. The following year, Utah won the Mountain West and went on to beat Alabama in the Sugar Bowl. Following the 2009 season, two non-AQs faced each other in a BCS bowl for the first time in BCS history as Boise State from the WAC met up with TCU from the Mountain West in the Fiesta Bowl. The next year, TCU beat Wisconsin in the Rose Bowl.

Non-AQs had shown they could compete on the field with AQ teams. They even showed they could fill the stands at bowl games. For the five BCS games played in by non-AQs from the 2006-2010 seasons, four of the five had attendance better than the five-year average for that bowl. However, the same was not reflected in the ratings.

As you can see in Chart 5.1, only two of the five times did a BCS game featuring a non-AQ team beat the five-year average television rating for that bowl, both in the Fiesta Bowl.

Chart 5.1

	Sugar Bowl	Fiesta Bowl	Rose Bowl
2006-2007	Notre Dame vs. LSU 9.29	Boise State vs. Oklahoma 8.40	Southern Cal vs. Michigan 13.94
2007-2008	Georgia vs. Hawaii 7.0	WVU vs. Oklahoma 7.70	Southern Cal vs. Illinois 11.11
2008-2009	Utah vs. Alabama 7.8	Texas vs. Ohio State 10.40	Southern Cal vs. Penn State 11.70
2009-2010	Cincinnati vs. Florida 8.5	Boise State vs. TCU 8.23	Ohio State vs. Oregon 13.18
2010-2011	Ohio State vs. Arkansas 8.2	Connecticut vs. Oklahoma 6.15	Wisconsin vs. TCU 11.26
AVERAGE	8.16	8.18	12.24

Source: Nielsen

The argument from the non-AQ camp and its supporters would be that the non-AQs drew higher ratings than the bowl games featuring schools from two of the AQ conferences: the ACC and Big East. From 2006 to 2010, the Big East and ACC played in eight different games, because two years they faced each other in the same game. Only three of those eight games garnered higher ratings than the bowl featuring a non-AQ team in the same year.

Because bowls rely more heavily on television ratings than attendance, they might be able to make the argument that hosting a non-AQ team hurts ratings more often than not, but they'd have a tough time arguing the same isn't true for the ACC or Big East, which receive automatic bids.

Despite increased access and revenue distribution since 2006, the rallying cry on behalf of the non-AQs has only grown louder. As you've seen the BCS was not a turning point in history where the lower-tiered conferences were suddenly cast outside the system. Instead, the BCS merely continued a long history of favoring the conferences that had traditionally performed better and commanded more market attention.

So why did the BCS create such a visible division between conferences? One problem identified with the BCS was the AQ vs. non-AQ language itself. The advent of the BCS had produced very little change in the way in which college football naturally divided into higher and lower-tiered schools, but it did create these new labels that made some conferences and schools feel inferior. What had once gone unspoken was now being made blatantly obvious: there was a class system in college football.

Although the AQ and non-AQ labels are being dropped with the new College Football Playoff, the division remains. The ACC, Big 12, Big Ten, Pac-12 and SEC are grouped together, while the other conferences are being called the Group of Five (the former Big East, now American Athletic Conference, C-USA, the Sun Belt, Mid-American and Mountain West). More details on the structure of the new College Football Playoff follow in Chapter 6.

There's no reason to believe that division will disappear with the advent of a college football playoff. There continues to be greater market demand for conferences like the SEC, Big Ten, Pac-12 and Big 12 on television. This is reflected in the deals conferences receive for the regular season. In chart 5.2 you can see the disparity in revenue received from regular season television contracts for each conference in 2009-2010. The amounts shown include rights for both football and men's basketball, and in some instances other sports, but are largely driven by football.

Chart 5.2

Big Ten	$232,000,000*
SEC	$153,300,000
ACC	$77,600,000
Big 12	$72,500,000
Pac-10	$58,200,000
Big East	$35,600,000
C-USA	$15,800,000
Mountain West	$11,700,000*
WAC	$1,900,000
MAC	$1,100,000
Sun Belt	$750,000

Source: Conference Form 990s filed with IRS

*Per year average of all conference television deals because Form 990 does not specify

Prior to a Presidential Oversight Committee meeting in June 2012 to approve a new playoff format, Western Kentucky president Dr. Gary A. Ransdell, said to expect only modest changes to revenue distribution under the new format. Despite being a president from the Sun Belt Conference, Dr. Ransdell acknowledged there's a reason revenue distribution has always favored some schools over others.

Referring to the ACC, Big 12, Big Ten, Pac-12 and SEC, Ransdell said, "It's those five conferences who have invested the most, have the largest stadiums, and create the television marquee."

He went on to add, "We just want to be sure we get a little more proportionate share. For the BCS to survive it's going to take all 120 institutions. The 50 to 60 in those five conferences can't just play each other. There has to be competition across all the conferences going forward."

In reality, there's no reason (outside of maybe antitrust law) those five conferences couldn't take their ball and go play somewhere else. Certainly there would be changes in scheduling, and expectations in terms of wins and losses would likely have to change as a result, but it is not outside the realm of possibility for those five conferences to form a separate tier.

When asked if a split of that sort would negatively impact television revenue, former CBS and ESPN programming executive Len DeLuca said, "In college basketball, media strength is determined by the numerator. However, college football is all about the denominator. What you're seeing is the denominator in football is shrinking, and it's shrinking to the power schools."

DeLuca added that throughout history the center of power in college football has hovered around 65 schools, all the way back to the days of the CFA. It's no coincidence, he says, that four 16-team super conferences would equal 64 schools.

Despite no formal division between the AQs and non-AQs, the FBS effectively operates as two separate levels with some interleague play thrown in. The system also has all the benefits of European soccer's promotion system without the disadvantages of a relegation system.

For those who are unfamiliar, European soccer (which they simply call futbol, but for ease of comprehension here we'll stick with soccer) uses a system of promotion and relegation to divide its teams into levels of competition. At the end of each season, teams are transferred between leagues based on their performance that season. The best-ranked teams in the leagues below are promoted to the league above and the lowest-ranked teams in the higher league are relegated to the league below. This can happen between levels 1 and 2, levels 2 and 3 and so on.

Generally, the number of teams moving up matches the number moving down. The exact mechanics of each system vary and can also include certain requirements for promotion such as stadium capacity and financial solvency.

Throughout college football's history there has been promotion as teams moved up from FCS, up from non-AQ and from one AQ into another higher-grossing AQ, but only a couple of times has there been true relegation: in 2001 when the Big East unceremoniously dumped Temple, which would cease playing in the conference following the 2004 season (but rejoin in 2012 for football and 2013 for all other sports). The Owls had never won more than 4 games since joining the conference in 1991 and annually had the lowest attendance in the conference. The other instance of relegation also involved the Big East. With the advent of the College Football Playoff, the Big East (which is being renamed the American Athletic Conference), will move from the AQ group to join the conferences formerly labeled as non-AQ, meaning far less revenue from the system.

Another way promotion or relegation could have occurred, but didn't, would have been if a seventh conference had become an AQ, like the Mountain West thought it might, or if the Big East had lost its automatic bid after conference realignment took its toll in 2010 and 2011. Both ended up being non-issues when it became clear the AQ and non-AQ labels were going away with the start of a playoff system in 2014.

Taking a look again at the 2011-2012 BCS bowls, this chapter began by showing 85 percent of all money paid out to AQ and non-AQ conferences went to AQs. However, AQs made up nine out of ten, or 90 percent, of all teams competing in BCS bowls. Fair or not?

Under the BCS system, you could argue access wasn't fair, but based on who played in the game the argument that the revenue distribution wasn't fair is a tougher one. What complicates the situation is that non-AQs have an agreement to share all BCS revenue, meaning the conference who had a team selected has to share with the other four conferences, albeit not equally.

As shown in Chart 5.2, BCS payouts aren't the only area in which non-AQs command less revenue. Television networks are willing to pay far less for non-AQ conference contracts, giving a glimpse of the marketplace. They also receive substantially smaller apparel contracts from companies like Nike, adidas and Under Armour.

For example, Boise State signed a new deal with Nike in 2012, the first time the athletic department has landed an all-sports contract with an apparel company. That contract calls for $850,000-1,150,000 in product each year, and cash payments of $30,000-50,000 annually. Meanwhile, Alabama is receiving product worth $2.3 to $3.0 million per year and cash payments of $750,000 per year. Even a school from an AQ conference without the brand value of Alabama receives far more than Boise State. Under its latest contract with adidas, North Carolina State receives $1.2 to $1.3 million in product per year and cash payments of $425,000.

AQ conferences also take home a far larger percentage of March Madness money than non-AQ conferences. From the 2011 tournament, the Big East brought home the largest share with $24.9 million. Conference USA, the largest earner of the non-AQ conferences, brought home $6.95 million.

Since AQs were given their label in 1998, only three basketball national championship games have featured a team from outside of those conferences. No non-AQ school has won the title during that period.

Chart 5.3 compares revenue received by conferences from the BCS to that received by the NCAA for March Madness. As you can see, the AQs take home the lion's share from both.

Chart 5.3

Conference	BCS (millions)	NCAA (millions)
ACC	$21.2	$18.2
Big Ten	$27.2	$18.5
Big 12	$21.2	$18.9
Big East	$21.2	$24.9
Pac-10	$27.2	$16.1
SEC	$27.2	$15.6
Mtn. West	$12.8	$5.0
Mid-American	$2.6	$1.7
Sun Belt	$1.9	$2.4
C-USA	$3.3	$6.9
WAC	$4.1	$2.9

Source: NCAA, BCS

The AQ conferences received 47.5 percent of all revenue distributed by the NCAA from performance in March Madness. Just 10.5 percent went to non-AQ conferences, with the remainder being distributed to conferences that do not play FBS football. If this doesn't sound like it adds up to the $771.4 million the basketball tournament produces each year, it's because all other March Madness revenue is distributed to conferences based on the number of sports the school sponsors and the number of grants-in-aid offered by each. Additional funds from March Madness are distributed for academic programs and financial aid.

The moral of the story is that AQ conferences benefit financially in a variety of ways, not only from the BCS. Some argue it's the structure of the BCS that perpetuates this problem. The line of reasoning goes something like this: because AQ conferences receive greater revenue under the BCS structure they are able to pay coaches more, recruit higher-quality student athletes and build grander facilities. This widens the gap between the AQs and non-AQs year after year. There's a question as to whether the financial disparity effects basketball recruitment, and therefore performance in March Madness and the resulting financial disparity there.

Is this any different than what we see in a variety of other industries? Even in professional sports, generally deemed to have greater parity than college football, there exists the notion of have and have-nots, largely due to market forces.

Major League Baseball's Oakland A's made a mere 36 percent of what the New York Yankees generated in 2011. Equal? No. Fair? Arguably, yes. By virtue of its location in New York, not to mention the team's history, the Yankees can command a higher price for everything from premium tickets to television. In addition, the Yankees franchise would be worth far more money on the open market than the A's, thus an owner would have to invest more in order to receive larger returns.

Let's make it even simpler. Should the founder of the company receive the same compensation as an entry-level employee or even a mid-level executive? Fair compensation, sure. But not equal compensation.

Comparing FBS football to a corporation presents problems. Corporations would find it hard to exist with only upper-level management and no lower levels to make the process more efficient. AQ conferences, however, could exist without the non-AQ conferences. Scheduling would be different, which would necessitate a change in expectations with regards to win-loss records, but it's plausible that AQ conferences could continue to enjoy a prosperous marketplace without non-AQ conferences.

As Keith Dunnavant said in his book, quoted earlier in this chapter, the market has time and again demanded certain conferences, while others seem to have merely had their wagon hitched along for the ride. It makes just as much sense to wonder why these conferences are included at all as it does to question why they are not treated equally. The answer to the former, as you'll see in the next chapter, is antitrust law.

NOTES

[1] The Southwest Conference champion was guaranteed an at-large bid in 1995, its last year as a conference. Four of its members then joined the Big Eight to become the Big 12.

[2] Barnes, Craig (August 5, 1994). "Alliance picks Sugar, Orange, Fiesta." Sun-Sentinel.com. Retrieved May 11, 2013, from http://articles.sun-sentinel.com/1994-08-05/sports/9408040701_1_carquest-bowl-alamo-bowls-sugar-bowl.

[3] Dunnavant, *The Fifty-Year Seduction: How Television Manipulated College Football from the Birth of the Modern NCAA to the Creation of the BCS,* 267.

[4] Crupi, Anthony (December 19, 2010), "ESPN's Bowling for Dollars," *AdWeek.com*. Retrieved March 27, 2012, from http://www.adweek.com/news/television/espns-bowling-dollars-bcs-104063.

CALL THEM WHAT YOU WANT, BUT THERE WILL ALWAYS BE NON-AQS

There's an argument to be made that the conferences known as the non-AQs during the BCS era are only part of the FBS because of the threat of an antitrust lawsuit. There were threats by Tulane president Scott Cowen in 2003, and more recently in 2011 Utah Attorney General Mark Shurtleff went so far as to have the State of Utah issue a "Request for Information" seeking law firms that might want to be involved in antitrust litigation against the BCS.

The argument by those who opposed the BCS, and are just as likely to continue to be unhappy with college football's postseason system, is that it's anti-competitive. In other words, the claim is that the BCS colludes to keep schools from smaller conferences out of the BCS bowl games, which prevents both access to the games and to the payouts that go with them.

As discussed in Chapter 4, the goal of antitrust law is to prevent *unreasonable* restraints of trade—not to prevent any and all restraints. In fact, courts have found some restraints actually benefit their industry. For example, although the NCAA television plan was found to be a violation of antitrust law, the court noted that because the NCAA markets competition among members there must be some restraints to define the bounds of competition. As recently as 2012 restraints on the number of scholarships that may be offered have been upheld by a federal court as a restraint that is not violative of antitrust laws.[1]

Sports, in general, have been treated uniquely under antitrust laws because regulation under a governing body actually creates a more competitive market than if everyone acted individually. For this reason, antitrust suits within sports are extremely unpredictable. In fact, antitrust laws haven't even been applied consistently from one sport to another, as was the case in the 1950s when antitrust laws were ruled inapplicable to baseball but applicable to boxing and football. In 1961 the Sports Broadcasting Act allowed for professional leagues for baseball, basketball, football and hockey to each enter into an agreement with a single network for national television coverage, yet, as you saw in Chapter 4, the NCAA's television plan was found to be an unreasonable restraint.

Before we explore whether the BCS could have survived an antitrust lawsuit, and why the College Football Playoff might still be susceptible to future antitrust claims, it's worth looking at the differences between the BCS and the College Football Playoff systems.

Through the 2013 season, the BCS consists of a national championship game and four BCS bowls: the Orange, Sugar, Rose and Fiesta Bowls. At the end of the regular season, rankings are determined by a formula that includes three components: the *USA Today* Coaches Poll, the Harris Interactive College Football Poll and an average of six computer rankings. The two highest-ranked teams compete against one another in the national championship game.

Next, the conference champion from the ACC, Big 12, Big East, Big Ten, Pac-12 and SEC are slotted into the BCS bowls, if they aren't one of the two teams chosen for the national championship game. The Rose Bowl is always the Big Ten champion versus the Pac-12 champion. If one of those teams is in the national championship game, then the Rose Bowl can choose from any available automatic qualifiers or at-large teams before any selection is made by other bowls. If not selected for the national championship game, the following conference champions are automatically slotted into the following games: the SEC into the Sugar Bowl, the Big 12 into the Fiesta Bowl, the ACC into the Orange Bowl. If any of those conference champions is selected for the national champion, the bowl follows the same procedure as the Rose Bowl defined above.

There are several other automatic qualifiers not contractually committed to bowls. They are teams that could be chosen if the Rose, Orange, Sugar or Fiesta Bowl loses its contractually committed team to the national championship. The Big East champion is guaranteed a spot in one of the BCS bowls, but it does not have a contract with a specified bowl like the other AQs. Notre Dame is guaranteed a spot in a BCS bowl if it finishes in the top eight in the final BCS standings. A conference champion from a non-AQ is guaranteed a BCS bowl berth if it is either ranked in the top 12 of the final BCS standings or ranked in the top 16 and higher than one of the AQ conference champions. No more than one non-AQ team can earn such automatic berth. A second team can be chosen as an at-large, however.

If after all that there are still spots open in BCS bowl games, the remaining slots are selected from bowl-eligible teams that have won at least 9 regular season games and are among the top 14 teams in the final BCS standings. No more than two teams from a conference can be selected for the national championship and BCS bowl games, unless two non-champions from the same conference end up ranked number 1 and 2 in the final BCS standings.

As you saw in Chapter 2, an automatic qualifier from an AQ conference for the 2011-2012 season received $22.3 million. An automatic qualifier from one of the five non-AQ conferences received $26.4 million (or 18 percent of BCS net revenue), but those conferences have agreed to share amongst all five non-AQ conferences according to a formula they've devised. If the non-AQs don't have an automatic qualifier, they receive $13.2 million, which is 9 percent of the net revenue. At-large teams received $6.1 million, as did Notre Dame, Army, Navy or BYU if one of them played in a BCS game. Notre Dame received $1.8 million if it did not play in a BCS game, while Army, Navy and BYU received $100,000 each.

For 2011-2012, final payouts worked out like this: $133.8 million to the automatic qualifiers from the AQ conferences, $24.4 million to the at-large teams from AQ conferences, $13.2 million to the non-AQ conferences, $1.8 million to Notre Dame, $100,000 each to Army, Navy and BYU, and $3.25 million to the 13 FCS conferences. That's 89.5 percent to the AQ conferences and 7.5 percent to the non-AQ conferences. The rest went to independents and FCS conferences.

The two major issues raised about the BCS were access to the BCS bowl games and division of the revenue. Is either problem solved by the new College Football Playoff system?

Let's look at access first. The new College Football Playoff will consist of a national championship game and two semifinal games. There are six Access Bowls: the Rose, Sugar, Orange, Fiesta, Chick-Fil-A and Cotton. The Rose, Sugar and Orange are Contract Bowls, meaning they have contracts with conferences. The Rose Bowl will continue to host the Big Ten and Pac-12, as it did under the BCS model. The Sugar Bowl has contracts with the SEC and Big 12. The Orange Bowl has a contract with the ACC and will feature either the SEC, Big Ten or Notre Dame as the other team. However, in a year when a Contract Bowl is hosting the semifinal, its contracted teams will be considered displaced and will be placed in one of the Host Bowls (Fiesta, Chick-Fil-A and Cotton). According to ESPN's Brett McMurphy, the conference commissioners have agreed that in the years when the Rose Bowl and Sugar Bowl are hosting semifinal games, and therefore the Big Ten and SEC champions are displaced and could be picked up by the Orange Bowl, the Big Ten and SEC champions will instead be placed in one of the other three Access Bowls in order to increase the value of those bowls.[2]

The Host Bowls do not have contracts with conferences. They will feature teams that are displaced from their Contract Bowl in a year that bowl hosts a semifinal game, the highest-ranked team from the Group of Five (The American Athletic Conference, C-USA, Mountain West, Sun Belt and Mid-American) or at-large teams chosen by a selection committee. It is anticipated the selection committee will consist of current and former athletic directors (with one current athletic director from each of the five power conferences), former coaches and administrators and possibly one retired media member. Early reports indicate the committee will operate in a fashion similar to the NCAA men's basketball tournament selection committee, but those details were not yet finalized as of July 2013.

The new system will offer opportunities for a total of 12 teams, two more than the BCS. The former AQs have 5 of the 12 spots locked up, down from 6 under the BCS because of the move of the former Big East, now American Athletic Conference, to the non-AQs now known as the Group of Five (the WAC having dropped football after the 2012-2013 season). That means 42 percent of the spots automatically go to the five power conferences, as compared to 60 percent going to the AQs under the BCS. Is that enough to satisfy those who claim antitrust violations? Is one guaranteed spot for all the teams in the Group of Five enough access? Those are questions left unanswered as we move away from the BCS era.

The other issue, division of revenue, has similarly received tweaks under the new system, but not a complete overhaul. As of the publication of this book, reports varied as to how revenue would be distributed. In December 2012, *USA Today* and ESPN had conflicting reports. An AP story in April 2013 differed even more.

The ESPN report, by Brett McMurphy, detailed a 12-year contract with ESPN that averages out to $470 annually. Off the top, $125 million would be used for expenses, "including an academic reward component, game participation, team expenses, allotment to Football Championship Subdivision conferences and other items." The remaining average of $345 million annually would be split 75 percent to the ACC, Big 12, Big Ten, Pac-12 and SEC and 25 percent to the Group of Five. The Big 12, Big Ten, Pac-12 and SEC also receive an additional $40 million each annually from ESPN thanks to their Contract Bowl deals with the Rose Bowl and Sugar Bowl. The ACC would receive an additional $27.5 million from ESPN for its Contract Bowl deal with the Orange Bowl. If the SEC or Big Ten played in the Orange Bowl, the conference would receive $27.5 million, but if Notre Dame played in the Orange Bowl it would be "substantially less." Notre Dame would receive approximately $4 million if it didn't play in an Access Bowl, but "a great deal more" if it played in one.[3]

In summation, $86.25 million would be split among the Group of Five. According to a CBS Sports report from January 22, 2013, the five conferences would split half of the revenue evenly. The rest of the revenue would be split into two tiers, with the first being distributed based on a conference's "body of work," with the top conference getting the most and so on down the line. The other tier would go to the conference that supplied the highest-ranked team.[4]

However, the split worked out amongst the Group of Five, each conference's share would pale in comparison to the money guaranteed to each of the other conference. The Big 12, Big Ten, Pac-12 and SEC would be guaranteed a minimum of $91.75 million ($51.75 million from the Access Bowl revenue, $40 million from Contract Bowl deals), with the SEC or Big Ten possibly receiving another $27.5 million if one of them played in the Orange Bowl. The ACC would be guaranteed $79.25 million ($51.75 million from the Access Bowl revenue and $27.5 million from the Orange Bowl deal).

The *USA Today* report from December 2012 had 71.5 percent going to the five power conferences and 27 percent to the Group of Five.[5] Meanwhile, the AP report from April 2013 had 85 percent to the five power conferences and 15 percent to the Group of Five.[6]

The Group of Five conferences, with the exception of the former Big East now American Athletic Conference, should each make far more than under the BCS—but is it enough to silence would-be antitrust lawsuit filers given the gulf that will still exist between those conferences and the ACC, Big 12, Big Ten, Pac-12 and SEC?

The new system going into place for the 2014 season, on its face, improves access by guaranteeing a spot for the highest-ranked team from the Group of Five but is not so different from the BCS as to remove all scrutiny, especially given that the lion's share of the money still goes to the five most powerful conferences. The new College Football Playoff is, however, less restrictive, as the BCS was less restrictive than the system that came before it. Accordingly, it's worth exploring whether the BCS could have survived an antitrust lawsuit. As you'll see, the mere threat of antitrust litigation has improved the college football postseason market. In fact, there's a strong argument it's done more than a lawsuit ever could.

Section 1 Analysis

Antitrust law is largely governed by federal laws under the Sherman Act. An antitrust case against the BCS, or its successor, could potentially be brought under either Section 1 or Section 2 of that Act. It's also worth nothing the suit wouldn't be against the BCS, as there is no legal entity in the form of a corporation but instead a series of scheduling agreements among conferences, independent institutions and bowl games. (This part of the analysis will change with the College Football Playoff, which will be a corporate entity.) Therefore, any suit would likely name conferences, schools and bowl games as defendants. A suit brought under Section 1 would claim collusion exists among the defendants in ways that are economically harmful, which could include claims of price-fixing and limiting output, amongst other practices. A claim brought under Section 2, covered later in this chapter, would claim an illegal monopoly exists.

Under a Section 1 claim, the plaintiff would likely first ask the court to find there had been a per se violation of antitrust law. "Per se" is a Latin phrase meaning "in itself," which is used in law to describe something that is a violation on its face, or because of its very existence. In antitrust law, a per se violation is one that has been predetermined to violate antitrust laws. Courts have found agreements that are inherently anticompetitive to be per se illegal, such as agreements for horizontal price fixing and market allocation. Certain practices, such as group boycotts, have also traditionally been found to be per se illegal.

Practices considered per se violations do not require the plaintiff to prove anything other than the existence of the agreement or practice and that the practice is inherently anticompetitive. Market power, a component of other types of antitrust analysis described later in the chapter which requires the plaintiff to present evidence about the defendant's role in the marketplace, is irrelevant in a per se case. Instead, the plaintiff would merely allege one of the practices recognized as a per se violation has occurred.

Horizontal price-fixing, which involves competitors at the same level coming to an agreement to set prices, is per se illegal. There's reason to believe the BCS (and the College Football Playoff) could be susceptible to a horizontal price-fixing claim. Collectively, the conferences and independents that constitute the FBS have established the amounts to be paid for participation in the highest-level bowl games. In addition, there may be an additional argument that selling television rights for Fiesta, Sugar and Orange bowl games along with the BCS title game together in a package constitutes horizontal price-fixing. That same argument would be applicable to the new College Football Playoff, which packaged together the rights to the title game and semifinal games.

Indeed, in the 1984 Supreme Court case brought against the NCAA for its television plan, discussed in Chapter 4, the Court found the limits on television appearances and the recommended fee schedule to be horizontal price-fixing. However, the Court declined to apply the per se test and continued on to the rule of reason test, described later in this chapter. In recent years, courts have been resistant to apply the per se test, instead choosing to allow defendants to provide evidence of procompetitive justifications for restraints.

In the NCAA television case, the Court reasoned college football was an industry in which some horizontal restraints were necessary in order to produce the product. There's every reason to believe courts would feel the same way in the case of the BCS, or its successor, and proceed to use the rule of reason to evaluate the system.

Group boycotts are also a per se violation, and many scholars have suggested the BCS fits the definition. A group boycott is when competitors conspire to cut off a rival's access to tools needed to compete, such as supply, facilities or the market. The argument here would be that the AQ conferences have conspired to limit non-AQ's access to BCS bowl games and the associated payouts. Although access is broader and payout percentages larger, there is still a distinction made between the ten conferences involved in the College Football Playoff, with two groups of five being treated differently as you saw in the discussion that began this chapter. Accordingly, it is foreseeable that the same claims could be made against the new system as against the BCS.

Analyzing the BCS, we see non-AQ teams receive less media attention and can be less attractive to recruits. It has also been alleged this leads to reduced revenue from regular season ticket sales, donations, television contracts and other sources of revenue. However, it's worth noting, as previous chapters have shown, that those schools have historically commanded less in the marketplace. The claim by many is that the BCS has reinforced and widened the gap between the so-called haves and have-nots.

Under the BCS's original formula, from 1998 to 2004, a non-AQ team only made a BCS bowl if it finished in the top six, which never happened. However, after restructuring in 2004, the BCS has featured several non-AQ teams in BCS bowls. Non-AQs were guaranteed a spot under the new regulations if a team either ranked in the top 12 in the final BCS standings or in the top 16 and ahead of at least one AQ conference champion. The resulting increase of non-AQ teams in BCS bowls led many commentators to conclude the BCS could survive a group boycott claim. Access has been improved even more with the College Football Playoff, where one team from the Group of Five (the equivalent of the former non-AQs) is guaranteed a berth every year.

However, some believed the group boycott claim was still valid with respect to the absence of access non-AQ teams have had to the national championship game under the BCS. Hawaii, Utah, Boise State and TCU were all left out of national championship games despite having undefeated seasons. The BCS would defend the system by pointing out that any team that finishes first or second has the opportunity to compete in the championship game, but opponents would say the BCS ranking system favors AQ teams. Again, it's unclear at this stage whether the new postseason system will present the same issues, as details of the selection committee and its process were not yet available when this book went to press.

Another important factor to note with regards to group boycotts is that they are not always per se violations. They are only illegal when they are not justified to increase overall efficiency and improve the competitiveness of the market. The BCS could argue its system is both more efficient and more competitive than the previous system, as will be shown later in the chapter.

Similarly, if the new postseason configuration is challenged, those in power will contend it improves upon the BCS.

Another per se violation the BCS might have been susceptible to is the existence of a tying agreement. A tying agreement is illegal when two or more products are grouped together and the seller conditions the sale of one product on the sale of all the products. The seller must have sufficient market power to force buyers to purchase the products together and must coerce the buyer to make the purchase in order for it to be a per se violation.

The claim here would be that the BCS packaged the national championship game and Fiesta, Orange and Sugar Bowls together for television. Indeed, during the BCS' tenure, all of those games were packaged together and sold to ESPN. However, the plaintiff would have to prove ESPN was forced into buying a product it did not want in order to get one it did. Given ESPN has long been an active bidder for college football, it would be tough to prove the network wasn't thrilled to get all of the games together in one package. The entire claim could be shot down with one statement from ESPN confirming it was happy to be able to purchase all of the games together.

In general, courts have been reluctant to find per se violations in the context of sports. In fact, in the 1984 case regarding the NCAA's television plan the court recognized that some restraints in sports are necessary in order to produce the product. More recently, in 2010, the Supreme Court ruled in *American Needle Inc· v· NFL* that per se rules are inapplicable when restraints on competition are necessary for the product to exist, as is the case in sports.

If the plaintiff was unsuccessful at having the BCS, or its successor, declared per se illegal, it would likely ask the court to use the "quick look" rule of reason. This test weighs the anticompetitive effects of the restraint against its procompetitive benefits. If the restraint is net anticompetitive—that is, if procompetitive benefits are outweighed by the anticompetitive effects, the court will rule in favor of the plaintiff. Basically, the defendant will attempt to show it does more good than harm. A restraint may also be held illegal if there are less restrictive alternatives to achieving the procompetitive benefits.

Using the quick look rule of reason, or the full rule of reason test described later in this chapter, requires a definition of the "relevant market." A market must be defined in order to measure the defendant's power over price and output. The court will define the relevant market both in terms of product and geographic coverage. It will then look to the defendant's power within the market. The Supreme Court defined market power as, "the ability to raise prices above those that would be charged in a competitive market," in its NCAA television decision in 1984, discussed in Chapter 4.[7] If a court applied the per se test in an antitrust case against the BCS or its successor, the plaintiff would not have to show the BCS or its successor has that market power.

Markets can be defined very broadly or more narrowly. The broader the market, the better the situation for the defendant. It's much tougher to have market power in a marketplace easily entered by competitors. A more narrowly construed market likely favors the plaintiff. Thus, definition of market is an important part of any antitrust case.

In the NCAA television case, the federal district court found the relevant market was "live college football television." That was a narrow definition, which did result in a favorable result for the plaintiff. The court found the NCAA virtually had complete control over televised college football from what was made available to the networks to the price for the product. In addition, the price was uniform with no differentiation for quality of the product or consumer demand. As was mentioned in Chapter 4, two teams ranked in the top five that played one another and appeared on 200 stations would receive the same amount of money as two lesser-ranked teams that appeared on just four stations.

The level of control within the narrowly defined market was impossible to ignore in the NCAA television case and resulted in a judgment against the NCAA. The market definition could have been much broader—it could have been any live sporting events on television. The outcome could have been very different if that had been the definition.

Accordingly, how a court defined the market in a case against the BCS or the College Football Playoff would be vitally important. There are an unforeseen number of possible markets, but two that seem most probable. The relevant market during the BCS era would likely be either the BCS National Championship Game alone or all five BCS bowl games together. Under the new playoff format, the relevant market would likely be either a combination of the semifinal games and the national championship game or those games along with the so-called Access Bowls (Rose, Orange, Sugar, Fiesta, Cotton and Chick-Fil-A bowls). The defendants would be smart to argue for an even broader market such as all of football (both collegiate and professional) or even all of sports or all of entertainment.

Once a market is defined, a court using the quick look rule of reason test will weigh the procompetitive justifications against the anticompetitive effects. A plaintiff can only be successful under this test if the anticompetitive effects significantly outweigh the procompetitive justifications. It's very similar to the per se analysis in that it allows for an expedited ruling and the burden is largely shifted to the defendant to show procompetitive benefit. Courts have used the quick look rule of reason test more in recent years as they seemingly move away from the per se analysis in order to examine the actual effect of the restraint. It's unlikely a court would find the case so clear cut as to allow for this method of review.

Instead, a court would analyze the BCS or the College Football Playoff under the "rule of reason" test, which requires the court to determine if the restraint's procompetitive qualities outweigh its anticompetitive aspects. Like the quick look rule of reason test, the court will have to define the market before it begins its analysis.

Another large piece of the analysis is going to be determining if and how consumers are harmed. The Supreme Court has repeatedly emphasized that antitrust laws are meant to protect competition, not the competitors themselves. That being the case, anyone bringing an antitrust suit would likely have to show consumers—not the competitors—are harmed by the way college football conducts its postseason. It's worth noting courts have put less emphasis on consumer harm in recent cases involving group boycott allegations, but since a suit in this case could involve other antitrust claims it's likely the plaintiff will have to show consumer harm. There are a number of potential consumer groups in an antitrust case against the college football's postseason, but as you'll see fans are the most likely subject of any antitrust case.

One option would be that bowl games are the consumers. A lower-level bowl could potentially attack the BCS or the College Football Playoff based on the fact that the top teams are reserved for BCS bowls, leaving teams that draw less attendance and ratings, and thus produce less revenue, for the other bowls. However, no bowl has exhibited any desire to bring such a suit. Even if such a bowl were to bring a suit, this chapter will later detail how it might be a tough case to prove when you consider the number of bowl games has increased during the BCS' tenure and television contracts have continued to increase.

It's possible that with the future playoff system, bowls could become less relevant or that some bowls might not survive. If bowl games are diminished or forced out of existence under the new system, this type of suit could be more likely.

Another potential consumer would be television networks. As you'll see, this would be a tough case to prove. The number of bowls has continued to increase under the BCS, including the addition of the BCS National Championship Game. The College Football Playoff beginning in 2014 increases the number of teams playing in top-tier games from ten to twelve. Another important factor is that there are no restrictions on how many bowls one network can televise. Like the bowl scenario above, there has been no discussion by television networks regarding proposed antitrust cases against the BCS.

Advertisers and sponsors could also be a potential consumer. They would likely need to show the BCS, or its successor, caused advertising and sponsorship rates to artificially rise. Another option would be for advertisers or sponsors to show there is a price-fixing arrangement between bowls or conferences that sets rates. The question is would any of those companies be willing to jeopardize future relationships with conferences, bowls or schools to bring a claim?

The last, and most obvious, is college football fans as consumers. One argument that has been made is that fans pay higher prices—for everything from game tickets to Coca-Cola—because of the BCS. Although tickets for regular season games, bowl games and the BCS National Championship Game might be seen as expensive for some consumers, those prices may very well reflect consumer demand given there are a limited supply of tickets.

Outside of ticket prices, arguments could be made that the BCS harms consumers by affecting prices for other products. Roger Noll, an economics professor at Stanford University and expert on antitrust law, has been quoted as saying, "I think the majority of consumers do not know that they pay higher prices for Coca-Cola as a result of the higher prices to promote inside the bowl championship game."[8] Given that Coca-Cola sponsors a wide variety of sports properties globally, it would be tough to prove the BCS alone impacts prices.

Another argument advanced here would be that consumers are harmed because output is limited, as was the case under the NCAA's television plan discussed in Chapter 4. However, the argument can be made that the BCS actually increases the output.

Although the BCS (and even its successor) may produce less games than fans would like, it does not reduce the previous output of games. What's more, there's no proof that without the current format more postseason games would be played. Instead, by consenting to the BCS, and in the future to the College Football Playoff, the relevant players have agreed to that specific output.

One last argument for consumer harm is that the BCS decreases the quality or competitiveness of college football games played by non-AQ teams. This would be a tenuous argument by the plaintiff, likely based on a 2004 decision in the U.S. District Court for the Southern District of New York regarding an NCAA rule preventing universities involved in the NCAA college basketball tournament from competing in the National Invitational Tournament (NIT).[9]

In that case, the court rejected the NCAA's argument that only competitors were harmed, not consumers. Instead, the court found it could not distinguish between harm to the NIT and harm to competition itself. Ultimately, the court decided the rule prevented the NIT from offering consumers the most competitive basketball possible and allowed the case to proceed. In the end, the case was settled when the NCAA purchased both preseason and postseason NIT events.

Opponents of the BCS would argue the BCS's revenue distribution system allows AQ teams to hire better coaches, obtain higher-quality recruits and build better facilities. They would point to this as proof that games played by non-AQs are less competitive, and therefore consumers are harmed. Based on the discussion that began this chapter about the new College Football Playoff, the same case could likely be made about the new system.

The BCS, and the College Football Playoff, would have at least two arguments in its defense. First, under the BCS non-AQs are receiving more revenue than they ever have before. Likewise, under the College Football Playoff those conferences are receiving more than under the BCS. Second, the decision in New York is only precedent in that jurisdiction, meaning courts in other locations can choose whether to follow the ruling. It is also not binding on the Supreme Court, should a case make it to that level.

Once consumer harm is established, the burden shifts to the defendant to show the procompetitive justifications promote competition. If the defendant, which would likely be some combination of the power conferences and those individuals who execute the restraints, show the restraints enhance competition, the burden shifts back to the plaintiff to show there is at least one less restrictive alternative. Courts have varied greatly in how they analyze the least restrictive means portion of the test, and the Supreme Court doesn't even recognize it, which makes antitrust litigation largely a crapshoot in this situation.

Early antitrust cases look at a set of prongs to analyze whether a violation had indeed occurred: the nature of the market or industry, the motives or goals that led to implementation of the restraint and a comparison of the competitiveness of the market both before and after the restraint was instituted. Courts today don't look at these each as separate prongs to be reviewed independently of each other, but instead use the rule of reason as a shortcut way to answer the questions.

In terms of the nature of the market, college football is one in which cooperation and restraints are necessary in order to produce a postseason. As shown in earlier chapters, it wasn't possible to produce even an arguable national champion before the BCS because the FBS was split into factions where some conferences chose not to participate, as was the case with the Big Ten and Pac-10.

In fact, prior to the BCS the nation's top two ranked teams met in postseason competition just eight times in 56 years, an average of once every 7 years. Since the BCS' inception, the top two teams (per BCS measurements) have played each other 15 times in 15 years. Twelve of those 15 years, the top two teams in the AP poll met in the national championship game, with a streak of nine consecutive meetings from the 2004-2012 seasons. Accordingly, the BCS would be likely to survive this prong of analysis. It remains to be seen how the selection process will work under the new College Football Playoff, but there's reason to believe it will be an improvement over the BCS.

The next prong would have the court look to the motives or goals that led to the system. Anticompetitive intent is not required in order for a court to find a violation, but instead help determine the anticompetitive effect of the restraint.

The stated goal of the BCS is to produce a "five game showcase of college football [which ensures] that the two top-rated teams in the country meet in the national championship game, and to create exciting and competitive matchups among eight other highly regarded teams in four other bowl games."[10]

The BCS isn't an actual legal entity, but instead a series of agreements between the FBS conferences, both AQ and non-AQ, and the independents who play at the FBS level. That means anyone bringing suit would name those parties as defendants. In many cases that might end up meaning a conference or state could end up suing itself. For example, if Utah Attorney General Mark Shurtleff brought suit, University of Utah and Utah State University would both be on the other side of the suit as members of BCS conferences. Since both are state institutions, Shurtleff would essentially be suing the state he represents.

Back to the analysis at hand, the BCS is governed in part by the Presidential Oversight Committee, which has representatives from each AQ and non-AQ conferences and independent Notre Dame. The selection process for the National Championship is based on a combination of both computer and human polls that in theory are meant to provide equal opportunity for all. Based on all this, there's an argument to be made that the goals and motives of the BCS is more pro-competitive than anti-competitive.

Additionally, the BCS can argue its only goal is to pair the top two teams for the National Championship, and that beyond that the bowls each operate individually and can choose their means for creating their game at their own discretion.

Bill Hancock, director of the BCS, told the *Salt Lake Tribune* in 2012, "The Sugar Bowl is an independent organization. It owns the game, presents the game, and arranges for the opportunities for student athletes, coaches, and fans to enjoy as part of the bowl experience. It makes no sense that, having created the event, the Sugar Bowl should not be able to select those teams that it wishes to invite to its game."[11]

As for the College Football Playoff, many of the stated motives and goals focused on increasing access to the system and including more teams. It remains to be seen how the selection process will work, so it can't be included in the analysis at this time. There's reason to believe the College Football Playoff's arguments would build upon those that could be made by the BCS in order to show there was no anticompetitive intent.

The last of the prongs used by courts in early antitrust cases may be the most important for the College Football Playoff, as it would have been for the BCS: comparing the competitiveness of the market both before and after the restraint. Today, it is the primary focus of the rule of reason analysis.

In the 45 years prior to the formation of the BCS, teams from non-AQ conferences participated in premier bowls only six times, or approximately once every 7.5 years. During the nine-year period from the 2004-2005 season to the 2012-2013 season under the BCS system, eight non-AQ schools played in seven of those bowls, an average of nearly one per year.

In addition, previous cases have affirmed that increased public interest is an important pro-competitive justification, and the BCS would have had no trouble arguing there was an increase during its tenure. When the BCS was instituted in 1998 total attendance for FBS was 27.6 million. By 2012, attendance had increased to 32.7 million. That's a 34.8 percent increase compared to a mere 8.6 percent increase over the previous 14-year period.

Ratings have increased as well, allowing the BCS National Championship Game to out-rate most other sports championships. The 2012 BCS National Championship Game drew 24.2 million viewers, a decrease over the previous year's 27.3 million attributed to the 2012 game being a rematch between conference rivals Alabama and LSU. Even with the decline, the BCS beat out the 2012 NCAA Men's Basketball Championship, which drew 20.9 million viewers. The 2011 MLB World Series averaged 16.2 million per game, although Game 7 drew 25.4 million. The 2012 NBA Finals averaged 16.9 million per game, with 18.5 tuning in for the Game 5 finale. The BCS National Championship Game pales in comparison to only the Super Bowl, which had 111.3 million viewers in 2012.

It's not hard to see the competitiveness of the market improved under the BCS. That would be an important part of the defense in a case like this. Opponents of the system would argue that non-AQ schools do not receive automatic berths in BCS bowls. It is important to note that those schools did not receive automatic berths prior to the BCS. Instead, bowls each operated independently and chose schools based on their own individual criteria. Many had conference tie-ins, generally with AQ schools. Therefore, the BCS does not restrain trade any more than the previous system—as shown, it has improved access and allowed for the creation of additional bowl games.

Based on these facts, it's possible the court would find the BCS had more pro-competitive effects than anti-competitive. The College Football Playoff would have an even better argument, as it does now guarantee one spot to the Group of Five.

Opponents of the system focus on there being what they perceive to be less restrictive, or better alternatives, such as a more comprehensive playoff. This is where making bets on the outcome of antitrust litigation gets risky. It'll take a little Law School 101 to understand this next issue.

Although there are state antitrust laws, a suit against the BCS or its successor would likely be brought in federal court under the federal antitrust laws. The federal court system is made up of three tiers: district court, court of appeals and the United States Supreme Court. A case starts in the district court, then can be appealed to the court of appeals for that circuit (there are 12 geographic circuits and one nationwide circuit that handles only specific types of cases, which would not apply here), and lastly can be appealed to the United States Supreme Court. The Supreme Court does not hear every appeal, with the justices voting on whether to hear a case or let the lower court ruling stand, so there's no guarantee a case would make it to that level.

Antitrust law is tricky because the rule of reason test varies from circuit to circuit. The lower courts have all added a final step to the rule of reason test, which asks whether a less restrictive alternative to the current system is available. This is where a plaintiff would have argued that a playoff would achieve the same result as the BCS, only through less restrictive means. The same could apply to the College Football Playoff going into effect after the BCS ends following the 2013 season. Plaintiffs could argue less restrictive alternatives to the selection process, revenue distribution or even the format in terms of number of game played.

However, the problem with predicting the outcome of antitrust litigation against college football's postseason is that the lower courts vary as to how they apply the less restrictive means prong of the test. For example, the D.C. Circuit has required defendants to show they are using the *least* restrictive means available. Meanwhile, the Tenth Circuit places the burden on the plaintiff to show the procompetitive benefits laid out by the defendant can be achieved through substantially less restrictive means.

The outcome could be entirely dependent on where the case was filed. Then what happens if the case is appealed all the way up to the Supreme Court? Well, it turns out the Supreme Court hasn't used the less restrictive means prong of the rule of reason test since a prominent 1918 antitrust decision.[12] The Supreme Court, in previous decisions, has made it clear that it will not evaluate business decisions once the court has determined the mechanism at issue is more beneficial than harmful to competition. Therefore, there's reason to believe the Supreme Court would not consider any alternatives—which would favor the defendant.

Even if a court were to find in favor of the plaintiff, the judge cannot and will not order a specified postseason system in football. Before college football announced in 2012 it would move to a four-team playoff format in 2014, many fans hoped an antitrust suit against the BCS would result in a playoff. However, a judge has no authority to order a playoff. It was just as likely college football would revert to the old bowl tie-in system. It also means that no future suit will result in an order for an 8-team or 16-team playoff.

Section 2 Analysis

Claims under Section 2 of the Sherman Act are less prevalent, because they're generally considered more difficult to prove than claims under Section 1. An allegation under Section 2 differs from Section 1, because the plaintiff must prove the defendant has illegal monopoly power within the relevant market. This has historically been challenging for plaintiffs. Existence of a monopoly alone is not enough to bring a successful Section 2 claim. Previous case law states an illegal monopoly is one which displays a, "willful acquisition or maintenance of that power as distinguished from growth or development as a consequence of a superior product, business acumen or historic accident."[13] The BCS, therefore, could argue its market power is simply a result of a superior product.

Even if the plaintiff could prove the BCS had illegal monopoly power, it would then need to prove the BCS excluded non-AQ schools from a meaningful opportunity to compete in that market. Under the BCS model, if a non-AQ team finishes in the top 12, or in the top 16 and ahead of at least one AQ conference champion, it will receive a BCS bowl bid. The plaintiff would have to convince the court that does not constitute a "meaningful opportunity."

The case would become more difficult for a plaintiff attacking the College Football Playoff, as it gives an automatic berth to the highest-ranked team from the Group of Five, guaranteeing at least one member of that group will participate in one of the Access Bowls (Rose, Sugar, Orange, Fiesta, Chick-Fil-A or Cotton).

Opponents of the BCS would likely point to the BCS ranking system, particularly the computer portion. The BCS computer rankings do not account for margin of victory. Some believe this disadvantages non-AQ schools, which often beat lesser competition by significant margins. The computers do, however, taken into account strength of schedule. This is also viewed as a disadvantage for non-AQ schools, because there are generally a small number that are competitive, meaning their conference schedule is full of opponents the computers deem weak.

The College Football Playoff being introduced in 2014 could still be vulnerable to an attack under Section 2 on many of the same grounds as the BCS. The selection process could be at issue, much as it was under the BCS, and again members of the ACC, Big-12, Big Ten, Pac-12 and SEC have contractual ties to the top bowls.

Although there are some arguments to be made under Section 2, most experts believe the best shot at an antitrust victory would be under Section 1, as Section 2 claims have historically been more difficult in every industry.

Hopefully what this chapter has shown is that the issue of whether the BCS, or the College Football Playoff, violates antitrust laws is anything but clear. Noted experts on antitrust law across the country have reviewed the merits of proposed cases and come to opposite conclusions, with some saying it simply depends on where the case is filed.

What we do know is that the threat of antitrust litigation is effective, even if there is no clear-cut violation. In addition to the hefty legal fees associated with bringing or defending against such a suit, the threat of treble (which means triple) damages is a deterrent and encourages parties to work toward resolutions out of court.

It's reasonable to believe the only reason non-AQ conferences were even included in the BCS was due to this unpredictable threat. Not only would an antitrust lawsuit have been costly, but a decision adverse to the BCS would have likely destroyed the power structure in college football that has existed for decades. It's no wonder the mere threat of a suit has been enough to effect change over the years, even if only little by little.

However, with each change we've moved further away from the possibility of an antitrust suit. During the BCS's run, it has increased payouts and improved access for non-AQs and has moved from a Presidential Oversight Committee with just one member of the non-AQ conferences represented to a committee comprised of a representative from each AQ and non-AQ conference. That committee ultimately voted to approve the playoff coming to college football for the 2014 season, including the revenue distribution and bowls involved and will ultimately decide the selection process for such bowls.

The increased inclusion of the non-AQ conferences, even if not on an equal basis in terms of revenue distribution, and their acquiescence to the system, makes an antitrust suit less and less likely in the future. However, it was likely the threat of antitrust suits that made the future possible.

NOTES

[1]   *Agnew v. National Collegiate Athletic Association* (7th Cir. June 18, 2012).

[2]   McMurphy, Brett. "Six Bowls in Playoff Format," ESPN.com, November 13, 2012. Retrieved May 11, 2013, from http://espn.go.com/college-football/story/_/id/8624387/six-bowls-pool-college-football-semifinal-games.

3. McMurphy, Brett. "Big earnings for power conferences." ESPN.com, December 11, 2012. Retrieved May 11, 2013, from http://espn.go.com/college-football/story/_/id/8736544/sec-big-ten-big-12-pac-12-acc-average-91-million-new-playoff-format-sources-say.

4. Fowler, Jeremy. "Smaller conferences crafting plan to share playoff revenue." CBSSports.com, January 22, 2013. Retrieved May 11, 2013, from http://www.cbssports.com/collegefootball/blog/jeremy-fowler/21599899/smaller-conferences-crafting-blueprint-for-playoff-revenue-sharing.

5. Schroeder, George. "College football playoff revenue distribution set." USAToday.com, December 12, 2012. Retrieved May 11, 2013, from http://www.usatoday.com/story/sports/ncaaf/bowls/2012/12/11/college-football-bcs-playoff-revenue-money-distribution-payouts/1762709/.

6. Russo, Ralph. "10 things to know about the College Football Playoff." AJC.com, April 25, 2013. Retrieved May 11, 2013, from http://www.ajc.com/ap/ap/georgia/10-things-to-know-about-college-football-playoff/nXXxw/.

7. *National Collegiate Athletic Association v. Board of Regents of the University of Oklahoma, et al.*, 468 U.S. 85 (1984).

8. Gara, Antoine, "BCS Challenge Would Need to Show Consumer Harm," *TheStreet.com*, September 23, 2011. Retrieved July 20, 2012, from http://www.thestreet.com/story/11258111/1/bcs-challenge-would-need-to-show-consumer-harm.html.

9. *Metropolitan Intercollegiate Basketball Ass'n v. National Collegiate Athletic Ass'n*, 339 F.Supp.2d 545 (S.D.N.Y. 2004).

10. *BCS Background*, BCSfootball.org. Retrieved May 12, 2012, from http://www.bcsfootball.org/news/story? id=4809699.

11. Gehrke, Robert (January 2, 2012), "Mark Shurtleff: Boise State snub helps BCS antitrust lawsuit," *Salt Lake Tribune*. Retrieved May 21, 2012, from http://www.sltrib.com/sltrib/home2/53206839-183/bowl-bcs-shurtleff-state.html.csp.

12. *Bd. of Trade of City of Chi. v. United States*, 246 U.S. 231, 238 (1918).

13. *United States v. Grinnell Corp.*, 384 U.S. at 570–71 (1966).

WHAT MAKES A GOOD AD?

Tom Jurich followed the normative pattern for becoming an athletic director: he was a student athlete, coached collegiate sports, served as an assistant and associate athletic director and then assumed the role of athletic director. He may have followed the roadmap, but Tom Jurich is not a cookie-cutter athletic director.

If Jurich finishes his current contract, he will have held the head position in University of Louisville athletics for nearly three decades. Having initially taken the job in 1997, Jurich signed an extension in 2011 that keeps him at the helm through 2023. It's an unprecedented contract, and Jurich has had unprecedented success at Louisville.

Louisville wasn't exactly a destination job when Jurich toured the campus in 1997. It was an urban commuter campus located adjacent to railroad tracks. Dog food stored in nearby silos owned by Purina permeated the air. Although it had achieved great basketball success in the past, its football program had only begun to make progress in the '90s under the guidance of Howard Schnellenberger. At the time Jurich was approached for the job, the school was excited to have broken ground on a new football stadium on the edge of campus to replace the aging fairgrounds stadium where it had played for 40 years.

Football didn't bring Jurich to Louisville. Neither did basketball. It wasn't anything Louisville had that attracted Jurich, it was what it didn't have: quality women's programs. Facilities for women's sports were decrepit and the school was out of Title IX compliance.

"The facilities when I first came to campus were probably the biggest disappointment I had with the university," said Jurich. "My wife, Terrilynn, leaned to me and said, 'What are we doing here?'"

"They had four shower heads in the basement of a building with the swimming pool and only two of them worked," Jurich said, recalling the absurdity of it. "That was to take care of all the female athletes."

Louisville didn't have a Title IX lawsuit yet, but it had hired a leading Title IX consultant who was preparing to deliver a scathing report. Another athletic director with whom Jurich was friends had used the same consultant and put Jurich in touch with the consultant so he could find out exactly what he'd be getting himself into in Louisville.

"I called and he went over the report with me on the phone. He said it was the worst Title IX situation he'd ever seen. He told me what he was going to write and that they were going to have to drop some sports."

Jurich was no stranger to Title IX issues. When he was hired at Colorado State, where he served as athletic director prior to taking the Louisville job, the school was being sued by members of the softball team for dropping the sport. He only caught the tail-end of the process, but it was enough to know he never wanted to be part of a Title IX investigation again.

Jurich's experience at CSU is certainly what attracted Louisville to him. What attracted him to Louisville was more personal.

As the father of young twin girls involved in athletics, Jurich was shocked by the state of the women's athletic facilities at Louisville when he first arrived. It's the first thing he'll tell you about when you ask him how he came to be at Louisville. He says right then and there was when he got the idea for what is now Cardinal Park.

When Jurich's achievements are touted, orchestrating the move from Conference USA to the Big East(and recently to the ACC), hiring basketball coach Rick Pitino and bringing an NBA-quality arena to Louisville are among the most prominent. Tour Louisville's athletic facilities with him, and you'll quickly realize building brand new facilities for every single women's sport during his tenure takes a back seat to no achievement. The new facilities include the field hockey stadium where his twin girls played for the University of Louisville in recent years.

Every men's sport has a new facility since Jurich's arrival as well, and all of Louisville's facilities have been built with private funds with the exception of the basketball arena, which was a joint venture with the City of Louisville. These new facilities replaced abandoned warehouses and rail yards, creating an attractive athletic village credited in part for the influx of students now living on-campus at Louisville.

Some athletic directors are hired because they own an impressive background in fundraising or hiring coaches or building facilities. Jurich is the total package. From hiring coaches who have a profound impact on programs, including John L. Smith and Rick Pitino, to ushering football into an AQ conference and building top-notch facilities, Jurich has made a lasting mark on Louisville.

University of Louisville President Dr. James Ramsey says Jurich's varied background has allowed him to have success in multiple arenas (no pun intended):

"He has the advantage of being able to see the world of collegiate athletics from the viewpoint of a coach, an administrator, an athlete and a parent because he has worn all of those hats in his career. He has the vision to create a model program, assemble an ambitious group of talented coaches and staff, build world-class facilities and create educational as well as championship opportunities for hundreds of student athletes. He is committed to creating a forward moving, competitive and compliant culture that reflects well on our university."[1]

Historically, there has been a pattern for becoming an athletic director: compete as an athlete in college, become a high school coach, move up to coaching at the collegiate level, become an associate or assistant athletic director and then be named athletic director. A step was skipped here or there, such as Jurich who did not coach at the high school level. Oftentimes it meant the head football coach went straight to athletic director or other times someone moved straight from college athlete to collegiate coaching, but through the 1970s, '80s and '90s all or most of this pattern was followed.

A 1983 study of 320 athletic directors across all divisions found 96 percent of male athletic directors competed in a sport at the college level, compared to 88 percent of female athletic directors. Nearly 67 percent of the male athletic directors had coached at the high school level and an overwhelming 94.1 percent coached at the college level. Just over 40 percent served as an assistant or associate athletic director prior to becoming athletic director.[2]

A study completed in 1987, which focused solely on Division I-A, showed a majority had coaching experience, although not as high as the previous study. Over 70 percent of the 58 Division I-A athletic directors in the 1987 study held head coaching positions prior to being named athletic director. Less than a quarter had served as assistant athletic directors and less than half as associate athletic directors.[3]

The percentage of athletic directors with coaching experience continued on a downward trend into the 1990s. A study completed in 1994, which covered 285 athletic directors across all three divisions, including 95 in Division I, found 65 percent of athletic directors had college coaching experience. The percentage with prior experience in the athletic department as an assistant or associate athletic director remained largely unchanged from previous studies at just under 40 percent. A whopping 80 percent of all the athletic directors studied competed as college athletes.[4]

By 2011, the percentage of athletic directors who had experience as both coaches and college athletes had dropped at the FBS level. Only 43 percent had held coaching positions and the percentage who were former college athletes dropped to 63.6 percent.[5]

Although having experience as a college athlete has diminished over the years, it still appears to be an important factor. In the 1994 study by Fitzgerald, Sagaria and Nelson, the authors noted a peculiar aspect of the culture in collegiate athletics hiring:

> The vast majority of ADs have been collegiate athletes. Thus the career patters of athletic directors do indeed indicate a portal of entry . . . or a prerequisite experience that may screen out some and permit access to others. Unlike most occupations, however, the AD position has as its portal not a first job or a required education, but rather a significant socializing co-curricular experience that cultivates leadership skills and athletic abilities and provides at least a glimpse into collegiate athletic administrators.[6]

Greg Byrne, athletic director at University of Arizona, says experience as an athlete, whether at the collegiate level or as a youth or high school athlete, instills a competitive spirit in someone. That competitiveness is a vital component of the athletic director's role.

"You have to know what it's like to compete. You have to," Byrne said. "When you have the inner ability to really commit and understand what it means to compete for something, that helps drive you. A great foundation to have in your life is the foundation of competition."[7]

Byrne didn't play collegiate athletics, though he did play baseball as a youth and credits that experience for his competitive instincts. As you'll see later in the chapter, what Byrne lacked in collegiate athletics experience as an athlete he made up for in other areas.

In addition to competitiveness, those who have been involved in athletic director searches say the experience of a former college football player can be important when it comes time to hire a new football coach. One went so far as to say hiring a head football coach represents the single biggest responsibility an athletic director can have. As you saw in the Chapter 2 discussion regarding Bobby Petrino at Arkansas, a football coach can have a profound effect on an athletic department. After all, there's no multimillion-dollar budget to balance if the football team isn't bringing in the money.

There are other reasons former college athletes make good athletic directors, at least in the minds of university presidents. UConn president Susan Herbst, who hired Warde Manuel to head her school's athletic department in February 2012, says Manuel's background as a Division I college athlete was an attractive part of his resume and something she sought out in candidates. It's worth noting Manuel had previously been a finalist for the athletic director job at his alma mater, Michigan, where fellow alum of the football program, David Brandon, was hired.

"For us, at least, at this point in time we liked the idea of someone who had been a Division I athlete themselves and could relate to our students and the athletic-academics balance," said Herbst.

Herbst believes Manuel, a former defensive end at Michigan, can use his experience as a student athlete to help her student athletes focus more on the student part of their title. Before hiring Manuel, UConn knew it was in danger of a postseason ban thanks to low Academic Progress Rate scores for its men's basketball team. The APR uses a formula to determine how student athletes are performing on a term-by-term basis, which predicts the probability of graduation. Each team is measured together, and any team not meeting a specified threshold is subject to sanctions.

A few months after Manuel's appointment UConn received official notification its men's basketball team, which has won three national championships, would indeed be banned from the postseason. It was the first time a school from an AQ football conference was banned from the postseason for its APR score.

The NCAA banned programs from the postseason in 2012-2013 based on four-year APR scores falling below 900, unless they had a two-year APR score of over 930. UConn had three years of falling APR scores before rebounding in 2010-2011, the last year of the assessment. Scores of 909 in 2007-2008, 844 in 2008-2009 and 826 in 2009-2010 meant its 978 score in 2010-2011 wasn't enough to save the program from a postseason ban. However, its 2011-2012 score of 947 was enough to remove the ban and allow for postseason play in 2013-2014.

Manuel was brought on board in part because of his understanding of the difficulties student athletes face balancing playing their sport with academics, and also because of his vast experience in college athletics.

Finding someone with that experience was a primary goal for Herbst during UConn's search.

"For us, at this particular point in time, we have a lot of work to do. We're a winning place and a great program, but we had some challenges with APR in men's basketball. We're over the hump and that problem has solved, but it needs constant attention," Herbst said of her inclination toward hiring someone with prior experience as an athletic director or senior administrator.

Jeff Schemmel, a former athletic director and managing director of JMI Sports LLC's College Division, which provides consulting services, says the real trend isn't everyone hiring one certain type of person, it's toward hiring someone that meets an immediate need. At UConn that was someone who could handle the APR issue and ensuing NCAA penalties. At Miami in 2011 it might have been someone with a wealth of compliance experience, as its athletic department was rocked by allegations of recruiting violations.

In addition, Herbst believed an experienced athletic director would have the requisite knowledge to improve other areas of need in the UConn athletic department. "Fundraising—we were behind where we should be. I think a sitting AD is used to working in the university's fundraising environment."

In addition to Manuel's ability to connect with student athletes from the perspective of having been one himself, his athletic department experience gives him a familiarity with the NCAA and its rules and regulations. With scandals involving recruiting and impermissible benefits seemingly at an all-time high, those in the industry say there's value in hiring an individual already familiar with the system.

Herbst isn't the only school president hiring an athletic director with prior experience working in a department. In 2011, 85.1 percent of then–current FBS athletic directors held assistant or associate positions first. In the 1994 study by Fitzgerald, Sagaria and Nelson, only 39.5 percent of athletic directors held positions as assistant or associate athletic directors prior to taking the chief position.

A major factor in the increase of department experience, and the corresponding decline on the importance of coaching experience, is likely the growth in degree programs specifically tailored to training students to work in sports, including programs geared towards college athletics. The first degree-granting sports management program was founded at Ohio University in 1966. By 1980 there were approximately 20 sports management programs. The presence of academic programs saw an enormous jump in the 1980s, thanks in part to Title IX increasing the number of teams and student athletes. As of August 2012, the North American Society for Sport Management listed over 330 undergraduate degree programs in the United States.

Today, students go to college with the goal of being an athletic director, a reality that largely wasn't true thirty years ago. Greg Byrne knew at age ten he wanted to be an athletic director, a job he already knew a great deal about thanks to his father, Bill Byrne. The elder Byrne was an associate athletic director and then promoted to athletic director at Oregon during Greg's childhood and continued to hold athletic director positions until he retired in 2012. No doubt the younger Byrne learned much from his father, though he amassed an impressive resume of his own by the time he assumed his first athletic director position.

Greg Byrne's first job in athletics was as a special projects coordinator for the Fiesta Bowl, a position he held from 1993-1995 while earning his bachelor's degree from Arizona State in 1994. He would take his first athletic department job at University of Oregon as regional director of development. While overseeing fundraising efforts in Portland, Southern and Central Oregon, Northern California and the Oregon coast, he achieved success by securing record donation totals for each region.

From there, he moved to Oregon State, where he served as associate athletic director for development. Annual giving increased from $1 million to $5 million, and he assisted in efforts to secure a $12.5 million gift for naming rights to the football stadium. Byrne moved from Oregon State to Kentucky after four years, again holding an associate athletic director for development position. Annual gift totals rose from $4 million to $9 million, and he led a capital campaign for a new basketball practice facility.[8]

By the time Byrne took over as the associate athletic director for external affairs at Mississippi State he had 11 years of experience in development. Once in Starkville, he increased annual giving and created the Road Dawgs Tour, which sent Mississippi State coaches out on the road during the summer months to interact with fans.

On February 1, 2008, Greg Byrne became the youngest FBS athletic director in history at just 36 years of age when Mississippi State promoted him to replace Larry Templeton, who'd led the program for two decades. Although Byrne was only athletic director at Mississippi State for two years, he amassed some major accomplishments. He hired Dan Mullen, an assistant on the national champion Florida staff, to be the new head football coach and lured baseball coach John Cohen away from Kentucky.

In 2010, Byrne was offered the chance to move west and take the athletic director job at Arizona, putting him back in a conference where he'd spent much of his childhood and early working years. Perhaps because of its success with Byrne, Mississippi State would look to another young, internal candidate: Scott Stricklin.

Stricklin says he knew at a young age he wanted to have a career in sports, but even when he entered college he wasn't sure what shape that future career would take.

"I went to college wanting to either coach or go the administrative route," said Stricklin. "I was the sports editor of my high school paper, so I had an interest in the media side of stuff. My older brother was already in school at Mississippi State and had a friend interning in the sports information office. He had press passes to all the sports, and I thought that was neat."

The first day of his freshman year, Stricklin walked into the SID's office and asked to volunteer. It was a match made in heaven.

"I remember going to work as a student worker in 1989 in Knoxville for the basketball tournament. I got to sit courtside and go to all these press conferences. For a kid who grew up around SEC sports it was nirvana. I remember coming back from that and knowing that's what I wanted to do."

Stricklin graduated from Mississippi State in 1992, having worked his final three years as the communications point person for the baseball team. Following graduation, he was named assistant media relations director, a position he held for one year. Stricklin moved on to Auburn, where he served as associate media relations director focusing on baseball for five years. From there, Stricklin went on to hold media relations and communications positions at Tulane, Baylor and Kentucky before returning to Mississippi State. He returned just in time to take Greg Byrne's job as the senior associate athletic director for external affairs when Byrne moved up to athletic director.

Not only was Stricklin not a college athlete or coach, his professional career largely consisted of media relations and communications positions. There's been a growing trend of athletic directors coming from development in recent years, but Stricklin doesn't fit that mold either.

Asked how important development experience is for an athletic director, Stricklin says, "It's important to understand how important development is."

Stricklin says it was a question he was asked when he interviewed for the external affairs position at Mississippi State.

"I said there are three things you have to do in PR or media relations and that's develop relationships, communicate relationships and have difficult conversations from time to time. That's what you do in development. The skill set translates."

It's just as important in Stricklin's world to know how to effectively communicate, especially in an age where athletic directors are often in the spotlight.

"The communications background has really benefited me, because my peers from a development background sometimes struggle with comfort level of how to communicate," said Stricklin. "Sometimes in development you're good at one-on-one, but struggle with this different style of communication."

While Schemmel doesn't believe there's any one prototype for athletic directors anymore, he does recognize the growing celebrity of the position.

"The AD position has become astronomically more visible than it used to be," said Schemmel. "There's media attention on everything you do."

That means it's not enough to be a superstar at fundraising or an expert at handling the media—today's athletic director has to be able to do it all. They have to surround themselves with a knowledgeable team, and also understand everyone's role.

I will tell you my own story about the first time I met Ross Bjork, then–athletic director at Western Kentucky University and the youngest athletic director of a BCS school. The minute I got into my car after my athletic facilities tour with Bjork I immediately knew he was going to be somewhere big one day. Not that Western Kentucky isn't a wonderful school with a strong athletic program, but I knew Bjork would get an opportunity with a bigger program in an AQ conference soon enough. There was something indescribable about the passion he had for his job and Western Kentucky. By the time I finished my tour, I was ready to get out my checkbook and donate to this school I previously knew nothing about. A school I never would have visited had Bjork not reached out to me on Twitter and invited me. Another example of how forward-thinking and proactive he is.

Clearly I wasn't the only one who felt that way about Bjork. Five months later, sooner than even I could have imagined, Bjork was named the new athletic director at Ole Miss after only two years of athletic director experience.

Mike Glenn, a vice president at FedEx and an Ole Miss alum who co-chaired the search committee with Archie Manning, had a similar experience when he met Bjork minutes before his interview at Ole Miss.

"We just talked about philosophy and vision," Glenn said, "and I knew right then and there that he was something special. I couldn't wait to get into the interview, because I knew it was going to be full of energy and passion. He was going to share his vision to take Ole Miss to a whole new level and that's exactly what he did."

Liberty Bowl executive director Steve Ehrhart had a similar experience meeting Bjork. In November 2011, Bjork contacted Ehrhart and asked to come speak with him about Western Kentucky getting an invitation to his bowl game.

"I explained to him before they came to see me that it would be a long shot since we had a three-way contract with the SEC, Conference USA and Big East," Ehrhart said. "But they came anyway, and he presented me with a plan on how he would market the Liberty Bowl to his fans if we chose his team."

Although the Liberty Bowl is not one of the premiere bowl games, it would have meant a great deal to Western Kentucky. Football teams from Western Kentucky have participated in only two bowl games in the program's history: the 1952 Refrigerator Bowl and the 1963 Tangerine Bowl. Neither were NCAA-sanctioned Division 1 bowl games. A Liberty Bowl appearance would have been a treat for the players, who would have participated in four days of activities in Memphis and played another game that season, and it would have meant national exposure before millions of viewers for Western Kentucky on ABC on New Year's Eve.

"He was very thorough, very proactive, very organized and very impressive," Ehrhart said of Bjork. In fact, Ehrhart was so impressed he drove down to Oxford when Bjork was announced as athletic director just to shake his hand.[9]

Bjork certainly had a strong background for someone his age when he was hired by Ole Miss. He had spent the previous two years at Western Kentucky as athletic director, and five years previous to that at UCLA. While at UCLA, Bjork was the senior associate athletic director for external affairs, handling everything from development to marketing and promotions, to ticket sales, to licensing, branding and merchandising. In his first year on the job, total giving to UCLA athletics doubled and both football and men's basketball experienced record ticket sales.

Prior to UCLA, Bjork spent two years at University of Miami, where he gained experience in development, renegotiated contracts with Nike and Gatorade, and directed the search process for a new men's basketball coach in 2004. For six years prior to Miami, Bjork oversaw development at Missouri.

As you can see, Bjork has an impressive resume to go along with his charismatic persona, and stands as a great example of an athletic director who sees and understands all the different facets of the athletic department.

Although there have been several hires in recent years from outside the world of college athletics, the perception that universities are moving to corporate America to fill the roles and manage the multimillion budgets is deceiving. Even those who haven't held prior athletic department positions do have strong ties to the school or collegiate athletics.

In 2011, there were only 15 FBS athletic directors who did not hold a position within a college athletic department immediately prior to their appointment as athletic director. Two of them held positions within college athletic administration previously in their careers, which means only 13 of the 120 athletic directors, or 11 percent, had never worked in college athletics administration prior to their appointment as athletic director.

Breaking it down further, however, none of these athletic directors were random leaders from corporate America. Of the 13 with no prior college athletics administration experience, 4 had collegiate coaching experience and 2 had served on the university's board. The most interesting number? Eleven of the 13 were alums of the schools that hired them to lead the athletic department.

Everyone on the list of 15 had one of the following: collegiate coaching experience, collegiate-athletics administration experience, student athlete experience or held a position on the university's board. Only two had just student athlete experience, but both brought more to the table. One is USC's Pat Haden, who in addition to being a former USC quarterback had careers as an NFL player, broadcaster and attorney. Then-Rutgers athletic director Tim Pernetti played football at Rutgers before going on to a career in television, working in programming at ABC Sports before joining upstart CSTV, which was eventually purchased by CBS.

Only 3 of the 15 took the athletic director post with nothing more than coaching experience in collegiate athletics: Barry Alvarez at Wisconsin, Tom Osborne at Nebraska and Mike Holder at Oklahoma State.

Alvarez is the most successful coach in Wisconsin history. Osborne is also a long-time coach with a national title, along with a PhD and six years as a congressman. Holder has an MBA and 32 years in the Oklahoma State athletic department as golf coach. Both Osborne and Holder are alumni of their respective universities.

One of the athletic directors who came in without any previous athletic administration experience was David Brandon, hired as athletic director at University of Michigan in January 2010. Prior to his appointment, he was CEO of pizza chain Domino's. This, people said, was a sign that college athletics was being treated like the big business it had become. Michigan, with one of the largest budgets in college athletics, was turning to someone from corporate America to lead its future.

What was rarely reported outside of Ann Arbor, however, was that David Brandon had been a football player at Michigan and had served on the University's board of regents from 1998 to 2006. Although he had no experience as an athletic department administrator, his relationship with the university as both a student athlete and as a member of the board of regents likely had more to do with his hire than his Domino's experience.

Increasingly, it is important for athletic departments to integrate with the university, whether it's partnering on sponsorships or simply because of the impact athletics can have on academics, as you'll see in Chapter 9. Someone like Brandon, who has relationships with university administration and the board, can play a pivotal role.

Not only did Brandon previously serve on the board of regents, he also made a $4 million donation to the university to help build the new Mott Children's Hospital. Along with his wife, and former Michigan head football coach Lloyd Carr and his wife, Brandon headed the fundraising campaign for both the children's hospital and the Women's Hospital Replacement Project. From being a student athlete at Michigan to his intimate knowledge of university affairs from his time on the board and his role in fundraising, Brand brought far more to the table than his corporate America experience.

"Dave Brandon has a deep knowledge of and appreciation for the university and its mission," said Mary Sue Coleman, the president of University of Michigan who hired Brandon. "He's been a student, a regent, a donor and now a senior administrator. He understands Michigan."

Similarly, Jack Swarbrick understands Notre Dame, even if he didn't hold any positions in collegiate athletics administration prior to being appointed Notre Dame's athletic director. Not only is Swarbrick an alum, he spent decades in the Indianapolis sports world, which included continuous interaction with the NCAA.

Jack Swarbrick, Notre Dame's athletic director hired in 2008, represents one of the three attorneys from the Arkansas study. While that position was his first on-campus job, he was no stranger to sports administration. From 1992 to 2001, Swarbrick served as chairman of the Indiana Sports Corp. Under his guidance, Indianapolis lured a number of impressive sports properties to town. For example, he served as vice president of the Indianapolis 2012 Super Bowl Committee, which won a successful bid to host the Super Bowl.

In his role with Indiana Sports Corp., Swarbrick also had a long history with the NCAA. Since 1991, Indianapolis has hosted the NCAA Men's Basketball Final Four six times. In addition, Swarbrick assured Indianapolis would host the event an average of once every five years through 2039. In 1999, he secured the City's relationship with the NCAA by leading what became a successful effort to relocate the NCAA headquarters to Indianapolis. Swarbrick would also be instrumental in securing rights to the Big Ten Conference men's and women's basketball tournaments for a five-year period that began in 2008.

As an attorney, Swarbrick represented owners of sports teams and organizations that sanction or conduct athletic competitions. He also served as general counsel for several national governing bodies for Olympic sports, including USA Gymnastics and USRowing.

While college athletic departments often deal with tens of millions of dollars, and sometimes in excess of $100 million, they remain unique business units, which you'll remember from Chapters 1 and 2 are not directly comparable to for-profit corporations. Perhaps that is why athletic departments continue to favor more relatable experience, such as that of a former athlete or lower-level athletics administrator.

There's no reason to believe there will be a dramatic shift to hiring athletic directors from corporate America. As demonstrated in this chapter, there have been no athletic directors hired for an FBS school with no ties to college athletics, whether it be through experience as a student athlete, coaching or working with college athletics and the NCAA in the private sector.

Being an athletic director has become a career destination. New sports management/marketing/administration programs are popping up every year, and students and professionals from a variety of other disciplines are just as eager to head up a college athletic department. At the convention for the National Association of Collegiate Directors of Athletics in 2012, a number of affiliated organizations such as the Collegiate Athletic Business Management Association and National Association of Athletic Development Directors held sessions for their members about how to become an athletic director.

The role of athletic director is specialized and requires working knowledge of a number of different areas within collegiate athletics from compliance to development to communication and more. An MBA or law degree adds a depth of knowledge, but it takes more than a degree or a few years working at a Fortune 500 company to have the knowledge and connections necessary to lead a collegiate athletic department.

NOTES

[1] "Tom Jurich, Director of Athletics/Vice President, U of L," GoCards.com. Retrieved August 2, 2012, from http://www.gocards.com/school-bio/lou-jurich.html.

[2] Williams, J.M. & Miller, D.M., "Intercollegiate athletic administration: Preparation patterns," *Research Quarterly for Exercise and Sport*, 54 (1982): 398-406.

[3] Hatfield, B.D., Wrenn, J.P. & Bretting, M.M. "Comparison of job responsibilities of intercollegiate athletic directors and professional general manager," *Journal of Sport Management*, 1 (1987): 129-145.

[4] Fitzgerald, M.P., Sagaria, M.A.D., Nelson, Barbara. "Career Patterns of Athletic Directors: Challenging the Conventional Wisdom," *Journal of Sport Management,* 8 (1994): 14-26.

[5] Dittmore, S.W. (advisor), White, E., Gates, E., Martin, D. C., & Sanders, C. J. *Predicting career patterns for becoming an NCAA Division I FBS athletic director: Revisiting the "normative" sequence.* Abstract presented at the 2011 College Sport Research Institute's Scholarly Conference on College Sport, April 19-22, 2011, Chapel Hill, N.C.

[6] Fitzgerald, Sagaria and Nelson, op.cit. at 22.

[7] Chandler, Annie (February 28, 2012). "Athletics Director Redefined." ArizonaWildcats.com. Retrieved April 1, 2012, from http://www.arizonawildcats.com/genrel/022912aaa.html.

[8] University of Arizona, Office of Communications (March 22, 2010), "Greg Byrne Named Athletics Director." ArizonaWildcats.com. Retrieved March 22, 2012, from http://www.arizonawildcats.com/sports/inside-athletics/spec-rel/032210aaa.html.

[9] Higgins, Ron (March 23, 2012). "Bjork sells AD committee at Ole Miss". *The Commercial Appeal*. Retrieved August 6, 2012, from http://www.commercialappeal.com/news/2012/mar/23/bjork-sells-committee-at-ole-miss/.

8

WHY NOTRE DAME GRADS ARE PAYING MORE FOR CABLE SO INDIANA GRADS CAN WATCH THEIR TEAM

What does Appalachian State have to do with the future of college football television? As you'll see in this chapter, probably more than you think. When the Mountaineers upset No. 5 Michigan on the first weekend of the 2007 season hardly anyone saw it outside of the 109,218 in attendance at Michigan Stadium. Instead of reaching 100 million fans on a network like ESPN, the game was the first aired by the startup Big Ten Network, reaching merely 17 million homes. Within the week, Dish Network had signed up, and within the month Big Ten Network became the first cable or satellite network in history to reach 30 million households in its first 30 days.

As of the start of the 2012 season, Big Ten Network was available in 80 million homes. Not only is it distributed across its footprint and the nation, it was profitable within two years of launching. No doubt, its success shaped the decisions made by the Pac-12, which launched not one but seven networks in 2012 , and the SEC, which launches its network in 2014. As you'll see in this chapter, the Pac-12 took what the Big Ten did and made the scale larger, both in terms of content and overall strategy.

It's become commonplace to say television is running college football, because of the hundreds of millions of dollars networks pump into the system. False. As you'll discover in this chapter, the conferences run the show. Television plays a role, but the conferences have built the stage and are casting the parts.

As you saw in Chapter 4, television has been an important supporting actor in the story of college football for the last three decades. The 1984 Supreme Court decision not only brought more college football coverage to the masses, fueling its popularity, it also created a divide between the CFA schools and the Big Ten and Pac-10 that persisted until the BCS era began in the late 1990s. Securing its own television deal has allowed Notre Dame to sustain independence and has been a catalyst for conference realignment.

How might television, and the emergence of digital technologies, shape the future of college football? Over the past decade we've seen the emergence of conference networks like The Mtn. - MountainWest Sports Network, Big Ten Network and Pac-12 Networks. Schools like Texas and BYU have created their own networks, and most schools offer a variety of both live and replay content on their websites. It's all meant more money and more exposure for college athletics, with football at the helm.

With a minimum of 16 sports required to participate at the FBS level, each school creates a plethora of content from games, meets and contests. Some of those, like football and men's basketball, hold tremendous value regionally or nationally, while others might only hold value locally or amongst friends and family of the program. Both conferences and schools are constantly looking for ways to package and monetize all this content, but is there really an appetite for it all?

In the 10 years following the Supreme Court decision to strike down the NCAA's television plan, it's been estimated $200 million in television revenue was lost. Supply increased and demand initially didn't keep up. With more and more content flooding the airwaves today from conferences and schools, both terrestrially and digitally, will the industry once again be on the wrong side of supply and demand theory?

In 2004 the Big Ten and ESPN decided to discuss a media rights extension three years prior to the end of their existing deal. Big Ten commissioner Jim Delaney didn't like the offer coming from ESPN's side of the table. He warned that without a significant increase he would considering launching a channel of his own.

ESPN executive vice president of programming and production at the time, Mark Shapiro, told the *Chicago Tribune*, "He threw his weight around, and said, 'I'm going to get my big [rights-fee] increase and start my own network.' Had ESPN stepped up and paid BCS-type dollars, I think we could have prevented the network."

Delaney confirmed that would have been the case. "If Mark had presented a fair offer, we would have signed it. And there would not be a Big Ten Network."[1]

The Big Ten did go on to sign a ten-year, $1 billion deal with ESPN/ABC in 2006 for its first-tier rights, which included up to 41 football games per season, approximately 60 men's basketball games per season and 100 women's basketball and volleyball games, including the Big Ten Women's Basketball Tournament.

The bigger announcement came the same day as the ESPN/ABC deal: the Big Ten would be partnering with Fox to create its own channel, which would later be named the Big Ten Network. The plan had been two years in the making. Once the conference decided to create a channel, it began searching for a partner. The conference talked to cable companies, venture capitalists and private equity firms. Fox Sports COO Larry Jones ran into Delaney at a BCS retreat in January 2006 and used the opportunity to pitch Fox as a potential partner.

In April 2006, Fox brought a full team of executives from News Corp. and various Fox units to convince the Big Ten it was the right partner. The group highlighted its experience, including building four of the six cable networks that had launched with a viewership of at least 20 million: Fox News, National Geographic, Fuel and Speed.

The Big Ten had found a partner. Fox agreed to cover all the startup expenses, including production and on-air talent. The network and conference formed a limited liability company to run the channel, later named Big Ten Network, LLC, to initially be owned 51 percent by the conference and 49 percent by Fox. The agreement is a 20-year joint venture, with an option for an additional 5 years.

Payouts over the 25-year agreement are based on profit projections by News Corp., starting low and increasing over the years. The network officially launched August 30, 2007, with the rights fee beginning at $50 million. In addition to the rights fee, the conference receives annual profits in proportion to its ownership percentage. At launch that percentage was 51 percent with Fox retaining 49 percent; those percentages were flipped sometime between June 2010 and August 2011. Total compensation to the Big Ten over the 25-year life of the agreement was projected at $2.8 billion by Fox.

Media experts believe the Big Ten could have received the same compensation by putting its second-tier rights out on the open market. The SEC signed a 15-year, $2.25 billion deal for its second-tier rights in 2009 with ESPN. The Big 12 sold its second-tier rights for $1.17 billion to Fox for 13 years in 2011.

The advantage with the Big Ten Network comes in providing the conference control over its programming. Whether showing academic programming, which it first included and then pulled due to low ratings, or highlighting more non-revenue sports, the conference can make every minute of every day all about them. The network also ensures every football and basketball game has a national television outlet.

The network replaced an ESPN Plus regional television package, where games were typically only seen on one station in the team's local market. For example, Illinois might only be on Champaign station WCIA. Minnesota says that from 2002-2006, 13 of its football games were not available on a major carrier, which it defined as ABC, CBS, ESPN, ESPN2, ESPNU, ESPN Regional or TBS. In addition, in 2005 and 2006, 13 Big Ten football games were not televised at all. Similarly, in 2006, 85 Big Ten men's basketball games were not televised. The goal of Big Ten Network was to ensure every home football and men's basketball game was produced for a national audience, and the channel should be available on expanded basic cable in all of the eight states within the Big Ten footprint.

Initially, the Big Ten Network would air at least 35 football games per season (with each team appearing at least twice), 105 regular season men's basketball games, 55 regular season women's basketball games, 170 Olympic sporting events, Big Ten championship events, coaches shows and archived Big Ten events, including bowl games. There would also be 660 hours of academic/institutional programming, 60 hours for each member institution that it would produce on its own. In 2012, however, academic programming was scaled back due to low ratings and limited resources for production at some institutions.

When the Big Ten Network launched in August 2007, it failed to meet its goal of being on extended basic cable in all eight of the states in its footprint. News Corp.-owned DIRECTV was the first to pick up the network after its announcement in 2006, and placed it on its Total Choice package, which had 15.4 million subscribers nationwide at the time. Later that same year, AT&T agreed to carry the network on the new U-verse service it was to launch in 2007. At the time the carriage deal was announced, AT&T U-verse was fairly new, having launched in San Antonio, with plans to launch in Houston soon thereafter.

Talks with multisystem operators (MSOs) like Comcast and Time Warner didn't go as well. In early 2007, multiple outlets reported Big Ten Network sent out an initial offer to the MSOs asking for close to $1.10 per subscriber per month for operators within Big Ten markets and asking for analog distribution, the highest level of distribution on an MSO. Those out of Big Ten markets were asked for around 10 cents per subscriber per month, and Big Ten Network would accept being on digital platforms with those operators.

The MSOs immediately balked at the prices. At the time, NFL Network was charging approximately 70 cents per subscriber per month. MLB Network, also preparing to launch at that time, was reportedly asking 25 cents per subscriber per month. The $1.10 the Big Ten Network was asking compared to regional sports network rates at the time, although well below a network like ESPN that commanded $3 per subscriber per month, but not only was

Big Ten Network a brand new channel, it was a new kind of channel—one that relied on one conference to provide all its content. Although it would feature at least 35 football games and 105 men's basketball games, these weren't going to be the best games, because they were reserved for ESPN and ABC.

The per subscriber fee aside, cable operators also took issue with the Big Ten's insistence that the channel be carried on extended basic cable in Big Ten markets. The Big Ten's position was that Comcast put its own regional sports networks on basic cable, so the Big Ten Network belonged there as well. However, operators like Comcast and Time Warner believed only a small percentage of their customers were interested in the channel, and thus it should be on the sports tier.

Comcast Midwest Division President Bill Connors told the *Chicago Tribune*, "It's a single-digit percentage who view [the net] as an absolute must-have. That's why the best landing place is on a sports tier."[2]

Time Warner Cable spokesperson Karen Baxter said at the time, "We know that these games are very important to a select group of our customer fan base. We do believe the best place for this network is on the sports tier so the customers who want it can get it, but we're not asking every customer to pay for it."[3]

The battle between Big Ten Network and the MSOs was very public throughout the spring and summer of 2007. The barbs traded between Comcast and Big Ten Network were perhaps the worst. It was pointed out that Comcast carried the conference channel it partially owned—The Mtn.—on expanded basic cable in some markets. Comcast shot back that its deal with The Mtn. allowed it to choose the tier on which it placed the network on a market-by-market basis, something Big Ten Network wasn't offering.

In July of 2007, the Big Ten Network would announce it had 75 carriage deals with smaller cable operators, which covered 500,000 subscribers. The MSOs, however, were still convinced they didn't need Big Ten Network as much as it needed them. Comcast decided to pull its sponsorship of University of Minnesota in August 2007. In a letter to the St. Paul Area Chamber of Commerce, Comcast withdrew its sponsorship of an upcoming football kickoff luncheon.

The letter was written by Comcast's Twin Cities Region Vice President Bill Wright, who wrote the decision was made "in light of reported plans by the Big Ten Network and Fox Sports to encourage Comcast customers to disconnect their service in favor of DirecTV, which is owned by the parent company of Fox."

The letter went on to say Comcast would be pulling all sponsorship arrangements with University of Minnesota. Comcast had been on a year-to-year contract with the University, which included signage and hospitality arrangements for football, basketball and hockey and was worth about $60,000 annually.

Industry analysts took notice of the ongoing battle between the Big Ten Network and the MSOs, pointing out significant portions of the MSOs' customer base would be affected by the impasse. For Mediacom, which serviced much of the smaller towns in the Midwest, it impacted more than 50 percent of its subscriber base. For Charter it was 20 percent, and for Comcast and Time Warner 15-20 percent.

On the eve of the Big Ten Network debut, the network inked a deal with Insight, the ninth-largest U.S. cable operator. This added approximately 660,000 subscribers, which brought the Big Ten Network's launch total to 17-18 million homes. The deal put Big Ten Network on expanded basic in Ohio and Indiana and on the digital tier of non-Big Ten market state Kentucky.

Comcast, with 5.7 million customers in Big Ten states and the provider on the University of Minnesota campus, refused to meet the Big Ten Network's demands prior to launch. The cable operator continued to publicly state it would place Big Ten Network on its sports tier, but would not force its entire subscriber base to pay what it was calling the "$13 Big Ten tax" (the approximate cost a subscriber would pay annually due to the channel's addition).

With major conference games not coming until later in the season, the MSOs didn't feel much pressure when Big Ten Network launched August 30, 2007. The tide turned only two days later due to an unpredictable event: FCS school Appalachian State came back to beat No. 5 Michigan to become the first FCS school to beat a ranked FBS opponent. The game was shown live exclusively on the brand new Big Ten Network.

Big Ten Network President Mark Silverman told the *New York Times* after the game he didn't know if the game would change the stance of the MSO, but, "[g]iven the various entities clamoring for highlights of the game, it goes to our point that there is a broad appeal for this type of programming. It justifies our contention that there is a demand for us."[4]

Perhaps coincidentally—but probably not—the Big Ten Network signed a deal with Dish Network the next week. That would extend the network's reach by 1.9 million subscribers within the Big Ten footprint and by 9 million nationally, bringing the Big Ten Network into a total of 28 million homes. It also meant the channel was available on both satellite providers, playing into the already existing competition between satellite and cable. It was a large reason the Big Ten was able to reach 30 million households within 30 days of its launch, the first cable network to do so.

Outside of the upset in Ann Arbor, the first big game to be featured on Big Ten Network and disappoint fans with its lack of availability on cable was an early November matchup between Wisconsin and Ohio State. The network lucked into the game thanks to a provision in the agreement that stated each school would have one conference game on the network. Over 40 percent of homes in Columbus, Ohio, would be unable to watch a game being played in their own backyard, because Time Warner and the Big Ten Network had yet to come to an agreement.

There were some indications the MSOs were suffering from their lack of Big Ten Network carriage as the year wore on. The Big Ten Network announced in October that among homes that received the network its college football games had ranked among the top 12 programs on ad-supported cable and satellite nine times. In addition, within its distribution, its Saturday afternoon games were averaging a 3.6 local Nielsen rating in the major Big Ten markets, putting it ahead of NBC (3.4) and CBS (1.8). Mediacom, with a significant portion of its subscriber base in the Midwest saw its stock decrease 35 percent from mid October through the end of the year, in part due to subscriber defections.

It would take until June 2008 for the Big Ten Network to land a deal with the largest of the MSOs. Comcast agreed to a deal estimated at 70 cents per subscriber per month on expanded basic service in Big Ten states. The deal gave Comcast the option to move to a digital service level in 2009 as long as still reaches at least 70 percent of its expanded basic subscribers. The deal meant the Big Ten Network had a total availability in more than two-thirds of homes in the Big Ten states.

It still left approximately six million homes in the Midwest without Big Ten Network. Comcast had no households in Iowa, and Time Warner, Mediacom and Charter covered portions of the Big Ten states. Roughly 60 percent of Ohio households remained without Big Ten Network.

Analysts predicted the Comcast deal would provide a template for other MSOs to enter agreements with the Big Ten Network, and they would turn out to be correct. The week prior to the start of the 2008 season, the dominos began to fall. First, the nation's second-largest MSO, Time Warner, agreed to a deal similar to the Comcast deal, including the provision allowing it to move the channel to digital service level in 2009. The very next day, Charter agreed to similar terms with Big Ten Network. Mediacom made its announcement the same week.

Cable systems analyst Rich Greenfield noted the Comcast and Time Warner deals did more than significantly increase Big Ten Network's distribution. "Comcast's agreement . . . enabled

[Big Ten Network] to eliminate its $70M-plus start-up losses from fiscal (June) 2008 and (Tuesday's) Time Warner Cable deal should enable the network to be profitable, particularly as it provides a meaningful advertising platform for the first time."[5]

By 2009, Big Ten Network was indeed profitable, generating $7 million per school annually. The annual revenue per school increased to $7.9 million for fiscal year 2011, and $8.2 million in 2012, but dropped back to $7.6 million in 2013 due to the addition of Nebraska. In addition to becoming profitable, the network achieved full distribution within its footprint by 2009, and was gaining ground outside of Big Ten territory, including its deal with Cablevision in New York. By the beginning of the 2012 season, the Big Ten Network was available in more than 80 million homes in the United States and Canada.

Although the business model relies heavily on subscriber fees, the ratings for Big Ten Network haven't been bad either in recent years. For example, on September 18th, 2010, four non-conference matchups on Big Ten Network (featuring "cupcake" games like Massachusetts vs. Michigan) averaged a 5.64 rating per Nielsen in the eight local markets, which rivaled the local ratings on ESPN and the broadcast networks.

Launching the Big Ten Network, and waging battles with the largest cable operators in the nation, wasn't for the faint of heart. There was no roadmap for a conference network, and the first year the network was on the air it failed to reach the majority of fans, creating a PR nightmare. A great deal of credit must go to commissioner Jim Delaney, who kept members of the conference calm and united and who never wavered from his position that the network should be carried on expanded basic cable within the conference's footprint.

Michigan's then–athletic director, Bill Martin, was asked in July 2007, a month before the network launched, if he was concerned about the network's status at that point, having no major carriage deals. He responded, "We anticipated this. Jim Delany counseled us on this a year ago. Fox counseled us on this." He went on to say his focus was on the long-term, where he seemed confident the network would be successful.[6]

Barry Alvarez, Wisconsin's athletic director, echoed Martin's sentiments in September 2008, after the network had secured deals with the major cable operators, crediting Delany for keeping everyone on the same page.

"There was some head-banging," Alvarez said. "But the fact that he was able to keep all 11 schools together is incredible. . . . It was absolutely worth it. This puts us out on the cutting edge of media."[7]

In hindsight, it's easy to say the Big Ten made the right decision launching its own network, despite the struggles early on. While Big Ten Network was able to withstand its early distribution issues, another network was not so lucky.

Many wrongly believe Big Ten Network was the first on-air channel to feature one conference exclusively. That title belongs to The Mtn., the Mountain West Conference's channel, conceived the same year as Big Ten Network and placed on air a year earlier.

In 2004, the five-year-old Mountain West Conference was preparing to enter the sixth year of its seven-year, $48 million deal with ESPN. Negotiations for an extension with ESPN weren't what the conference had hoped for, and the presidents of the conference members tasked commissioner Craig Thompson with finding an alternative. Chris Bevilacqua, a founder of CSTV says the conference wanted to play the majority of its football games on Saturdays, instead of the Tuesdays and Wednesdays ESPN was proposing, wanted better start times for its men's basketball games, which ESPN set at 10 P.M., and ultimately more exposure and more revenue.

A former director of licensing at a Mountain West institution during The Mtn.'s formation and launch said his school was concerned about having football games start at 5:00 or 5:30 P.M. local time on weekdays under the ESPN proposal.

"The few times the school had played on television during those timeslots, attendance had suffered as people still had to go to work, go home and get their family, and then try to get to the game. It wasn't a good brand message to show a half-filled stadium on television, and that was a concern for athletics."

Bevilacqua's 18-month-old CSTV gave the Mountain West the money and game times it wanted and more. It began with a seven-year $82 million deal, which ESPN did not match, citing declining ratings. Less than a month later, the Mountain West and CSTV would announce the launch of the first-ever network devoted to one conference: The Mtn. - MountainWest Sports Network. The original plan was to feature as many as 40 conference football games and up to 120 men's and women's basketball games per year. Between CSTV and The Mtn., virtually every conference football game and men's basketball game would be televised and women's sports would have increased air time as well.

In addition, the network would produce and air exclusive and original sports programming, including news and highlight shows and replays. During the day, the network would air educational programming from continuing education classes to lectures and theatrical productions from all member institutions.

The partnership made sense for CSTV, which already represented 6 of the 9 Mountain West members on an institutional level prior to the conference deal. It was a young network built on college sports content. It owned CollegeSports.com, the most-trafficked college sports website and SIRIUS College Sports Radio satellite radio station. CSTV also built a substantial part of its business running college sports websites, and would have approximately 250 by the time CBS acquired CSTV in 2005. When the CSTV deal with the Mountain West was announced, CSTV had 8 million satellite and cable subscribers and hoped to have more than 40 million by the time the conference deal began in the fall of 2006.

Prior to launching The Mtn., CSTV announced Comcast had acquired a 50 percent stake in the new channel. That meant initial distribution in parts of Utah, Colorado and New Mexico, where the conference had members, but not San Diego or Las Vegas. The deal also meant some games would be carried on Comcast-owned OLN, which would be rebranded as Versus that fall.

On the surface, the CSTV deal paid dividends for the Mountain West in its very first year in terms of exposure. In 2006, all 55 football games were televised, including 8 games on Versus, which had 72 million subscribers nationally at the time. One hundred and fifty men's and women's basketball games were televised during the 2006-2007 season, quadruple the number shown in any previous year. In addition, 200 men's and women's Olympic sports contests were carried on The Mtn., including conference championships. Comcast also offered some of the content on its Video On Demand platform.

Despite those numbers, there were problems, not the least of which was the fact that the channel launched in a mere 1 million households. Projections during the network's formation had been around 52 million—less than ESPN's over 92 million at the time, but still a wide reach.

On November 11, 2006, CSTV had the rights to air Notre Dame at Air Force thanks to its Mountain West deal. It was the first time since 1992 a Notre Dame game wouldn't be shown on either NBC, ABC, CBS or ESPN. Although CBS had purchased CSTV the year before, the network still had limited carriage and was available in only 15 million homes. CSTV offered its programming to cable operators for free that weekend, although not all operators accepted, leaving it available to approximately 30 to 40 million homes. The only other way Notre Dame fans could watch the game was by paying $14.95-19.95 to watch on CSTV.com.

Although CSTV was excited to have a game of such magnitude, it didn't go over well with the Irish faithful. Notre Dame has not scheduled another away game against a Mountain West opponent since.

There were other problems with distribution. The CSTV deal ended local telecasts of BYU and Utah on KSL and KJZZ, channels available in nearly all 839,000 homes in the Salt Lake City television market (which includes all of Utah and parts of Nevada, Idaho and Wyoming). A telecast on The Mtn. reached 66 percent fewer people than a telecast on KSL or KJZZ. In addition, instead of watching the games for free on the local stations, fans were forced to purchase a $45 cable package to get The Mtn.

The Mtn.'s reach improved modestly over its first couple of years. Following the 2006 football season, its first, CSTV and Cox reached an agreement for the cable company to air The Mtn. on cable systems in San Diego and Las Vegas. The deal included some interesting guarantees with regards to San Diego State.

Cox received the rights to any SDSU game not aired on CSTV, The Mtn. or Versus. In addition, the deal required a commitment that 80 percent of SDSU's home football games and 60 percent of its home basketball games would appear on CSTV, The Mtn. or San Diego Channel 4. Cox also received rights to simulcast approximately one-third of all SDSU football and basketball games carried by CSTV or The Mtn. on San Diego Channel 4. The real kicker though was a guarantee Cox sought on behalf of SDSU. Bill Geppert, vice president and general manager of Cox San Diego, told the *San Diego Union-Tribune* half the "substantial amount of fees paid for the carriage" of CSTV and The Mtn. would be guaranteed to return to SDSU athletics.[8]

During The Mtn.'s tenure, TCU, Utah, BYU and Boise State all had success on the football field that helped fuel the network in terms of distribution. In 2008, DIRECTV signed on to carry the network on its Sports Pack, but the nation's other major satellite provider, Dish Network, never carried The Mtn. When the conference lured Boise State away from the WAC, there were high hopes for The Mtn. In Boise State's first year in the conference, Comcast added The Mtn. to its lineups in a number of cities, including Greater Atlanta, Boston, Indianapolis, Detroit, Chicago, Nashville, Houston and Jacksonville, Florida. The network's reach expanded to 32 million.

The Mtn. continued to struggle to please fans, even with increased distribution. Regular season conference basketball games were only offered in standard definition with the rest of the sports world moving on to high definition. Non-conference basketball games weren't shown at all on The Mtn., and football games didn't make the move to high definition until the end of the 2008 season. In addition, there were complaints about on-air talent and production quality, including returning from commercials late and not being able to keep up with which team had possession of the basketball on the court. Displeasure with distribution led to speculation amongst fans that BCS voters couldn't find The Mtn. to watch games, and therefore relied on box scores alone when evaluating Mountain West teams, putting those teams at a disadvantage.

When conference realignment heated up from 2010 to 2012, TCU, Utah, Boise State and SDSU were all attractive candidates and all announced their intention to leave the Mountain West. BYU decided to go independent, a move that was attributed to both Utah heading for the Pac-10 and ongoing disagreements with Comcast about rebroadcasting rights. According to BYU athletic director Tom Holmoe, there was a verbal agreement with Comcast that games not televised by The Mtn. would be available for BYUtv, the university's television channel, and BYU would be able to rebroadcast games on their own channel as well. BYUtv had larger distribution than The Mtn. and fans across the country thanks in part to their association with The Church of Jesus Christ of Latter-day Saints.

BYU would return to ESPN upon declaring its independence, signing an eight-year deal reported to be worth $800,000 to $1.2 million per home game. Under the Mountain West's television agreements, BYU was receiving $1.5 million for the entire year. The ESPN deal also guaranteed BYU exposure. All of its home games would appear either on an ESPN affiliate or on BYUtv.

In BYU's first year of independence it had 6 football games aired on ESPN, including its appearance in the Armed Forces Bowl, 4 games on ESPN2, two games on ESPNU and a game each on BYUtv and Fox College Sports Pacific/KBYU-Ch. 11. Total exposure was estimated at

1.2 billion households. A far cry from the exposure it received as part of the Mountain West television deals.

The importance of BYU and Utah to The Mtn. can't be underscored enough. A former director of licensing at a Mountain West institution during The Mtn.'s formation and launch who reviewed the contract said there was a clause in the The Mtn.'s contract that if BYU and Utah ever left the conference, the deal was over.

"The Mtn. realized that market, besides San Diego and Colorado, was the only market with viewers that mattered. Without that footprint the deal wouldn't be worth it," said the former licensing director.

The loss of TCU, Utah, Boise State, SDSU and BYU, on top of the ongoing problems with distribution and production, would doom The Mtn., and it went dark May 31, 2012. Even if it didn't last, what the Mountain West did with CSTV, and eventually Comcast, was revolutionary. They created the very first channel devoted to a single conference. It was trial and error, but it provided valuable lessons for the conference networks that have and will come after it.

The former licensing director said looking back there was definitely a learning curve.

"When you look back at the contract now, it is evident the [university] presidents who oversaw the deal didn't have any media rights experience, and the first example of a conference network contract would be radically changed today. It wasn't that the deal was bad, it was just that they didn't know how to maximize the revenue and just gave everything to CSTV/CBS.

"Looking back, I think it was still visionary in its conception and The Mtn. learned along the way. The day-to-day execution of the network for the benefit of the schools was what probably needed improvement."

The same year The Mtn. went dark, a new conference network was born: Pac-12 Networks. "Networks," because in a very different model from Big Ten Network, the Pac-12 decided to launch six regional networks simultaneously and a national network.

With negotiations set to begin in 2011 for the Pac-12's media rights, commissioner Larry Scott let it be known in late 2010 that his conference was pursuing its own network. By that time, the Big Ten Network was turning a profit, and Scott could model his conference's network off an already successful model.

Except he didn't. He saw what the Big Ten Network had done and imagined what another successful model might look like. Scott spoke with media executives at the NFL and NBA, cable operators and, of course, the Big Ten Network and remained open to a variety of ideas. As of June 2011, media analysts believed there were three different models were on the table. The first would involve partnering with an existing programmer to flip an existing channel, which could eliminate distribution risks but would likely require the conference to allow the partner to have an equity stake in the network. An alternative would be to partner with an existing cable or satellite operator, much in the same way the Mountain West partnered with CSTV and then Comcast, but it wouldn't guarantee distribution outside of the partner. Another option was to partner with a non-traditional provider like Google or Apple for an all-digital model. That would only produce advertising revenue and no subscription revenue.

Which one did the Pac-12 go with? None of the above. In July 2011, the Pac-12 announced it would create not one, but seven channels: a national channel and a channel for six regions (Washington, Oregon, Northern California, Southern California, Arizona and Mountain). The vision was that the regional networks would be carried on expanded basic cable in Pac-12 markets, and the national channel on digital basic. In states outside the Pac-12 footprint, the national channel would be available on digital sports tiers.

Larry Scott told the *Los Angeles Times*, "We've had a national brand, but the tribal nature make college sports very local. So this is an attempt through the unique structure of our conference and the cable industry to super-serve fans in a hyper-local way."[9]

As if launching seven channels wasn't enough of a game-changer, the Pac-12 also announced it would wholly own Pac-12 Networks. No partner, despite reported interested from a number of parties. It would bear all of the start-up costs (estimated at $50-100 million) on its own, but in the future it will reap all of the financial reward alone as well.

The Pac-12 entered a new television contract with ESPN and Fox (unique in its own right, as discussed later in the chapter) in May 2011, and because it already had its sights focused on a conference network held back content it knew would make the network indispensable to carriers. ESPN and Fox would have rights to 44 football games a season, with the Pac-12 Networks receiving 36 games. The conference negotiated the right to feature the best game of the week a couple of weeks each season, and in other weeks chooses either second or third behind ESPN and Fox. In total, the Pac-12 channels would carry 350 conference events nationally and 500 on the local channels, including approximately 100 men's basketball games and 40 women's basketball games.

Between the ESPN/Fox deal and the Pac-12 Networks, every home football and men's basketball game will be televised in 2012. Only one year earlier, 13 of Arizona State's 31 men's basketball games weren't televised. Olympic sports will see a boost in exposure as well. In 2011, just 15 women's volleyball games were televised. That number was expected to increase to 90 in 2012 with the debut of the Pac-12 Networks.

As if acquiring the content to make a television channel successful wasn't hard enough, Scott had ambitions of buying back digital and sponsorship rights from multimedia rights holders IMG College and Learfield Sports. Scott successfully worked out a deal that cost the conference approximately $15 million a year to require those rights, previously sold off by schools individually. That amount will decrease over the years as the contracts expire. Having those rights allows the conference to explore distribution categories like wireless and multiplatform video distributor, and makes the Pac-12 the first conference to control all those rights.

Unlike the Big Ten Network, which didn't land the nation's biggest MSOs until after its first year, the Pac-12 already had deals in place with Time Warner, Comcast, Cox and BrightHouse a year before its launch believed to be in the $0.90-1.00 per subscriber per month range. Thanks to TV Everywhere, a free service available through most of the larger cable providers, customers of those providers can watch the Pac-12 Networks away from home on their laptop, smartphone or tablet. However, as of one week prior to its August 15, 2012 launch, the conference still had no deals with DirecTV, Dish Network, Verizon or AT&T. Even so, the networks had the potential to reach 48 million homes, although not all the carriers that signed on were to show the Pac-12 Networks outside the Pac-12 footprint. Pac-12 Networks added more households with a Dish Network deal shortly after the 2012 football season began. At the time of the announcement, Dish Network reported having 14 million subscribers.

Also in a departure from the experience of the Big Ten with its network, schools won't receive a distribution from the Pac-12 Networks right away. The conference will bear the start-up costs without burdening individual members thanks to upfront money in the ESPN/Fox deal, but likely won't turn a profit that could be distributed to schools for several years. Industry analysts predict the network could distribute as much as $10 million per year per school in a few years once the network is up and running at full distribution and bringing in advertising revenue.

You'll find at least one football game a year on the Longhorn Network, which it seems the University of Texas chose over the Pac-12 Networks. There were any number of conversations in 2011 between the Longhorns and the Pac-12 about Texas becoming a member of the conference, but the Pac-12 was consolidating all of its members' rights at the same time Texas was exploring starting its own network. In the end, Texas would choose to strike out on its own.

Texas began mulling its own network as early as 2007 after watching the Big Ten Network's formation, which could be one reason it was reluctant to give up the idea two years later when it discussed Pac-12 membership. In the fall of 2008, Texas began having discussions with AT&T, Time Warner and Fox Cable Networks about potential partnerships. Unlike the Pac-12, the Longhorns had no intention of going at it alone and preferred a model similar to the Big Ten where a partner would take on start-up and production costs.

At the time, Texas already had a video on-demand channel with Time Warner, which had launched in 2004. The channel was on air in four markets and aired highlights, game replays, interviews and the Longhorn Sports Center show. It would be important for Time Warner to at least have a carriage deal with the new network, because it covered 1.8 million subscribers, or approximately 25 percent of Texas homes, including Austin. Time Warner had only signed on with Big Ten Network a week or so prior to Texas' announced intentions of forming a channel.

By the fall of 2010, Texas athletic director DeLoss Dodds was announcing the Longhorn Network would be up and running by the fall of 2011, but he still had no partner. Fox was originally reported as the frontrunner, although ESPN was also acknowledged as being in the mix. Both made sense because they had deals with the Big 12 conference, but some thought Fox might flip one of its existing Texas channels—FS Houston, FS Southwest or Fox College Sports—and secure the Longhorn Network instant carriage.

The speculation ended in November of 2010 when Texas announced it would be partnering with ESPN for the Longhorn Network. The two signed a 20-year deal worth a guaranteed minimum $300 million to the Longhorns. The rights fee paid to the school began at $10.98 million and would increase by 3 percent annually, averaging out at $15 million over the life of the contract. Once ESPN has received aggregate revenue exceeding $295 million, Texas would begin receiving 70 percent of Longhorn Network's adjusted gross revenue. Reports had Fox Network only offering a deal worth $2 million per year to Texas.

Initially, the Longhorn Network sought a 40 cent per subscriber per month rate to be on expanded basic cable in Texas and parts of Louisiana, New Mexico and Oklahoma, which would have made it one of the 30-40 highest-priced cable channels but would have kept it priced well below Big Ten Network's rate within the Big Ten footprint. In addition, cable operators haven't been swayed by the one guaranteed football game and eight guaranteed men's basketball games the Longhorns can feature on the network.

Time Warner, the largest distributor in Texas, reportedly sought a 20 percent ownership stake in the network in exchange for carriage in early 2011. However, that deal never came to fruition. Reports involving Time Warner surfaced again in the summer of 2012—this time that Time Warner might purchase the network from ESPN. However, Time Warner denied the reports about purchasing Longhorn Network and said it wasn't even having distribution conversations with the network at that time.

The Longhorn Network has experienced more than just distribution issues. It's been blamed for Texas A&M and Missouri splitting for the SEC. Both had likely been unhappy with the unequal revenue sharing in the Big 12 (changed only after Texas A&M announced it was leaving) and a myriad of other issues stemming from Texas' influence in the conference, but the Longhorn Network was viewed by many as the final straw. First, it meant a significant revenue increase for Texas, which already had the largest revenue of any athletic department in the country. Second, when details of the Longhorn Network surfaced they included the airing of high school games. That issue became extremely contentious, with many claiming it gave Texas an unfair recruiting advantage. The NCAA finally stepped in just prior to the network's launch and declared high school games could not be shown on university or institution-related networks.

Even after the high school issue was resolved, other issues remained. Longhorn Network wanted to air two games a year on the channel: one non-conference and one conference game. The conference agreed to allow it as long as the conference opponent and the conference approved the game.

Texas Tech was asked in 2011 and declined. It was reported by multiple outlets that Texas Tech turned down an offer from ESPN to carry two of Texas Tech's non-conference games over the next four seasons, broadcast other non-football programming and provide $5 million cash. In addition, reports said the network would help Texas Tech attempt to arrange a home-and-home series with a top BCS school. However, ESPN spokeswoman Keri Potts said those reports are inaccurate.

Fellow Big 12 member Kansas did agree to have its game against Texas shown on Longhorn Network during the 2011 season. Pursuant to a revision of the Big 12 Handbook, Texas would forfeit $200,000 from its annual conference distribution for each conference game shown on Longhorn Network beyond the one game Texas retains rights to each year.

The Longhorn Network tussled with Texas Tech again prior to the 2012 season. It all started because the WAC recognized Longhorn Network as an ESPN platform after Longhorn Network agreed to air the last five UT-San Antonio home games of the 2011 season. Texas State, a member of the WAC, was scheduled to play Texas Tech in 2012 and rumor had it Longhorn Network wanted the game. Sources told multiple outlets Texas Tech would rather cancel the game and play an 11-game schedule in 2012 than play on Longhorn Network.

In response to the reports, ESPN spokeswoman Keri Potts said having the Texas Tech vs. Texas State game on Longhorn Network was, "never a serious consideration." In the end, the game was not scheduled for Longhorn Network, and the disaster was averted. Texas did get conference member Iowa State to agree to play on Longhorn Network in 2012, meaning the channel would air a conference matchup in each of its first two years on the air.

Longhorn Network launched to approximately 20,000 households on August 26, 2011, with an agreement in place with Verizon's FiOS nationwide service and several smaller local distributors that would take distribution to 4 million households prior to the first game on September 3rd. Unlike Big Ten Network, which was able to come to terms with the major carriers after its first year, Longhorn Network was unable to secure any significant deals prior to the 2012 season. With much of the State of Texas left in the dark, fans voiced displeasure when they missed softball and baseball games on Longhorn Network previously seen on more widely distributed platforms. Branding experts began to fear the university was beginning to do harm to the brand as fans routinely booed Longhorn Network announcements during football games. The university and ESPN, however, remain committed and ask for patience, much like the Big Ten Network did in its first year.

In order to become a channel fans can't live without—and therefore, a must-have for cable operators—experts say the Longhorn Network needs improved content. It needs additional, or at least better, football games. Unfortunately, that's tough to get, because conference members are reluctant to assist Texas in amassing greater fortune given it's already the highest-revenue program in the country. Others in the conference must compete against Texas in everything from recruiting to facilities, and a successful Longhorn Network will only benefit Texas.

That being said, in both 2011 and 2012 the Longhorns and ESPN met the stated goal in their contract to have two football games on the channel by getting Kansas and Iowa State to agree to having their games against Texas on Longhorn Network. Its distribution levels don't rival the Big Ten Network or Pac-12 Networks, but a channel featuring one school cannot be compared to channels featuring an entire conference.

Fellow conference member Oklahoma signed a deal with Fox shortly after the 2012 season began, choosing a different route than Texas. Instead of a school-branded channel in existence 24/7/365, Oklahoma will have an expanded presence on Fox's regional sports networks and nationally on Fox College Sports separate from the conference's deal with Fox. No football games outside of the conference deal will be aired, but the spring game is part of Oklahoma's deal with Fox, as are pregame and postgame football shows and football coach Bob Stoops's weekly show. In addition, a selection of men's and women's basketball, baseball, softball and Olympic sports will broadcast live.

Oklahoma's deal will be worth nearly $60 million over 10 years as compared to the Longhorn Network's $300 million over 20 years.

Sports television consultants don't expect another school to try an around-the-clock channel like Longhorn Network any time soon though. Most of the schools that could attempt a channel of that magnitude are in conferences like the Big Ten, Pac-12 and SEC, which have or are planning conference channels to carry the programming that might otherwise fill a school-branded channel.

Both the then–Big East and Big 12 have explored conference networks and declined to pursue one for the time being. The Big East considered its own network before signing a six-year deal with ESPN in 2006. At that point in time, the risks were fairly high and there was no roadmap or precedent given The Mtn. wasn't due to launch until later that fall.

In 2010, Big East commissioner John Marinatto made it public that his conference was once again considering its own network. He noted the Big Ten Network's success, which at that point had become a profitable enterprise. He also mentioned the presence of his conference's members in 7 of the top 13 television markets in the country. With three years left on its then–current television contracts, the conference went into research mode, hiring former NFL commissioner Paul Tagliabue as a consultant.

Unfortunately, the Big East lost a few of its more powerful members in the realignment of 2010-2012, causing its commissioner to resign. Entering the fall of 2012, its last year under its current television contract with ESPN, the conference had to turn its attention to hiring a new commissioner and either renegotiating with ESPN or finding a new television partner, and plans of a conference network were put on the backburner.

Similarly, the Big 12's plans for a conference network were pushed to the side as realignment and its commissioner's resignation forced it to focus on other matters. With two schools gone (Texas A&M and Missouri) the conference needed to look for replacements, which it found in TCU and West Virginia. The conference also decided it was time to make the move to equal sharing of television revenue from its ESPN/ABC and Fox deals. In an effort to improve the conference's stability, the members also agreed to grant their first- and second-tier broadcast rights (those with ESPN/ABC and Fox) to the conference for six years, meaning if any member left its broadcast rights would stay with the conference. Amidst all the realignment activity in the Big 12 (both actually and rumored), the Longhorn Network starting up and Oklahoma looking to start its own network, the conference's focus was on stability and finding a new commissioner, not starting its own network.

If the Big 12 once again considers a network, it faces an interesting problem. Back in 2006, Fox Sports Net president Bob Thompson pointed out that a Big 12 Network would likely move product away from Fox. At that time, FSN had the conference's football rights until 2012 and exclusive national cable rights, meaning any network would almost certainly have to include a Fox partnership, and Fox would essentially be taking content from one of its channels and moving it to another. That wasn't the case when Fox partnered with the Big Ten, where it gained rights ESPN had previously held. While the conference's television deals have changed slightly since then, the base issue still exists. Fox would likely have to be a partner given it is part of long-term deals for both the first- and second-tier rights in the Big 12, and it would have to take content away from one of its channels to form the other. That's not to say it can't be done, or even that it can't be done in a fashion that's advantageous to Fox, but it would likely limit the Big 12's options for partners and structure of the channel.

The ACC has chosen a different route, not creating its own channel but branding a package of games and other content as the ACC Network. The ACC currently has an all-inclusive deal with ESPN for all of its rights, with a sublicensing arrangement in place with Raycom for games not broadcast on an ESPN platform. Beginning with the 2011 season, the Raycom package of football and basketball games was branded as the ACC Network.

The partnership between the ACC and Raycom also included plans for a digital network, which became a joint venture that included Silver Chalice, a digital sports and entertainment media firm. As of early 2013, the ACC Digital Network presents both live and on-demand programming, including a live studio show.

In addition, members of the ACC have indicated there is some interest in pursuing a cable channel for the conference.

"I think the members were very excited about the potential," said Georgia Tech then–acting athletic director Paul Griffin when asked about talk of an ACC cable network at a meeting of ACC athletic directors in February 2013.[10]

SportsBusiness Daily reported in January 2013 that the ACC hired Wasserman Media Group "to explore the financial benefits" of such a conference network.[11] Since announcing its members' grant of rights in April 2013, as discussed in Chapter 4, both athletic directors and presidents throughout the conference have acknowledged discussions of creating a cable network dedicated to the conference. As of July 2013, the ACC is researching and analyzing the potential for a conference network.

The SEC has a similar syndication package branded the SEC Network, which predates the ACC by a couple of years. When the SEC began a new contract with ESPN in 2009, ESPN Regional Television branded a package of football and basketball games as the SEC Network, shown on local broadcast channels, regional sports networks and ESPN platforms like WatchESPN.com (formerly ESPN3.com).

As of August 2014, however, the SEC Network will be its own cable channel, a partnership between the SEC and ESPN. SEC Network will be the fourth different type of conference network we've seen.

"[W]hat's unique and never been done before is partnering with our primary rights-holder, which will allow us to move events and content seamlessly between various platforms," said SEC commissioner Mike Slive at the May 2, 2013 press conference to announce the launch of the network.

At the press conference, executives from the SEC and ESPN announced SEC Network had already reached a distribution agreement with AT&T U-verse. ESPN's senior vice president of programming for college sports networks Justin Connolly described the carrier as, "the fastest growing multi-channel provider in the U.S." A release from AT&T U-verse in early 2013 showed the carrier had 4.8 million subscribers.

The press conference was held approximately 16 months from the network's launch, plenty of time to increase distribution according to Connolly.

"We feel good about the opportunities that exist on that horizon, and we're literally just getting into those conversations and discussions right now."

At launch the plan is for the SEC Network to feature 1,000 live sporting events each year, of which 450 will be televised on the cable channel, with the rest being distributed digitally. Forty-five football games will be aired on the channel, three each week, with CBS having given up exclusivity for the 3:30 P.M. timeslot on Saturdays. In addition, the network will carry more than 100 men's basketball games, 60 women's basketball games, 75 baseball games and championship games and events from the conference's 21 sports will air, along with other original content.

Beyond conference and university-affiliated channels, the past few years have brought interesting developments in television as it relates to college football. Perhaps the most groundbreaking was the ESPN/Fox partnership for the Pac-12's first- and second-tier rights. This marked the first time the two rival networks had partnered for college football rights, and it was all thanks to NBC/Comcast (which were newly merged at the time).

Having only Notre Dame rights in major college football, NBC/Comcast made a strong push for the Pac-12 rights. Plans were in place to flip Comcast-owned Versus to NBC Sports in the future, and college football would be a profitable way to place content on the channel. NBC/Comcast made its pitch to the Pac-12 to pay $225 million annually for the conference's rights. Neither ESPN or Fox could bid that kind of money and place the content alone.

The Pac-12 had a long-standing relationship with both ESPN and Fox, however, including a historic relationship with ABC (owned by Disney like ESPN and often a partner on deals) through the Rose Bowl. The Pac-12's media consultant, Chris Bevilacqua, went to ESPN's John Skipper and proposed something outside of the box: what if ESPN and Fox partnered on the deal?

Crazy as it sounded on the surface, it made all the sense in the world in the bigger picture of the college football landscape. Outside of CBS's deal with the SEC, ESPN and Fox controlled the rights to every BCS conference. Teaming up was more appealing than letting NBC/Comcast into the market. Skipper called Fox Sports co-president Randy Freer and it wasn't long before the two were seeing eye-to-eye.

Together, ESPN and Fox were able to offer the Pac-12 $3 billion over 12 years, averaging $250 million per year. NBC/Comcast eventually came up to $235 million per year, but ESPN and Fox would win the day. The networks agreed to split the rights equally, each taking 22 football games per year. They'll alternate rights to the championship game.

Now the networks seem poised to do it again. In 2012, details of a deal for the Big 12's rights surfaced and once again saw ESPN and Fox teaming up. The deal is reportedly worth $2.6 billion over 13 years, averaging $200 million per year. The networks are expected to share the rights much in the same way they're sharing the Pac-12 rights.

There's one thing all the stories in this chapter—from the conference networks to the groundbreaking ESPN/Fox partnership in the Pac-12—have in common: conferences are now the ultimate powerbrokers in college football.

Media headlines and fans alike wonder if television has taken over college football. Quite the opposite appears to be true. It's not the networks who have all the power these days, it's the conferences. How else do you explain the unlikely partnership of ESPN and Fox on not one but two conference deals? What about the fact that the Pac-12 now controls all of its members broadcasting rights, and therefore its collective future? Unless and until there are fewer network options for conferences, or the unlikely event live sports become less popular, there's every reason to believe conferences will continue to dictate their future in this realm.

Some decry the increasing dependence on television for financial security, but it can ultimately mean less dependence on subsidies from the university in the form of direct payments and student fees. Across the Big Ten, subsidies averaged at $3.4 million per school in 2005-2006. By 2010-2011 that number had decreased to $2.7 million, a trend not seen across college athletics.

Don't believe the Big Ten and Pac-12 have secured their financial futures by having ownership in their respective conference networks? Look no further than the Yankees and YES Network. Ten years into its run, YES Network was valued at $2-3 billion in 2012. The Yankees, the sole basis for YES Network's development, are worth $1.85 billion according to Forbes's 2012 valuation, a number that would significantly lower if the team didn't own 34 percent of YES Network.

NOTES

1. Greenstein, Teddy (July 2, 2011). "ESPN's low-ball offer triggered conference expansion." *Chicago Tribune*. Retrieved July 29, 2012, from http://articles.chicagotribune.com/2011-07-01/sports/ct-spt-0701-big-ten-nebraska--20110701_1_commissioner-jim-delany-john-wildhack-espn-officials.

2. Greenstein, Teddy (June 22, 2007). "Big Ten, Comcast in "taxing" fight." *Chicago Tribune*. Retrieved July 29, 2012, from http://articles.chicagotribune.com/2007-06-22/sports/0706211112_1_big-ten-network-btn-comcast-officials.

3. Nagel, Kyle (June 22, 2007). "Big Ten still pushing for an agreement with Time Warner." *Dayton Daily News*. Retrieved July 29, 2012, from http://www.daytondailynews.com/b/content/region/story/sports/college/osu/2007/06/22/ddn062207bigten.html.

4. Sandomir, Richard (September 2, 2007). "A Prime Time-Worthy Upset That Hardly Anybody Saw." *New York Times*. Retrieved July 29, 2012, from http://www.nytimes.com/2007/09/02/sports/ncaafootball/02sandomir.html?pagewanted=print.

5. Ourand, John. "Big Winner." *SportsBusiness Daily* (August 27, 2008). Retrieved July 29, 2012, from http://www.sportsbusinessdaily.com/Daily/Issues/2008/08/Issue-236/Sports-Media.aspx.

6. Carty, Jim (July 23, 2007). "Bill Martin Talks Adidas, Part 2." *MLive.com*. Retrieved August 3, 2012, from http://blog.mlive.com/jim_carty/2007/07/bill_martin_talks_adidas_part_1.html.

7. Ourand, John. "How BTN cleared last hurdle." *SportsBusiness Journal*. September 8, 2008. Retrieved July 29, 2012, from http://www.sportsbusinessdaily.com/Journal/Issues/2008/09/20080908/This-Weeks-News/How-BTN-Cleared-Last-Hurdle.aspxhttp://www.sportsbusinessdaily.com/Journal/Issues/2008/09/20080908/This-Weeks-News/How-BTN-Cleared-Last-Hurdle.aspx.

8. Posner, Jay (December 21, 2006). "At last, Cox, mtn. sign deal." *San Diego Union-Tribune*. Retrieved August 4, 2012, from http://www.utsandiego.com/uniontrib/20061221/news_1s21mtn.html.

9. Sandomir, Richard (July 27, 2011). "Pac-12 Conference to Create Seven TV Channels". *Los Angeles Times*. Retrieved August 7, 2012, from http://www.nytimes.com/2011/07/28/sports/ncaafootball/pac-12-conference-to-create-seven-tv-channels.html.

10. Sugiura, Ken. "Griffin addresses ACC network possibility." *The Atlanta Journal-Constitution*. February 11, 2013. Retrieved May 4, 2013, from http://www.ajc.com/news/sports/college/griffin-addresses-acc-network-possibility/nWLsF/.

11. Michael Smith and John Ourand. "ACC panel will study whether to launch net." *SportsBusiness Journal*. January 14, 2013. Retrieved May 4, 2013, from http://www.sportsbusinessdaily.com/Journal/Issues/2013/01/14/Colleges/ACC.aspx.

WHAT HAS FOOTBALL DONE FOR US?
8 Reasons Football Raises the University

Much of the commentary on the business of college sports today focuses on a perceived battle between a school's academic mission and its athletic program. When correlations are drawn between the two, it's generally in order to show how athletics degrades academics.

It's interesting to examine how the two became intertwined and then regarded as divergent. Murray Sperber, in his book *Beer and Circus: How Big-time College Sports Is Crippling Undergraduate Education*, details how the academic side called upon athletics to save it after building to accommodate the baby boomers of the 1960s and 1970s and then finding classrooms and dorms empty in the early 1980s:

> In a period when most institutions of higher education had many more places in their undergraduate classes than students to fill them, and schools desperately needed to increase the flow of tuition dollars, they marketed themselves in every way possible, many emphasizing their big-time college sports programs and party atmosphere, usually depicted as "collegiate good times." This marketing game plan succeeded, and, as a result, it continues in a mutated form in the twenty-first century.[1]

Even researchers and economists who are critical of the relationship between academics and athletics admit athletic programs have an "advertising effect," serving as a de facto marketing campaign. They don't question the effectiveness of the advertising effect; their concerns range from students making ill-informed academic decisions based on athletic performance to whether athletics is the most cost-effective way to market to students.

Research suggests having a successful football or men's basketball program can have a substantial impact on the university as a whole. The most recognized impact is dubbed the "Flutie Effect."

In 1984, Boston College's Doug Flutie threw a 48-yard touchdown pass as time expired to defeat then–football powerhouse University of Miami. The game was nationally televised and the pass received extended national coverage. Flutie went on to win the Heisman Trophy and Boston College experienced a 30 percent increase in applications.

Since then, the Flutie Effect has been observed at numerous universities following a winning season, particularly one that culminates in a postseason berth.

Research has shown those increased applications can lead to either increased enrollment, and thus increased tuition dollars, or can allow a university to become more selective. In addition, funding from donors, state governments and licensing efforts have all been shown to rise following a successful season. Studies have even shown increased ranking in US News and World Report as the result of a successful season that receives national attention.

Since the focus of much of the research is on success, and those accomplishments cannot be duplicated every year, many wonder if the short-term impact realized as a result of that success is the most cost effective way to produce these results for universities.

Athletic department expenditures can run upwards of $130 million annually and average $51 million across all Division I programs, large sums for sure. As you learned in Chapter 1, operating athletic spending accounted for an average of 6 percent of total higher education spending for Division I schools in 2007.[2] In 2003 the percentage was lower at 3.8 percent, with the authors of the study believing it was due in part due to updated survey/data collection methodology.

Media reports often focus on the increasing costs of operating athletic departments, particularly football programs. However, research indicates growth in average athletic spending has only slightly outpaced overall educational and general spending: 4.5 percent to 2.7 percent.[3] In addition, athletic operating expenditures have not outpaced athletic revenues on average amongst public FBS schools. From 2004-2005 to 2010-2011, operating revenues increased by 58 percent across public FBS schools, while expenses rose 54 percent.

Football spending has increased less rapidly than total athletic operating spending from 1985 through 2001, with women's sports having the most rapid growth.[4] Meanwhile, revenues associated with football have grown by larger percentages, which is attributable to rising television contracts. For example, in 1996 the SEC signed a five-year deal that averaged out to $25 million per year. Compare that to 2009 when the SEC began two 15-year deals worth an average of $205 million per year.

From 1993-1997, football revenues across FBS athletic departments rose by 6 percent. From 1997 to 2001 it leaped another 28 percent.

Numerous articles and books have been devoted to examining how athletic programs have degraded the academic mission of universities. This literature is almost entirely written by university professors and administrators, who one would imagine are often times competing for the same dollars as the athletic department.

An important question becomes what alternative methods are available for producing the same positive results as studies have shown athletics to produce?

Brian Goff, a professor of economics at Western Kentucky University, included the impact of adding or dropping football on student enrollment in his 2000 study by looking at three schools that added or dropped football. The three schools were Wichita State University and University of Texas-Arlington, which dropped football in the mid-'80s, and Georgia Southern University, which added football.[5]

Examining the years 1960-1993, Goff found an average decline of 600 students per year during "no football" years at Wichita State and UT Arlington. In contrast, he found an average increase of 500 students at Georgia Southern after adding football.

In a study by brothers and economists Devin G. Pope and Jaren C. Pope, football success in the form of being ranked in the top 20 in the AP Poll was found to increase the quantity of applications to a school by 2-8 percent. In order to achieve that same increase by lowering tuition or increasing financial aid, an adjustment of anywhere from 2-24 percent would have to be made. The study also found finishing in the top ten produced increased applications approximately equivalent to a school's rank being improved by half in US News and World Report (e.g. 20th to 10th or 8th to 4th).[6]

From both number and quality of applicants to increased enrollment, retention, faculty recruitment and licensing and sponsorship revenue, studies conducted over the past decade have increasingly found athletics, particularly big-time college football, can have a positive impact on the university at-large. While competing in football at the highest level isn't for every school, you'll see how many have embraced college football's place on campus and experienced tremendous results.

Advertising Effect

In short, no university can afford the kind of publicity it gains from an appearance in a major sporting event, such as the BCS National Championship Game.

Consider the 2012 Allstate BCS National Championship Game, which was played in New Orleans, Louisiana. ESPN, which televised the event, logged more than 36 hours of programming on sets around New Orleans in the week leading up to kickoff, not counting the game itself, pregame or postgame shows or the halftime show.

Asked to estimate the value of the advertising New Orleans received around the BCS National Championship Game, Malcolm Turner of Wasserman Media Group said, "There's no question we're talking in the tens of millions of dollars."

Turner says the same applies to the universities participating in game. "[F]or a participating school, their participation with major events for a national title, for example, is a tangible proof point of a commitment to excellence that corresponds with all the institutional brand messaging each school runs in and around the broadcast."

Goff explores the advertising effect in his study, focusing on instances of coverage in eight leading newspapers.[7] He focuses on Northwestern University and Western Kentucky University during the time period of 1991-1996, which saw Northwestern go to the Rose Bowl and WKU men's basketball make the Sweet Sixteen and women's basketball make the Final Four.

Articles about Northwestern increased by a whopping 185 percent during 1995, the football season that ended with a Rose Bowl invite. WKU had a similar experience with articles about the university jumping from "2 or 3 in typical years to 13 and 30 in 1992 and 1993 when the men's and women's basketball programs enjoyed atypical successes."

The study showed it wasn't athletic success driving the coverage, it was athletics in general. In 1992, 70 percent of the articles written about Northwestern in those publications were about athletics. In contrast, articles related to university research accounted for a mere 5 percent. Fascinating when you consider Northwestern is a leading academic institution.

What makes the advertising effect important?

In the most recent study by the Pope brothers, two economists studying this area, ". . . the results we present suggest that students can be affected by events that do not change the quality or cost of a school but that capture a student's attention."[8]

Texas Christian University experienced the advertising effect firsthand on New Year's Day in 2011 when they played in the Rose Bowl. The school's website, tcu.edu, had more than 100,000 unique hits from people who had never visited the website in the past. Since its football website is gofrogs.com, the hits were attributed to general interest in the university.

Goff underscores the importance of the advertising effect by concluding, "Athletics is an integral source of name exposure for almost every university and often the only frequent source of exposure for schools possessing little in the way of academic reputation."

Their hypothesis for why college sports affect student application decisions rests on prospective students not being fully educated about their college choices. Students are most likely to be educated about universities within their state and those where friends or family members have attended.

The Carnegie Foundation completed extensive polling in the late 1980s and found college applicants to be influenced greatly by the athletic reputation of universities to which they were applying. One question asked of students enrolled at Division I schools was, "When applying to colleges for admissions, how well informed were you about the intercollegiate football and/or men's basketball teams of the schools to which you applied?" Eighty-eight percent of males and 51 percent of females answered either "very well informed" or "moderately well informed." The Carnegie Foundation says they haven't completed a similar survey since.

In contrast, when asked, "When applying to colleges for admission, how well informed were you about the undergraduate education programs of the school to which you applied?" only 39 percent of males and 42 percent of females chose the affirmative answers.[9]

Athletic contests covered by the media, particularly high-profile ones like the BCS National Championship and bowl games, have the capability of capturing a prospective student's attention and making them aware of schools they hadn't considered, which might ultimately lead to an application. As you'll see in the next section, this is especially true for out-of-state applicants.

Increased applications/enrollment

Numerous studies show the Flutie Effect is still alive and well. It doesn't seem to matter whether the school is already recognized for its academics or previously successful in football, a bowl appearance can impact application rates.

Following its ten victories and Rose Bowl appearance in 1995, Northwestern saw applications rise by 21 percent. Penn State, which had a solid academic reputation and a successful football history, saw 15 percent more applications following its Rose Bowl appearance the previous year.

A national championship can have an even larger impact. Georgia Tech shared the national football title in 1990, and subsequently experienced a 28 percent increase in applications from 1991-1993 as compared to 1988-1990. The average increase from 1991-1994 was 34 percent higher than the average from 1983-1990.[10]

On average, the most recent study by the Popes shows winning the national championship in football results in a 7-8 percent increase in applications. Finishing the season in the top 20 in the AP poll results in a 2.5 percent increase in applications the following year and a 3 percent increase if the team is ranked in the top ten.

As was stated previously in the chapter, the Popes study found that in order to achieve the same results, a 2-24 percent adjustment would have to be made to tuition/financial aid.

At an even more basic level, increasing the team's winning percentage from one season to the next has been shown to increase application rates. A 1998 study found teams whose winning percentage increased by .250 over the previous season saw an average 1.3 percent increase in applications.[11] A more recent study in 2005 found that number to be larger when in-conference winning percentage increased. A .250 increase in conference winning percentage was associated with a 6.1 percent gain in applications the following year. A decrease in winning percentage was found to produce a 0.4 percent decrease in applications.[12]

A new study, released in mid-2012, found a large increase in wins, such as three wins to eight, was followed by a 5 percent increase in applications.[13]

Some of the largest impacts found by many researchers were in relation to out-of-state students. The Popes 2012 study concludes, "While a sports victory for a given school may not change the awareness of in-state students regarding its existence, the sports victory may present a significant shock in attention/awareness for out-of-state students."

One study showed mere membership in NCAA's Division I increased the number of out-of-state students at a university by 2-4 percentage points.[14]

In recent years, TCU experienced the impact BCS bowl appearances could have on out-of-state applications. They experienced a 200 percent increase in applications from Oregon students following their 2011 Rose Bowl appearance. Applications from California rose by 109 percent.

"[N]ow we get more applications from California than we do from Houston," said Ray Brown, dean of admissions.[15]

Although the impact is not permanent, studies show the afterglow of football success tends to last for three application cycles.[16]

Increased applications allow for schools to either enroll a higher number of students, thus increasing revenue, or become more selective in the class they admit.

Following University of Florida's national football championship in football, just ten months after the men's basketball team won a national title and only two months before they would go on to win another national title, the university saw a spike in the number of accepted students choosing to enroll.

Prior to the championships, approximately 50 percent of accepted students enrolled at UF. However, after the basketball title in March of 2006 and the football title in January 2007, 63 percent of accepted students enrolled. As you'll see later in this chapter, UF chose to become more selective in the years that followed.

As discussed earlier, Goff's study examined schools that added or subtracted football and found a direct impact on the number of students enrolled. There was an average decline of 600 students per year at the schools dropping football and an average increase of 500 students at the school that added football.

The Popes found that while basketball success did not lead to enlarged enrollment at most universities, football success did. Their results showed the champion, on average, enrolled 10.1 percent more the following year. Teams finishing in the top 10 and top 20 in the AP Poll enrolled 4.4 percent and 3.4 percent more students the following year.

The study showed public schools were more likely to increase enrollment as a result of football success. The Popes concluded this was due to the majority of those schools being public institutions, which in some instances give guaranteed admission to in-state students with specified class rank or test scores.[17]

Boise State experienced spikes in applications following both its 2007 and 2010 Fiesta Bowl appearances, which led to increased enrollment. A 9.1 percent increase in applications after the 2007 bowl game resulted in a 4 percent increase in enrollment the following fall, the first time enrollment had ever exceeded 19,000 students.

The story was similar after Boise State's 2010 Fiesta Bowl win. A 5.6 percent increase in enrollment led to the largest enrollment in school history.

Instead of increasing enrollment, some schools focus on using athletic success to increase selectivity.

Following its 2006 national football title, then–UF provost Janie Fouke said, "When a university is still trying to build its academic reputation, this kind of windfall is a blessing. Suddenly it allows you to be more selective because you have a bigger pool."[18]

UF had an unprecedented run of national championships in both football and basketball. The Gators won the national basketball title in 2006 and 2007 and the football title in 2006 and 2008.

A look at UF's freshman classes over the years 2006-2011 shows a significant increase in the quality of students as measured by high school GPA. In 2006, there were 1,603 entering freshman whose high school GPA was below a 3.69, which amounted to 15.3 percent of the class. By 2011 there were only 396 freshman with high school GPAs below 3.69, accounting for 3.4 percent of the class.

A look at US News and World Report rankings show UF's acceptance rate has gone from 53 percent in the 2006 rankings to 39 percent from in the 2010 rankings.

Results of studies that have focused on the SAT scores of applicants and enrollees have been mixed. One study found that a school with a "big-time athletic program" could expect a 33 point, or 3 percent, jump in the SAT scores of incoming freshman.[19] Another focused on schools that finished in the top twenty of the AP Poll for the years 1980-1989 and concluded those schools would attract a freshman class with SAT scores an average 3 percent higher than schools that never finished in the AP top twenty during those years.[20]

However, a later study using new SAT data attempted to imitate one of the previous models and found no relationship between athletic success and increased applicant SAT scores.

Even without a direct correlation between athletics and SAT scores, one could reason the increased selectivity possible via increased applications could lead to improved enrollees, and years of these increases could improve a university's academic profile and ranking.

Increased retention/graduation rates

Several studies have shown that beyond attracting prospective students, athletics has an impact on students once they're on campus in the form of increased retention and graduation rates. One reason may be that students with higher credentials are admitted as application rates rise and a university is able to become more selective.

The authors of one study label the phenomenon "football chicken soup," which they define as football helping students "deal with the psychic costs of leaving home." The authors say the social development encouraged by football, which they say could also be achieved through involvement in other activities on campus, leads students to do better in the classroom as they acclimate to university life.[21]

That study found both freshman retention rates and overall graduation rates rose along with a school's football team's winning percentage over a ten-year period. For each 4 percent increase in winning percentage they found a correlating 1 percent increase in graduation rate.

Another study concluded both undergraduates and student athletes have higher graduation rates at schools with major athletic programs. According to those authors, this is due in part to "superior academic resources" at those institutions.[22]

Increased ranking

Researchers have also found athletic programs to have an impact on a university's academic ranking, specifically in US News and World Report. Hypotheses about this phenomenon range from the increased profile of entering classes discussed earlier in this chapter to simple advertising effect.

The reason the advertising effect may impact rankings in US News and World Report is that one factor of the ranking is peer assessment, which involves a survey of university presidents, provosts and deans of admission and high school counselors. It is the most heavily weighted factor at 25 percent.

A recent study examined the impact of a football national championship on US News and World Report ranking from 1992-2006. It found that on average a school's ranking increased by 6.87 from two years before the championship to two years after.

In addition to any impact the advertising effect might have on the subjective peer assessment portion of a school's ranking, the study also found improvement in a number of the other factors taken into account by the ranking system. A championship was found to decrease acceptance rates by an average of 3.6 percent as schools received more applications and became more selective. Average SAT scores for the incoming class rose 26.5 points. Retention rates improved by nearly 1 percent, and graduate rates improved by 3.42 percent.

However, the study found no evidence that SAT scores, freshman retention rates or graduation rates followed improved football performance without a championship.[23]

Increased donations/ state appropriations

Multiple studies have found athletic success increases donations, both to the athletic department and the university. In recent years, Boise State has seen the impact firsthand.

Boise State's first comprehensive fundraising campaign was announced in 2007 following its first BCS bowl appearance in the Fiesta Bowl. Its goal of $175 million was reached, and exceeded by $10 million dollars, by the close of the 2011 fiscal year.

A new business building on campus, the Micron Business and Economics Building, received funding support as a direct result of the athletic program. Following the 2007 Fiesta Bowl win, the university sent a mailing to potential donors that included a copy of the USA Today cover story on Boise State's win. It inspired an alumnus in California to pledge $250,000 to the new building.

Head coach Chris Petersen and his wife also made a gift to the building in the amount of $150,000. The subsequent media coverage of that gift inspired another donor and football fan in Salt Lake City to match the donation.

The impact is also felt in more obvious ways, like game revenue and contributions required in order to purchase premium seating. From 1992 to 1996, football game revenue at the University of Florida remained fairly stagnant around $7.5 million. Following Florida's 1996 national title (and a stadium expansion), game revenue climbed to nearly $10 million by 2000. Then from 2000 to 2004, game revenue again leveled out at around $10 million. By 2008, following the Gator's 2006 national title and Tim Tebow's 2007 Heisman Trophy, game revenue had exceeded the $15 million mark. That number has continued to climb, although not at the same rapid pace as it did in the years the Gators were competing for national titles. Ticket revenue for the 2010 season was $17.6 million.

Ticket-related contributions saw a jump from 2002 to 2004 when Florida's Ben Hill Griffin Stadium expanded. They saw an even greater rise following the 2006 national championship. In 2002, ticket-related contributions were over $10 million. By 2008, they passed the $20 million mark, and in 2011 that amount exceeded $37 million.

The impact of a winning football season or a bowl game appearance on giving is not unique to these schools. Multiple studies have found athletic success to be directly linked to both athletic giving and general giving to the university.

One study focusing on Clemson University from 1979-1993 found a 10 percent increase in athletics giving corresponded with a 5 percent increase in general contributions, debunking the myth that increased athletic giving precipitates decreased donations to the university.[24]

A study of how athletic success impacted giving at Mississippi State from 1962-1991 revealed a $200,000 increase for each 10 percent increase in winning percentage in basketball and a $200,000-300,000 increase for television appearances, most closely related to the College World Series.[25]

Another study, which examined general giving at 167 institutions from 1973-1990, found increases of 40-54 percent following a football team's bowl game appearance.[26]

Along the same lines, a later study looked at 87 universities with both a Division I football and basketball team and found alumni contributions per student rose 7.3 percent when the football team won a bowl game. Using the mean alumni contributions per student for all universities ($487), the study found that each football bowl win is worth an additional $35.55 per student. Mean enrollment at the universities in the study was 24,132, which equated to an additional $858,000 following a football bowl victory.

A recent study in 2012 found donations significantly increased following a sharp increase in wins, controlling for other variables. An improvement from three to eight wins correlated to donation increases of 28 percent.[27]

Another interesting discovery in the study was the level of athletic success necessary to make up for certain academic lacking. It found a university would need 24 additional bowl appearances or 58 basketball tournament berths to compensate for the lack of Carnegie Research I status[28] or admission of weaker students. It also found it would take 10 additional football bowl appearances or 24 basketball tournament appearances to compensate for each 50-point reduction in average SAT scores for entering freshman.

The study concluded by finding that year-to-year changes in athletic success have no impact on giving by non-alumni, but do impact donations by alumni. A history of football bowl appearances and basketball tournament appearances was found to have an impact, but not as great as being a Carnegie Research I university.

However, the study concludes athletics may still be the most efficient way to improve contribution rates:

> Despite this outcome, university presidents seeking to expand educational contributions still may find it advantageous to support athletic programs at their institutions. For example, building or maintaining quality athletic programs may be less costly when compared to the resource requirements to build up academic programs. Additionally, the payoff from establishing an athletic tradition may come more quickly, particularly if prospective donors have difficulty judging academic improvements and if changes in academic reputation lag behind actual improvements.[29]

While most studies have found athletic success, specifically in football and men's basketball, to increase contributions, some have found that only to be true in relation to the athletic department and not general giving to the university. One dividing line appears to be alumni versus non-alumni donors. In Sperber's book he says fewer than 2 percent of alumni donate to the athletic department, instead focusing on general giving. He posited non-alumni give almost exclusively to the athletic department, although that has not been substantiated by studies on the subject.

In examining US News and World Report rankings for alumni giving, Sperber found the highest-ranked schools for alumni giving coincided with the highest-ranked academic schools, while schools more widely known for their athletic prominence had fewer alumni contributing.

None of the ten highest-ranked universities for alumni giving in the 2012 US News and World Report play football at the FBS level. Princeton ranks first with 61 percent of alumni giving, with the remaining nine all being national liberal arts universities.

Below are the ten highest-ranked academic universities in the 2012 US News and World Report with FBS football programs and their respective alumni giving rates:

#5	Stanford University (34%)
#10	Duke University (36%)
#12	Northwestern University (30%)
#17	Rice University (32%)
#17	Vanderbilt University (23%)
#19	University of Notre Dame (41%)
#21	University of California – Berkeley (12%)
#23	University of Southern California (39%)
#25	University of California – Los Angeles (13%)
#25	University of Virginia (22%)

As a comparison, here are the ten highest-ranked football teams according to the AP Poll following the 2011 season, their overall US News and World Report ranking and their respective alumni giving rates:

#75	University of Alabama (34%)
#128	Louisiana State University (14%)
#132	Oklahoma State University (15%)
#101	University of Oregon (13%)
#132	University of Arkansas (23%)
#23	University of Southern California (39%)
#5	Stanford University (34%)
#67	Boise State University (8%)
#111	University of South Carolina (17%)
#42	University of Wisconsin (11%)

The ten FBS universities ranked the highest in US News and World Report have an average of 28.2 percent of alumni giving. The ten highest-ranked football programs came in at 20.8 percent alumni giving.

In Sperber's book in 2000, he asserted that athletic departments "actively undermine efforts to raise money from alumni for educational programs." However, a 2001 study, which focused on eight Division I universities concluded, "There is certainly no indication in the data we have collected that private giving to athletics today is so substantial (in either the number of donors or the size of the average gift) that it is likely to detract in any substantial way from fundraising for broader educational purposes."

That study has been marginalized by others in academia because it focused on private universities seen as academically elite. A study of the University of Oregon sought to see if the theory extended to public institutions. It focused on donors giving $1,000 or more from 1994-2002. Although these donors constituted only 4.3 percent of total donors, they contributed 72 percent of all charitable revenue.

The study was thought to have ideal conditions, as there were no major changes in academics at the university while the football and men's basketball teams experienced success unparalleled in previous years. The study found non-alumni gave less to academics and more to athletics as the athletic programs flourished. From 1994 to 2002 the average academic gift by a non-alum fell $671.35, while the average non-alum gift to athletics increased $962.88.

No significant change in alumni giving to academics was noted, but alumni giving to athletics increased from an average of 40.4 percent of a donors' gift to 56.7 percent.[30]

One correlation none of these studies has examined is how the financial relationship between the university and the athletic department changes as general giving and athletic giving fluctuate. As athletic giving increases, does the university provide less financial support to the athletic department? Does the athletic department's budget rely less upon student fees?

One thing football success, and even the mere presence of football, has been shown to do is impact state appropriations for public universities. A study published in 2003 by Brad R. Humphreys examined data from 570 public institutions of higher education at the Baccalaureate level or higher from 1976-1996 and found some direct correlations between football and state appropriations.

It's important to understand the role state contributions play in a public university's budget. Humphreys' study found from 1974-2000, appropriations from state governments accounted for 32 percent of each institution's current fund revenues, with amounts into the hundreds of millions of dollars. Meanwhile, tuition and fees accounted for 19 percent of current fund revenues and charitable donations an even smaller percentage at 4.7.

Simply having an FBS football team produced larger appropriations for schools, according to the study. On average, those schools received 6 percent higher appropriations. Humphreys says this could be because ". . . a big-time football program allows a universities' administration, alumni and athletic boosters to produce political pressure more efficiently, because of the visibility of the team and the lobbying opportunities generated by home football games."

Winning what Humphreys calls the "big game," which he defines as an annual or frequent game between two public universities from the same state (think Florida vs. Florida State or Michigan vs. Michigan State), was found to increase appropriations by nearly 7 percent, or $2.1 million in 1982 money.

His results, he says, support the model of competition for political influence amongst pressure groups described by Gary S. Becker in "A Theory of Competition among Pressure Groups for Political Influence," published the *Quarterly Journal of Economics* in 1983. Humphreys says:

In states with two prominent public institutions of higher education, these two institutions and their alumni and boosters, will be continually competing for political influence in the state legislature and other bodies governing higher education. Head-to-head competition in a high profile football game might provide one pressure group with an edge in the following year, allowing the winner to produce pressure more efficiently.[31]

As you can see in the following chart from Humphreys study, total wins, bowl game wins and "big game" wins led to appropriation increases of up to 9.5 percent.

Table 9.1

Average Annual Impact Percent Change in Real Annual State Appropriations

# of Wins	Wins Only	+Bowl	+ Big Win	+ Both
1	1.2%	-	3.6%	-
2	2.1%	-	4.5%	-
3	2.6%	-	5.1%	-
4	2.9%	-	5.3%	-
5	2.9%	-	5.3%	-
6	2.5%	7.0%	4.9%	9.5%
7	1.8%	6.4%	4.3%	8.8%
8	0.8%	5.4%	3.3%	7.8%
9	-0.5%	4.1%	2.0%	6.5%
10	-2.1%	2.5%	0.4%	4.9%

As depicted in the chart, there is a point of diminishing returns when it comes to wins alone. There's even a decrease in appropriations for teams with 9-10 wins and no accompanying bowl game or big game win. The study did not attempt to explain this occurrence.

In short, success on the football field, and sometimes even the mere presence of an FBS football program, can result in increased donations and state appropriations. No study examined whether there were more cost-effective ways to accomplish these increases.

Increased licensing/branding

Prior to winning the national championship in football in 2003, LSU had never received licensing revenue in excess of $1 million. However, just one year after winning the title, the Tigers experienced an increase of over 200 percent to nearly $3 million. When LSU brought home another title in 2007, they were bringing in more than $5 million.

Brian Hommel, a member of LSU's trademark licensing department, told *SportsBusiness Journal* a national title can increase licensing revenue by $1-2 million.[32]

The Gator logo is surely one of the most recognizable in college athletics today. Indeed, the athletic department received nearly $6.1 million in 2010-2011 from licensing revenue. From

2004-2006 that number was $2 million, having only seen modest increases from just over $1.5 million in 2001. National championships have certainly helped those licensing revenues more than triple since 2006.

In 2005, prior to the Broncos big appearances in the 2007 and 2010 Fiesta Bowl games, Boise State had approximately 100 merchandise licensees through the Collegiate Licensing Company and generated about $210,000 in royalties. In 2012, Boise State has over 350 licensees and generates more than $1 million in royalties.

The Boise State Bookstore, which ships Bronco merchandise to all 50 states, returns more than $1 million annually to the university in the form of scholarship funding and operating costs due to the sales of Bronco insignia merchandise.

"Our model is that proceeds from the Bookstore are returned to the university," said Frank Zang, director of communications and marketing for Boise State.

TCU, which met Boise State in the Fiesta Bowl in 2010 and went to the Rose Bowl in 2011, saw revenue from royalties rise 56 percent following its Fiesta Bowl appearance and rise another 84 percent following its Rose Bowl appearance.

Giving back

Many of the most financially healthy athletic departments give back to the university beyond funding student athletes' scholarships and sharing licensing revenue. Some have helped build libraries while others have endowed faculty chairs or funded a shortfall in the university budget.

Louisiana State University's athletic department has a history of giving back to the university that spans more than a decade. It's given over $5 million for campus beautification projects, over $4 million for classroom repairs and renovations, including the purchase of thousands of chairs and desks to replace items that were more than 50 years old, more than $3.5 million for the construction of a new band practice facility, $1.8 million for the construction of a new building complex for the College of Business and over $3 million for the Chancellor to use at his discretion.

The Tigers' athletic department has also spent over $5 million on parking lots for both sporting events and student use, and shares athletic spaces for university classroom use. When the athletic department received a $1 million bonus under the most recent SEC television deal, it donated those funds to the university.

In September of 2012, LSU's athletic department announced a formal agreement with the University to provide a minimum of $36 million over 5 years to support the University's academic mission. In addition to the minimum commitment, the athletic department will share 25 percent of any surplus revenue over $3 million and 50 percent of any surplus over $5 million.

Fellow SEC member University of Tennessee has also made commitments from the athletic department to the university. For the 2010 fiscal year, the athletic department funded $1.375 million in academic scholarships for non-athlete students. It also subsidized $1.125 million in annual debt service on five university parking garages and $1.73 million in operating deficits on university buildings.

As an example of the transfer pricing discussed in Chapter 1, the athletic department also allocated $140,000 of the proceeds from its Aramark concessions contract to the university and $1 million from its SEC television contract. In total, the athletic department sent over $10 million back to the university, not including student-athlete scholarship costs.

Notre Dame also has a long history of using athletic revenue to support university initiatives. Following the 2005 season, the Irish received a payout of $14.5 million for playing in the Fiesta Bowl. Those monies were not deposited by athletics but used to fund academic priorities: undergraduate and graduate financial aid, library acquisitions and purchasing of scientific instruments for the Jordan Hall of Science, which opened the following year.

Currently, Notre Dame athletics commits to giving $20 million per year back to the university, in addition to funding student-athlete scholarships, according to senior associate athletic director for business operations, Tom Nevala.

The University of Florida says it has contributed over $60 million to the university since 1990. In both 2011 and 2012, the athletics department gave $6 million to the university to cover budget cuts by the State of Florida.

The Ohio State University's athletic department gave $9 million for the renovation of the William Oxley Thompson Memorial (Main) Library, the largest academic building project in the university's history.

While every athletic department isn't financially successful enough to contribute to its university at these levels, it's not uncommon for athletic departments that operate in the black.

Degree Completion Programs

For all the commentary on what happens to student athletes who lose their scholarships due to injury or simply not making the cut, little press is given to degree completion programs. Yet, these programs have graduated over 19,000 former student athletes in the past two decades.

There are a number of degree completion programs from the NCAA down to the individual school level. The NCAA's program was founded in 1989 and is currently funded from March Madness revenue. To be eligible, a student must have competed at the Division I level, have received athletics-related aid and be within 30 semester hours, or 45 quarter hours, away from degree completion.

Approximately 45 percent of applicants are chosen for the award each year, which covers tuition and fees and an allowance for books. To date, over $18 million has been awarded to approximately 2,500 former student athletes. Of those, 92 percent have gone on to earn a degree.

Established at approximately the same time as the NCAA's program, another degree completion program was founded by the National Consortium for Academics and Sports. What began as a meeting of the minds among 11 member institutions has grown to include over 240 member institutions. The program allows former student athletes to return to their original institutions, tuition free, in exchange for community service and outreach. To date, nearly 16,000 former student athletes have attained a degree through NCAS's program.

In addition, many university athletic departments sponsor their own degree completion programs. Well-established programs exist at Clemson University and University of Nebraska, which both have programs over 20 years old. Others are newer, such as Arizona State's program, which administrators say is "a couple of years old" and has already enrolled six former–student athletes.

Nearly all of the programs are fully funded by the athletic department or booster club. University of Kentucky, for example, budgets $200,000 per year for its program. Bob Bradley, the associate athletic director for student services, has been around since the program began in 1989. He estimates the total number of student athletes who have completed their degrees under the program at 150, with over half of those being former football players.

University of Tennessee's athletic department has funded a degree completion program since the mid-'90s and has seen over 50 former football players complete their degrees. Administrators say those who come back to complete their degree vary from a former student athlete who returns almost immediately upon losing eligibility under their athletic scholarship to former student athletes who left the program over twenty years prior.

Eligibility for the programs vary by school. Many programs require applicants to be within 30 hours of degree completion, while others only require the applicant have a "reasonable" chance to complete their degree. Some require program recipients to work in the athletic department or complete volunteer work, while others have no such requirement. Although the format varies, a survey completed by athletic department administrators for this book shows these programs are increasingly being founded and supported by athletic departments.

Negative Correlations

Because of its visible profile, athletics can also negatively impact a university when scandal arises. The most notorious example occurred at Southern Methodist University in the late 1980s. In 1987, SMU's football program received the "death penalty" from the NCAA as a result of major violations from the mid-1970s through 1986. The football program also chose to forego the 1988 season after finding it difficult to field a competitive team.

SMU had experienced large growth in its endowment from 1982 to 1986 as the football team prospered. Although it did not fall following the death penalty, growth rates fell back to pre-1982 levels. From 1985-86 to 1987-1988, applications fell by 12 percent.

SMU quickly rebounded thereafter. By 1989-1990 applications had increased 30 percent over that low point. Goff posits this could be because of a variety of factors, including "positive exposure associated with reestablishing the program on a more reputable footing."[33]

Other studies have found contributions suffer following NCAA sanctions. Grimes and Chressanthis's study on Mississippi State found football sanctions led to a $1.6 million decrease in contributions.[34] Rhoads and Gerking's study found when a university's basketball program was placed on probation contributions were reduced by 13.6 percent.[35]

In 2004, Robert H. Frank, a Cornell economist, authored a report for the Knight Commission on Intercollegiate Athletics entitled "Challenging the Myth: A Review of the Links Among College Athletic Success, Student Quality and Donations," which countered the assertions made in many of the studies cited in this chapter.

It's important to understand what The Knight Commission is before diving into Frank's report. It's an organization that describes itself as follows: "Working to ensure that intercollegiate athletic programs operate within the educational mission of their colleges and universities since 1989."

Frank does note many of the studies discussed here that have shown increases in indirect benefits, such as alumni donations and applications. However, he feels those same benefits could be obtained by reallocating money from athletics to financial aid, direct marketing or improved academics.

The question then becomes one of efficiency. Each individual university would have to look at its own unique circumstances and determine the most efficient, cost-effective way to achieve its goals. Not every football program can be ranked in the top 20 of the AP Poll, but not every university can be ranked in the top 20 in US News and World Report either.

University of Chicago represents an interesting example of trying to find its place in both the academic and athletic worlds. In 1939, then–university president Robert Maynard Hutchins disbanded the football program. Although few would know it today, at that time Chicago was a well-respected football program. It had a national championship, a Heisman trophy winner and a legendary coach. Then, like flipping off a light switch, it was all gone.

What you probably know Chicago for today is its academic reputation. However, the university found being one of the highest-ranked universities in the country wasn't enough to attract students. Modern day students wanted more than just classroom experiences.

Reenter football at the University of Chicago in 1969. It wasn't the big-time program of the early 1900s though. Instead of playing at the original 55,000-seat Stagg Field, which was demolished to add a library, the new team would play at a new Stagg Field seating a mere 1,600. The program returned to compete in Division III (meaning no athletic scholarships) and limped along with players who had little to no football experience.

"In the '80s we were losing students who wanted a better quality of student life, and part of the solution was athletics, more coaches, better facilities," Tom Weingartner, athletic director at Chicago for more than 21 years, told the *New York Times* in 2011.[36]

Dick Maloney, who had experience in the Ivy League and Canada, was hired to coach the football team in 1994. Going into the 2011 season, Maloney's teams had a .545 winning percentage and had won three conference championships. According to its 2010-2011 EADA report, Chicago ran its entire athletic department for $3.4 million.

For University of Chicago, perhaps the right place is being the 4th ranked academic university in the country and playing Division III football. For Boise State, football success has attracted better students and faculty and the university seems to be improving its rank as a regional university with the long-term goal of transforming into a nationally ranked university.

Frank finds positive results experienced by institutions through athletics are "very small" when viewing results in the aggregate. As you've seen in this chapter, however, for individual institutions the results can be staggering. His analysis seems to imply institutions have no means by which to equip themselves to capitalize on those short-term gains in order to experience long-term results.

His suggestion? All schools roll back expenditures on athletics by half.

"Any institution that made such a cutback unilaterally would substantially increase its risk of fielding consistently losing teams," Frank said in his report. "But if all institutions cut back in tandem, competitive balance would be maintained."

The likelihood of all schools agreeing to roll back in tandem is hard to imagine, and any attempt by the NCAA to do so would likely result in antitrust litigation.

In the end, athletics can be an effective attention-getter. It can influence a student's decision to apply, their decision to visit campus and maybe even in some cases their decision to attend. However, when that student arrives on campus for a visit, the university likely has to meet expectations of both parents and students regarding degree programs, class sizes, graduation rates and the prospect of the student going on to graduate school or being placed in a job in their profession.

Beyond attracting students, athletics can attract others interested in a relationship with the university. One university administrator tells a story about a refuse and recycling company the athletic department called on to explore sponsorship opportunities. In the initial meeting, the company indicated what they really wanted was to get involved campus-wide and become the official waste/recycling partner of the entire university.

This story is not unique. Athletics is often the most visible part of a university, meaning it can be an entry point for many. It's important for athletic departments and universities to act as a cohesive unit and not as competitors in order to maximize the value athletics can provide.

Universities are not a single-product entity that only specialize in an education in traditional disciplines like English and mathematics. They are multi-product entities possessing assets from big-time college athletics to world-renowned medical centers to theatrical programs capable of putting on Broadway-quality shows.

Although the studies vary in scope and results, one thing they all have in common is that none provides conclusive evidence that athletics harms academics over the long term. In fact, the trend seems to be the more recent the study, the more likely positive impacts were found.

At worst, some athletic departments misallocate resources and overspend. At best, it's a national marketing campaign. Athletics can transform a commuter or regional school into a household name nationally, improving the quality of students. For some, it's a money generator that can send money back to the university at large. Each individual institution has a President/Chancellor, board of trustees and others who are entrusted with ensuring their program maximizes its ability to achieve.

NOTES

[1]   Sperber, Murray, *Beer and Circus: How Big-Time College Sports Is Crippling Undergraduate Education* (New York: Henry Holt and Company, 2000), 52.

[2]   Litzan, R.E., Orszag, J.M. and Orzag, P.R. (2003). *The Empirical Effects of Collegiate Athletics: An Interim Report*. Unpublished study commissioned by the National Collegiate Athletic Association; *see also* Orszag and Israel, op.cit.

[3]   Litzan, Orszag and Orszag, op.cit.

[4]   Litzan, Orszag and Orszag, op.cit.

[5]   Goff, op.cit.

[6]   Pope, D.G. and Pope, J.C., "The Impact of College Sports Success on the Quantity and Quality of Student Applications," *Southern Economic Journal* (2009).

[7]   Goff, op.cit. The eight newspapers included in the study were the *New York Times, Wall Street Journal, Washington Post, Boston Globe, Atlanta Constitution, Los Angeles Times, Chicago Tribune* and *The Christian Science Monitor.*

[8]   Pope, D.G. and Pope, J.C., "Understanding College Application Decisions: Why College Sports Success Matters" (out for publication, March 2012).

[9]   Sperber, op.cit.

[10]   Goff, op.cit.

[11]   J.D. Toma & M.E. Cross. "Intercollegiate Athletics and Student College Choice: Exploring the Impact of Championship Seasons on Undergraduate Applications," *Research in Higher Education* (1998).

[12]   McEvoy, Chad, "The Relationship Between Dramatic Changes in Team Performance and Undergraduate Admissions Applications," *The SMART Journal* (2005).

[13]   Anderson, Michael L., "The Benefits of College Athletic Success: An Application of the Propensity Score Design with Instrumental Variables," *National Bureau of Economic Research Working Paper No. 18196*, June 2012.

[14]   Mixon, F. and Hsing, Y., "The determinants of out-of-state enrollments in higher education: A Tobit analysis," *Economics of Education Review* (1994).

[15]   *Fort Worth Magazine*, July 2011.

[16]   Pope and Pope, op.cit. (2012) and Toma and Cross, op.cit. (1998).

[17]   See Pope and Pope, op.cit. (2012).

[18]   Shannon Colavecchio-Van Sickler and Elena Lesley (January 9, 2007). "For UF, here comes the love." *St. Pete Times*. Retrieved August 7, 2013, from http://www.sptimes.com/2007/01/09/news_pf/State/For_UF__here_comes_th.shtml.

[19]   E. McCormick and M. Tinsley, "Athletics Versus Academics? Evidence from SAT scores," *Journal of Political Economy* (1987).

20 Tucker, I.B. and Amato, L.T., "A Reinvestigation of the Relationship Between Big-Time Basketball Success and Average SAT Scores," *Journal of Sports Economics* (2006).

21 Mixon, F.G., Jr. and Trevino, L.J., "From Kickoff to Commencement: the positive role of intercollegiate athletics in higher education," *Economics of Education Review* (2005).

22 Rishe, Patrick. "A Reexamination of How Athletic Success Impacts Graduation Rates: Comparing Student Athletes to All Other Undergraduates," *American Journal of Economics and Sociology* (2003).

23 Cox, S.R. and Roden, D.M., "Quality Perception and the Championship Effect: Do Collegiate Sports Influence Academic Rankings?" *Research in Higher Education Journal* (2010).

24 McCormick, R.E. and Tinsley, M., "Athletics and academics: a model of university contributions." In B.L. Goff and R.D. Tollison (Eds.). *Sportometrics*, 193-206 (1990).

25 Grimes, P.W. and Chressanthis, G.A., "Collegiate Sports, NCAA sanctions and alumni contributions to academics," *American Journal of Economics and Sociology* (1994).

26 Baade, R.A. and Sundberg, J.S., "Fourth and down and gold to go? Assessing the link between athletics and alumni giving," *Social Science Quarterly* (1996).

27 Anderson, op.cit.

28 Carnegie has since renamed the category, "Doctoral/research universities-extensive."

29 Rhoads, T.A. and Gerking, S., "Educational Contributions, Academic Quality, and Athletic Success," *Contemporary Economic Policy* (Vol. 18, No. 2, 2000).

30 Stinson, J.L. and Howard, D.R., "Scoreboards vs. Mortarboards: Major Donor Behavior and Intercollegiate Athletics," *Sport Marketing Quarterly* (2004).

31 Humphreys, Brad R. "The Relationship Between Big-Time College Football and State Appropriations to Higher Education," *International Journal of Sport Finance* (2006).

32 Michael Smith, "For BCS winner, licensing boom is just the start." *SportsBusiness Journal* (January 9, 2012). Retrieved August 7, 2013, from http://www.sportsbusinessdaily.com/Journal/Issues/2012/01/09/Colleges/LSUBAMA.aspx?hl=brian%20hommel&sc=0.

33 Goff, op.cit.

34 Grimes/Chressanthis study: Grimes, P.W. and Chressanthis, G.A., op.cit.

35 Rhoads, T.A. and Gerking, S. , op.cit.

36 Bearack, Barry, "South Side Odyssey," *New York Times*, September 17, 2011, D1.

ACKNOWLEDGMENTS

This book would have never come to fruition without the education, advice and support given by so many. My first foray into college athletics finance was met with a phone call from Ben Jay, then–CFO of the athletic department at the Ohio State University. After he finished telling me that everything I'd written in a recent blog post was wrong, he went on to teach me what I needed to know to write the piece better the next time. Over the years, he's spent innumerable hours answering my questions about the business side of college sports. He taught me to ask questions, which no doubt led to much of the material in this book.

Saturday Millionaires would have never been more than my catchy idea for a title without Laura Bradford, my literary agent. Although she's much more at ease representing authors of paranormal and erotic romance, and has yet to spend an entire Saturday watching college football, her excitement for this book was palatable from the day she responded to my proposal. In lawyer-speak, she was a zealous advocate for me and my book from the jump, and for that I will always be eternally grateful.

Next, I'd like to thank my first editor on this book, Stephen Powers, who always understood my vision for this book. He reminded me it was okay to make strong statements when the facts supported it, and he came up with some great chapter titles. Also, thank you to Christina Roth, the editor who finished up my book and helped ensure it came out before another college football season passed.

When I set out to write this book, I vowed to myself that I wouldn't talk about a school's financial situation unless I had their cooperation. There are just too many variables and differences in reporting to attempt to analyze an athletic department's finances alone. Thank you to the following athletic department and university administrators who were always available to answer my questions: Susan Parish of University of Florida, Lisa Rudd of Virginia Tech, Shane Hinckley and Jason Cook of Texas A&M, Scott Stricklin of Mississippi State, Tom Jurich of Louisville, Frank Hardymon of Georgia Tech, Craig Pintens of Oregon, Frank Zang of Boise State, Kay Hargrave of Auburn, Brad Sutton of SMU and Tom Nevala of Notre Dame. Also, a big thank you to Christopher Radford of the NCAA for tracking down the answers I needed from the governing body of intercollegiate athletics.

There were also a number of professors and other experts around the country who answered questions, read chapters and generally acted as a sounding board. Thank you to Brian Goff, Paul Creasy, John Colombo, Andrew Giangola, Christian Dennie, Steve Dittmore, Gabe Feldman, Jaren Pope, Jon Orszag, Chad McEvoy, Burke Magnus, Jeff Schemmel and Len Deluca.

Several of my interns of the last couple of years have also been a huge help when it came to researching some of the more obscure data in this book. A big thank you to Lauren Nevidomsky, Tyler Jamieson, Rick Davis, Drew Balis, Victoria Conners and Jonathan Nehring.

Another person without whom this book would not be the same is Tim Brando, who was kind enough to write the foreword. I first went on Tim's radio show three years ago when I was still a full-time practicing attorney trying to figure out if there was room for me in the sports media world. We became fast friends, and I'm thrilled each and every time he asks me to come on his show. He's been supportive of this book since day one, and he has graciously allowed me to tell his listeners about it every time I'm on the show. In addition, he's always willing to lend an ear and has been a great mentor in the sports media industry for me and many others.

Then, of course, there's my family. My parents each gave me something very different for this book. Thank you to my father for instilling in me a love of sports at a young age, one Braves game at a time. And to my mother, thank you for marking up my work in red pen—since kindergarten! I'm sure the copy editors thank you too.

And last, but not least, thank you to my fiancé, Chadd, who despite having to put up with me while I wrote this book every weekend for a year still wanted to propose to me two days after I turned in the first draft. He read dozens of drafts and engaged me in lively debate on the subjects, which I know made this a better book. He's been my biggest cheerleader since the day I met him, and I can't wait to spend the rest of our lives together . . . at least a few days of which I'm sure will be at college football games.

INDEX

Kristi Dosh is the sports business reporter for ESPN. Prior to joining ESPN, she was a practicing attorney and a sports business analyst for Forbes.com, Comcast Sports Southeast, and The Pulse Network. She is also a frequent guest on shows such as the *Tim Brando Show*. Kristi founded BusinessofCollegeSports.com, a nationally recognized news source for the business of college sports.